Camping's Top Secrets

Camping's Top Secrets

A Lexicon of Modern Bushcraft

Fifth Edition

CLIFF JACOBSON

FALCONGUIDES

GUILFORD, CONNECTICUT

FALCONGUIDES®

An imprint of Globe Pequot, the trade division of
The Rowman & Littlefield Publishing Group, Inc.
4501 Forbes Blvd., Ste. 200
Lanham, MD 20706
www.rowman.com
Falcon and FalconGuides are registered trademarks and make your book a trademark of The Rowman
& Littlefield Publishing Group, Inc.

Distributed by NATIONAL BOOK NETWORK

British Library Cataloguing in Publication Information available

Library of Congress Cataloging-in-Publication Data
Names: Jacobson, Cliff, author.
Title: Camping's top secrets : a lexicon of modern bushcraft / Cliff Jacobson.
Description: Fifth edition. | Guilford, Connecticut : FalconGuides, [2022] | Includes bibliographical
   references and index. | Summary: "Seasoned camping veteran Cliff Jacobson shares insider tips and
   shortcuts to comfort and security in the bush"— Provided by publisher.
Identifiers: LCCN 2021032075 (print) | LCCN 2021032076 (ebook) | ISBN 9781493062942
   (paperback) | ISBN 9781493062959 (epub)
Subjects: LCSH: Camping. | Hiking.
Classification: LCC GV191.7 .J33 2022 (print) | LCC GV191.7 (ebook) | DDC 796.54—dc23
LC record available at https://lccn.loc.gov/2021032075
LC ebook record available at https://lccn.loc.gov/2021032076

♾™ The paper used in this publication meets the minimum requirements of American National
Standard for Information Sciences—Permanence of Paper for Printed Library Materials, ANSI/NISO
Z39.48-1992.

The author and The Rowman & Littlefield Publishing Group, Inc., assume no liability for
accidents happening to, or injuries sustained by, readers who engage in the activities described
in this book. The health information expressed in this book is based solely on the personal
experience of the author and is not intended as a medical manual. The information should not
be used for diagnosis or treatment, or as a substitute for professional medical care.

Contents

Acknowledgments

In my book *Expedition Canoeing: A Guide to Canoeing Wild Rivers in North America,* I wrote, "Canoeing the wild rivers of the far north makes one understand why primitive man felt so close to God." I am not a religious man, but I have brushed with death often enough in the bush to appreciate the caring spirits who guide my actions. I have spent nearly a lifetime canoeing remote rivers in northern Canada and neither I nor anyone in my charge has ever suffered a serious illness or injury. I believe that I owe much of my good luck to a kindly spirit who watches my back and helps me make wise decisions. I often feel the presence of my "river angel," and I wish to say thanks.

I also wish to credit and say thanks to the following people for their support and encouragement and use of their photos: my friend Dr. Bill Forgey, for his practical tips on wilderness medicine; Alv Elvestad (www.pakboats .com); Gabriel Branby; Sharron Chatterton; Dan Cooke; Chris Coleman; Bob Dannert; Darrell Foss; Bill Friedlander; Toni and Ria Harting; Rod Johnson; Rob Kesselring; Paul Kirtley; Tim Lynch and Mark Matheny; UDAP Industries, SPOT LLC and Globalstar; Jim Mandle; Heather Novaday Maier (HMS Wilderness Experience); Dick Person; Steve Piragis; Scott Power; Mike Rapatz; Thomas Rapatz; Larry Rice; Larry Ricker (www.lhrimages.com); Tom Schwinghamer; Bill Schwen; Paul Swanstrom; Tony Way; Alan Wenker; David Wescott, author of *Camping in the Old Style*; Wes Rusk; and my patient wife, Sue Harings.

What! Another Camping Book?

Camping out has changed considerably since the good old days of pine-bough beds, bonfires, and fresh-cut trail shelters. No longer is it ethical to shape the land to suit our whims. There are just too few wild places and too many of us!

As a result, a whole new style of camping has evolved, one geared to the high-tech, lightweight equipment of today. Forty-pound canvas tents have been thoughtfully replaced by equally spacious nylon models of one-fourth the weight. Camp stoves have taken over where fires once ruled, and a deluge of new fabrics—polypropylene, polyester pile, Orlon acrylics, and Gore-Tex—have challenged traditional fibers. Packsacks, hiking boots, rain gear: Everything has become lighter, more compact, and reliable. Surprisingly good outdoor gear can now be purchased at big-city discount stores—testimony to the growing interest in camping out. Regrettably, even new technology has brought disappointments. Outdoor clothing and footwear have become more stylish and less adapted for use in the wild outdoors. Tents have become exotic, difficult to pitch, and less rainproof than old designs. And today's thick-bladed, serrated knives are better adapted to cutting through metal doors than slicing salami and pine. Have we forsaken old ways that work for fashionable new styles that don't?

Amidst the generally welcomed improvements in gear, the one thing that has not changed at all is knowledge of the sport. The wise old scoutmaster who could sniff a coming storm and rig a tight camp in a driving rain has all but been replaced by the well-meaning leader who atones the night in his pickup camper . . . or more likely, doesn't camp at all. Everyone, it seems, has plenty of gear to cope with the elements, but precious few know how to use it. If misery loves company, you'll find plenty of it in the backcountry. Just watch the campers roll home (or to the nearest motel) at the first sign of rain. The notion that bad weather spells bad times afield is so firmly entrenched in the minds of contemporary campers that it is probably pointless for me to argue the truth in the pages of this book. Nonetheless, I shall try.

This book is not intended to take the place of a sport-specific text on backpacking, canoeing, family camping, or the like. Rather, it details hundreds of ideas and procedures that are never found in traditional camping texts—ideas that will make your next campout safer and more enjoyable. Main topics have been alphabetized, everything is indexed for your convenience, and space-consuming anecdotes have been eliminated to make room for the obscure but important things you really need to know.

Some of you may recognize procedures from my books *Canoeing Wild Rivers* (Fifth Edition) and *Canoeing & Camping: Beyond the Basics*. These procedures are repeated here for the benefit of those who don't canoe. After all, the rules of backcountry comfort are the same whether you travel by foot, ski, canoe, or truck camper. Foul weather can make you just as miserable in a state park campground as on a remote canoe trail.

I encourage everyone who loves camping to read *Camping and Woodcraft*, by Horace Kephart, which was published in 1917; and *Woodcraft and Camping*, by "Nessmuk" (George Washington Sears), which appeared in 1920. Fortunately, reprint editions of these old classics are now available. The theme in both is that the old-timers were not bungling idiots who slashed and trashed the backcountry. They knew it took a long time to build a bough bed or a snug shelter, so they devised surprisingly good (and ecological) alternatives. For example, Kephart carried a 1-pound mattress tick; Cal Rutstrum—author of *The New Way of the Wilderness* (a must read!)—had a down-filled air mattress and a "convertible A-tent." And every woodsman felt that a light tarp was essential for rain—something modern voyagers are just beginning to admit. If you asked a turn-of-the-century woodsman for advice, he'd have been more apt to tell you about the method than the gear. Now, as every modern camper knows, the emphasis is on "things" not "skills." At one of my seminars, a man wryly suggested that my camping ideas were old hat. "You've just taken the good ideas of Nessmuk, Kephart, and Rutstrum and updated them with new technology," he said. "Shhh," I replied. "Promise me you won't tell a soul!"

What's New in the Fifth Edition?

In a word, plenty! What was intended as a light revision morphed into a substantial rewrite with dozens of new color photos. Why so many revisions when the basic tenets of camping haven't changed in years? The answer is that if you take camping as seriously as I do, you are always on the prowl for better ways and better stuff.

For more than 30 years, I outfitted and guided canoe trips on remote rivers in northern Canada, where having one's act together is a tenet of survival and a prerequisite to having a good time. Each new adventure tested old methods and encouraged me to think outside the box. When I discovered a better way, I adopted it immediately and threw past practice to the wind.

Finally, those of you who have read earlier editions of this book have surely noticed that some of my recommendations have changed. Good! That's the price one pays for continued learning.

Here's wishing you warm winds, fair weather, bug-free days, and enough good camping skills to cope with the worst of times on the best of terms.

Note: New equipment comes and goes. What is state-of-the-art this year may be "old hat" the next. Some of my favorite (recommended) products from the last edition have been replaced this time around. The buyer's dollar determines what hangs around. Website addresses of companies change too, so to make future edits easier, I have removed them from the text and placed them in appendix B.

A

Accident Avoidance

My dad was a quality control engineer. A sign in his office read, "Accidents don't just happen; they are caused!" The villains are speed (doing a task too fast), impatience, and not following safety rules.

In 35 years of guiding canoe trips on some of the toughest rivers in North America, I've never needed more than Band-Aids, Tylenol, and antibiotics. I believe I owe my good luck to a plan that emphasizes avoiding accidents.

Appropriate Clothing

Everyone gets a detailed equipment list. There's a full field inspection—those who don't have the "right stuff" don't go! Not allowed are plastic rain suits, cotton socks, and blue jeans. Wool, fleece, polyester, and nylon are the respected fabrics. Sneakers are fine for camp but won't substitute for boots. Everyone carries a knife, matches, compass, and whistle.

Downplay Your Skills

Underestimating your skills—and those of your crew—keeps you humble and out of trouble! For example: Many people consider me an expert canoeist; I prefer "intermediate." Indeed, the best compliment I ever received was from a young woman who was trying out for the US Whitewater Canoeing Team. She asked me to paddle with her on a practice run through a qualifying whitewater course. We did fine. Afterwards, she said to me: "Cliff, you're pretty good; why don't you try out for the team?" I answered, "No, big rapids kinda freak me out." She responded: "Cliff, you have more skill than guts!" I couldn't have been more proud!

Wait for Good Weather

The book *Into Thin Air* reveals the high price you may pay if you continue on when you should stay put. Better to hunker down until conditions improve, even if the wait plays havoc with your schedule. Experienced wilderness travelers plan one "down day" in five for the unexpected.

Familiarity May Breed Contempt

If you have boated a river or hiked a trail many times, you develop a vision about what lies ahead. However, a heavy rain can make an easy rapid dangerous; it can flood a well-used trail and create mud slides that send trees and boulders crashing down, etc. Safety demands that you approach familiar routes with "fresh new eyes."

Slow Down and Smell the Pines

Most accidents occur late in the day when people are pushed and tired, or when the pace is too fast for slow hikers. Solution? *Slow down* and camp early if you can; fuel up on high-energy snacks and take frequent breaks if you can't.

Review Skills and Safety Procedures Each Day

Begin each day by reviewing skills and safety procedures. Is everyone dressed appropriately? Are there blisters or small cuts that *will* become infected? Are water bottles topped off, rain gear and warm clothes handy? Boaters may review paddle strokes and river safety signals.

Patience

Long before the white man discovered the recreational value of rivers, native North Americans used them as highways. Families often traveled together, with their elders, children, and dogs. By today's standards, their boats were fragile and their paddle skills marginal. Certainly, there were accidents. But native accounts don't dwell on them, any more than we do when we drive our cars. How is it, then, that even poor paddlers usually got downriver safely? The answer is "patience"—a commitment to not take chances!

Most modern outdoorspeople don't have much patience. They offer these reasons why:

1. *Bad weather/behind schedule*—gotta keep truckin' or we'll lose our layover day at the big falls.

2. *A macho attitude.* Other parties paddled these difficult rapids, climbed the high mountain, so can we!

3. *We're prepared for the worst!* Dangerous rapids, difficult climb, bad weather ahead? No problem; we have superior equipment.

Here are some examples of how patience pays:

Behind Schedule

The wind was blowing bloody murder when we arrived at Otter Lake (Fond du Lac River, Saskatchewan), so we put ashore around noon to wait it out. The waves continued through lunch, so I suggested that we camp and try again tomorrow. We were snuggled under a tarp, sharing hot buttered rum and popcorn, when we saw two canoes—wind in their face—plugging toward our camp. I waved them in and suggested they share our camp. They said they were behind schedule and had to keep going.

The wind quit around noon the next day and we paddled off with a smile, determined to make up lost time. The sun sets around 11 p.m. at this latitude (59 degrees), so we agreed to canoe until dark. Around 2 p.m. we passed

"their camp." Everyone was asleep. We logged 31 miles that day and 29 the next, which put us ahead of schedule. We never saw the other canoe party again.

Moral? Nature rules! Stop when you must; run when you can.

The Canyon

The MacFarlane River (Saskatchewan) rushes through a 3-mile canyon just before it breaks out into Lake Athabasca. There's serious water here—you have to be nuts not to portage. But where? There was no sign of a portage on river left so we crossed to the right and took out at a narrow trail that ran up a steep bank. There was a tree with an ancient axe blaze on top. Aha. The portage!

Hardly. The trail ran a quarter mile along the canyon rim then petered out. Perhaps it continued in the woods? Four hours of searching revealed nothing.

We were shot so I suggested we "sleep on it" and have another look tomorrow. We did, and drew another blank. Bickering began. Pressure grew to canoe the canyon, dangers be damned.

I suggested we pair off and keep looking. Shortly, someone found an old animal trail that went in the right direction. But it was overgrown with young trees—canoes and packs could not be carried through.

Sure enough, it was a portage, albeit one that hadn't been used in many years. It took us more than a day to clear the route and complete the carry. Our patience paid off.

Big Bear

We had just finished breakfast when I heard someone yell, "Bear! Big bear!" Sure enough, a huge cinnamon-colored black bear (or maybe it was a grizzly) was circling our camp. I hollered and blew a whistle. He didn't even look up. So I grabbed my rifle and amassed everyone into a tight group. He circled closer. When he was 50 feet away I fired a warning shot over his head. He just sniffed the air then ambled down the bank and came in from another direction. He paused behind a large rock and stood up to see us better. He was just 20 feet away!

I was plenty scared, even with a powerful rifle in hand. But I did not want to kill this gray-whiskered old boy. So we talked. I looked unthreateningly into his eyes and told him I didn't want to hurt him, that we'd be gone soon, and he could have his way. I said I respected him and wanted him to go on living. But I calmly emphasized that I would shoot him if he came over that rock.

We stared at one another for some time. I could sense the wheels turning in his head. There was no fear or animosity. Only the question of what to do next. Then, after what seemed like an eternity (I learned it was barely 1 minute) he turned and proudly walked away. As soon as he was gone, some crew members said they would have shot him before he got so close. But as the fear wore off, all agreed that my patient plan was the right one.

Patience is like a secure eddy in the middle of a raging rapid. It gives you time to formulate a plan before you dash dumbly downstream.

Alum

The water in many western US rivers and some Canadian and Alaskan tundra rivers is too silty to drink. If you attempt to filter out the silt, your filter will quickly clog. For this reason, most people just carry their drinking water in plastic jugs, but at roughly eight pounds per gallon, the weight adds up quickly. A lighter solution is to use alum to settle the silt, then purify the clear water with chemicals or a filter. Alum is used in home pickling to add crispness and as a settling agent in water treatment plants. It is non-toxic and tasteless. Most pharmacies have it. A 12-ounce (340-gram) bottle contains enough alum to settle about 24 gallons of silty water.

"Chocolate malt"–colored water from the Green River in Utah. A bucket of this silty water may need a day or more to settle. Use the alum "trick" described here and you'll have crystal-clear water (ready for purification) in about 20 minutes.
Larry Rice

Procedure

1. Fill your bucket with the silty water.

2. Add about a heaping teaspoon (the measurement isn't critical) of alum per gallon of water.

3. Use a long stick to *very slowly* stir the water. Stir in *one direction* only. Continue stirring until a "flocculent precipitate" (it looks like snow) forms on the surface of the water—it takes about 5 minutes.

4. When you see the snow-colored precipitate, stop stirring. Allow the water

Alum is being used to settle this silty river water. Stirring will continue for about 5 minutes until surface floc (it looks like snow) appears. The water will then be allowed to settle until clear (about 20 minutes). Note the clear water in the green bucket and the bottle of alum on the ground nearby.

to settle for about 20 minutes. At the end of this time, the water will be clear and the silt will have settled to the bottom.

5. Use a sierra cup or ladle to gently dip the clear effluent from the top of the bucket. You can now boil, filter, or chemically treat this water to make it potable. I've used this method to remove silt from river water on the Green River, Rio Grande, and Little Missouri River. It works great!

Anchor

Here's a slick way to make a light, portable anchor for fishing in a canoe. All you need is a basketball net and a carabiner (an aluminum link used by mountaineers, available at most camp shops). Tie off the net bottom with cord. Fill the net with rocks, then gather the net perimeter and clip it together with the carabiner. Attach a rope to the "biner" and you're set for action.

You can also make an anchor out of the nylon mesh bags you buy at camping shops. However, few of these bags are as tough as a basketball net.

Animals—Bears and Other Beasts

Bears are extremely smart and they are excellent climbers. A tree *is not* a safe place to store your food!
Rob Kesselring

Protecting Foodstuffs

Each year thousands of campers lose food and equipment to persistent critters. The common advice is to protect foodstuffs by one of these three methods:

1. Store food inside your car.

2. Place food in a critter-proof container.

3. Suspend food from a tree limb at least 15 feet off the ground.

Let's look at these three methods.

Store food inside your car. Not a good plan! Steven Thompson, a Yosemite National Park biologist, says that mother bears teach their young ones how to break into cars. They insert their claws above the rear side door and pull the door frame down to knee level. They climb this "stepladder" into the car. Then they claw through the backseat and into the trunk. Bears have also developed tricks to break into vans. They look for a van that has a car parked close by, then they lean against the car for leverage to bash in the van's windows. Or they break off the van's bolted windows and get in that way.

Park rangers say that bears often break into cars that contain no food. Perhaps they simply enjoy it. And why not? Animals like to have fun too!

Bears are extremely smart. Case in point: The BearVault 500 is a tough polycarbonate container that was built to be bearproof. It was tested on bears at the Folsom City Zoo in California and on grizzlies in Yellowstone National Park. None of the test bears could open it. But in New York's Adirondack Park, a shy female black bear named Yellow Yellow figured out how to release the double-tab lid to get at the contents. Then she set out to teach her friends! Scores of Adirondack bears are now successfully educated, and the BearVault 500 is no longer recommended for use in the Adirondacks. Interestingly, some humans have to read the instructions in order to figure out how to open the lid on this product! Again, I emphasize that bears are very smart.

Use a critter-proof container. A plastic or metal ice chest will deter ravaging raccoons and ground squirrels. Squirrels have sharp teeth and will bore right through a nylon packsack.

A thick-walled PVC plastic pipe with threaded end caps makes a reliable "food safe" that will deter bears. There are some commercial steel bearproof containers that are heavy, bulky, and expensive.

Commercial Bear-Resistant Containers

Search the web and you'll find scores of "bear-proof" food containers for sale. With rare exception, they are, at best, "bear-resistant." The story of Yellow Yellow on this page testifies as to how smart and capable bears are. This said, the Kevlar Ursack and stainless-steel mesh Outsack are two soft containers (bags) that have merit. Both are light enough for backpacking and will resist small animals. They may or may not deter a determined bear. The BearVault 500, mentioned earlier, has proven reliable everywhere except in parts of the Adirondacks where bears have learned to open it. None of these containers is 100 percent bearproof or waterproof. Plastic olive and pickle barrels are *not* bearproof! Some US national parks provide metal barrels that are.

Note the hole this bear chewed through the plastic "bear-barrel." Plastic barrels ARE NOT bearproof! Bill Schwen

If you want to know the current technology, check with the managers of national parks like Yellowstone and Glacier, which have large populations of bears.

Hang your food in a tree. Expert campers usually do not store their food in trees to

Plastic olive and pickle barrels *will not* discourage bears, but government-approved steel barrels will. The approved bear barrels are heavy, strong, and not waterproof—they don't have straps or handles that a bear can grab. Note the bear barrel to the right of the author, which doubles as a handy table. Some national parks will provide these barrels (they come in different sizes) free of charge to campers. A gravel-bar campsite along the Noatak River (Arctic National Wildlife Refuge) in Alaska.

protect it from bears. Instead, they seal their food tightly in plastic to eliminate odors, then they remove the food from the immediate camp area. Setting food packs outside the campsite perimeter is usually enough to foil hungry bruins and other animals. The rationale for this procedure is based on the fact that bears are creatures of habit—they quickly learn that camps, packs, and tin cans contain food. In each campsite there is seldom more than one or two trees with limbs high enough to deter a bruin. Bears aren't stupid; they learn the location of these trees and make daily rounds to secure whatever is suspended from them. When they find something (anything!) hanging from "their" tree, they'll get it down,

one way or another. All black bears (even fat old sows) can climb to some degree. And cubs climb like monkeys. If momma can't get your food, the kids will!

Young grizzlies can "claw climb" like black bears until they are about 4 years old, when their hooked claws straighten out. Then they will "hug climb" trees, just like people do. Adult grizzlies have climbed trees and pulled people down! Polar bears are the only bruins that don't climb trees.

Steve Thompson at Yosemite says bears have elaborate schemes for getting food. In an article by Suzanne Charle for the *Milwaukee Journal Sentinel* (November 30, 1997), Thompson described some of these schemes:

One time-honored precaution, hanging bags of food from a rope high in a tree, is now seen as useless. Local residents call the food bags "bear piñatas." The bears chew off the rope that has been attached elsewhere, or chew off the branch that is supporting the bag. If the limbs are small, they'll send the cubs out. If that doesn't work, they'll just climb above the bags, launch themselves out of the tree, and grab the bags on the way down.

Black bears often climb trees in search of food (insects, bird eggs, acorns, etc). Bears in the Great Smoky Mountain National Park are unique: They hibernate in winter in nests they build in the cavities of large trees. Really!

Question: If black bears climb trees, why do federal authorities ask campers to tree their food?

Answer: To discourage a possible mauling. The feds don't care if a bear gets your food or tears up your car, but they DO care if a bear gets you! The solution is to keep humans and their food a safe distance apart.

Recommendation: Double-bag (in plastic) all foodstuffs, especially meats. If possible, ask your grocer to vacuum-seal smelly foods. Or buy your own vacuum-sealing machine. Set food packs on low ground (to minimize the travel of odors), well away from the confines of campsites and trails. As an added precaution, separate food packs by 50 feet or more. Do not put food packs in trees!

If you're camping in grizzly or polar bear country, locate your kitchen at least 50 yards downwind of your tents. Naturally, cooking areas must be scrupulously clean—free of the last Rice Krispie. Nonetheless, human odor is stronger than most food smells: Don't be surprised if the bear smells you before he smells your food!

If taking your food out of camp and hiding it in the woods works, why don't federal authorities support this method?

Mostly, it's a matter of keeping people safe (i.e., "people here, food over there, yonder in that tree"). If a bear gets your food, it's no big deal; if he gets you, it's a very big deal! Federal authorities need a formula they can rely on—one that keeps people and food at a safe distance.

As mentioned, I never hang my packs in bear country (it bears repeating that bears climb trees!). And unless required by law, I don't use bearproof containers. But I keep a scrupulously clean camp, and at night I put my food in a place where a bear is unlikely to see or smell it—thick bushes, a tight grove of trees, a depression, beneath an evergreen tree, etc. The bottom line is that if a bear can't see or smell your food (vacuum-sealing will eliminate most odors), he won't get it! I've lived by my rules for fifty years, and in that time, neither I nor anyone in my charge has ever lost food or equipment to any animal. And that, friends, is the "bear" truth!

Bear Encounters

Here's the recommended procedure in the event you meet face-to-face with . . .

Black Bears

Blackies are timid and will ordinarily run away at the first smell of you. Bears don't see very well—what most people interpret as a "charge" is usually nothing more than simple curiosity. Screaming, blowing whistles, and other noise-making will usually send a wild bear running, but an experienced camp bear will remain oblivious to the racket.

The best plan is to hold your ground, spread your arms wide (so you look bigger), talk authoritatively but unthreateningly, and back off slowly. Do not run! Take off your pack and put it on top of your head. Place a child on your shoulders. Group your friends together. Bears are intelligent bullies. They assess their odds of success and go for it if they think they have the upper edge. Do whatever you can to make yourself look bigger and more powerful.

The danger signs are "woofing" and "clacking." If the bear goes "woof, woof, woof" and you hear loud hiccuping sounds with the clacking of teeth, the situation is deteriorating. The bear is mad and unpredictable. If you can beat a path to safer ground or climb a tree, do it. But remember, your safe haven better be close because you can't outrun the bear by far!

The pamphlet *Bears Are Dangerous*, published by the Government of the Northwest Territories, recounts a story of two young people who hiked to Hidden Lake outside of Yellowknife, in Canada's Northwest Territories:

Suddenly, a black bear appeared, forcing the campers to climb trees. The bear ate all the food in camp, then it attempted to climb the trees in which the two campers were hiding. They managed to keep it away by striking it with branches. Finally the bear left, but the campers remained in their trees for 5 hours before making good their escape.

If you are up a tree and a bear climbs after you, poking it in the face with a branch is a proven plan. Remember, bears climb as well as you!

If you are attacked by a predacious black bear, fight like mad! Do not play dead with a determined black bear! Use all your might—and whatever tools (knife, ax, rock, log) you have—to fend off the attack.

To retreat or fight: Your reaction will depend on whether the attack is *defensive-aggressive* or *predatory*. A bear in a defensive-aggressive mode is trying to protect its interests—its young or food source. Basically, the bear just wants to get you out of the way (eliminate the threat) and as quickly as possible get back to what it was doing before you appeared. In this type of attack, you are best off to play dead and thereby indicate you are no threat. The bear may rough you up some, but if you stay still, it will usually leave quickly.

A predatory attack is another matter. Here, *you* are the food and you will survive only if you fight like mad. The old advice to "play dead with a grizzly and fight back with a black bear" was based on the fact that most black bear attacks are predacious while most grizzly attacks are defensive-aggressive. In any case, you will have just seconds to determine the true motive of a bear attack.

Grizzlies

- Grizzlies have been clocked at 45 miles per hour on flat terrain. No way can you outrun one. Grizzlies are shy animals; they will usually run away from you. Nonetheless, grizzlies are king of the hill in their domain—it's doubtful you can bluff them. I was once charged by three grizzlies on the open tundra of Canada and I can vouch for the effectiveness of this procedure: Talk in a moderate, nonthreatening tone to the bear as you slowly back away. *Do not* make eye contact! Let the bear know that you made a mistake and are trying to skedaddle.

- If the bear runs toward you, interpret this as curiosity, not a charge. Remember, bears don't see very well, and they can't smell you if you're downwind.

- When the bear is within 50 feet, drop to the ground, *face down, nose in the dirt,* and clasp your hands tightly behind your head. Spread your legs wide so the bear can't turn you over easily. **Note:** Until recently the recommended method was to assume a tight fetal position, hands behind the head. I did this, and it worked for me. Discouraging bears is not an exact science!

Research by Stephen Herrero, author of *Bear Attacks: Their Causes and Avoidance,* suggests that the "face down" plan is best. Herrero found that the face is where most serious injury occurs. If the bear bites and claws you, try to remain quiet and passive. If the bear tries to flip you over, do a complete roll and maintain the face-down position. You will probably survive the attack.

In case you're wondering, "my" grizzly bear came within a dozen feet, checked me out, then hightailed it over the next hill. "Your" bear will likely do the same.

What if you see a bear who doesn't see you? Simply leave the area as quickly and as quietly as possible. It's best if you don't advertise your presence.

Polar Bears

Good luck! These are fast on the flats and they can swim 4 or 5 mph for hours on end in ice

Bears can be scary when they come into your camp. This big grizzly was just 25 feet away when the photo was snapped. Note that his ears are up and he's listening—considering his options. We "talked" for more than a minute; then he stately walked away. Along the Fond du Lac River, northwestern Saskatchewan.

Polar bears are fast on the flats, and they can swim 4 to 5 mph for hours on end in ice water. They move silently. Most people who have survived polar bear attacks said they never heard the bear or saw it coming! This photo was taken on a canoe trip at the mouth of the North Knife River where it flows into Hudson Bay.

water. They will, on rare occasions, eat human flesh. They have been known to stalk humans. Nonetheless, most polar bears will do their best to steer clear of you. It's best you do likewise. You cannot intimidate or outrun these animals. And in their habitat there is usually no place to hide. You are at their mercy.

I have had several scary polar bear encounters on my canoe trips to Hudson Bay. The most frightening was when a huge male bear slid down a muddy riverbank and followed my canoe across a rapid to the opposite bank. I quickly snubbed the canoe ashore, jumped out, and grabbed my rifle, praying I would not have to shoot. The bear swam to within a dozen feet of me, looked straight at me, then turned and continued downstream. It was quite a rush!

Some General Protective Thoughts

Bears don't like large numbers of people. Two people are more likely to be attacked than six. If a bear comes into your camp, huddle together and spread your arms wide, so as to make a large presence. Do not throw rocks at the bear, as advised in the Boundary Waters Canoe Area training film *Leave No Trace—A Wilderness Ethic.* I did this once years ago, and the bear nearly had me for dinner. Regrettably, space does not permit details.

You are safer to sleep inside a tent than on open ground, especially in grizzly country. Evidently, the big bears mistake a human in a sleeping bag for their natural food.

Women who are menstruating may be at greater risk from bear attacks, though there is no clear evidence to support this. Stephen Herrero addresses this topic in detail in his acclaimed book *Bear Attacks.* Bear-wary travelers will want to read it!

Protective Devices
Guns

Mention guns and wilderness trips in the same breath and some folks are apt to go ballistic. Still, if you're traveling among dangerous bears, it may be wise to go armed.

Shotguns

Residents of Churchill, Manitoba, who have had lots of experience with polar bears, always carry a high-powered rifle or 12-gauge shotgun when they go out on the land. If you're hiking or canoeing near Hudson Bay, especially after mid-July when the bears are off the ice—it's smart to do likewise! A 12-gauge pump-action shotgun with a short "slug barrel" is a good choice. With an average velocity of 1,470 fps and 2,888 ft. lbs of energy at the muzzle, 602-grain Brenneke Black Magic slugs are the clear choice for close-range bear encounters. No other slug compares! **Caution:** Avoid standard slugs like those used for deer hunting—they may not stop a charging bear! Again, remember that you'll probably get just one shot!

A grizzly has been sighted near this camp along the Noatak River, Alaska. The gun is a 12-gauge shotgun.

Rifles

The slim, short-barreled lever action Marlin and Winchester "Guide Guns," which are chambered for the powerful .45-70 and .450 Marlin cartridges, carry easily and stow well. My preference is a .450 Marlin Guide Gun, which I hand-load with 350-grain Swift A-frame bullets to a velocity of 1,920 fps. You don't need high-velocity at 15–20 yards. What you do need is a big heavy bullet that won't disintegrate at close range.

Handguns

It's not easy to hit a baseball-size spot on a fast-moving target with a handgun. For this reason, you're best off with a shotgun (with slugs) or high-powered rifle. However, a handgun can be useful if a bear attacks you while you're in a tent.

A bit about bullets: Be aware that most factory ammunition available at sports shops is designed for thin-skinned game like deer (it may fragment at close range if it hits a bone!) Dangerous game bullets are an absolute must!

God forbid you should ever have to shoot a bear. But if you do you better not have a misfire—a possibility if your bullets are wet from pouring rain or a boat capsize. Military ammunition is sealed against the elements; factory ammo is just "reasonably watertight." A thin layer of lacquer (clear nail polish) painted around the neck and primer of each cartridge will ensure ignition even in a torrential rain.

Bear-bangers are a popular bear-deterrent device. They are fired into the air from a single-shot, pen-sized launcher and sound like a gunshot when they explode. It's important to land/explode the "banger" between you and the bear!

If you over-shoot—and you may if you don't practice—the sound may drive the bear toward you! Bear-bangers are available at sports shops in Canada, and on the web here in the United States. Range is about 40 meters.

Firecracker Shells

Firecracker shells are fired from a 12-gauge shotgun. They explode on impact with a loud bang. They are available on the internet. **Caution:** Cracker shells can start a forest fire if they impact on dry grass!

Plastic "Stinger" Shells and Rubber Bullets are generally available only to law enforcement and wildlife management agencies. Your local police or wildlife management department may help you find them. Experiments in the Churchill area have shown that these non-lethal slugs deter bears (without injuring them) nearly 100 percent of the time.

Air Horn

A compressed gas air horn like that used on small boats can be useful. I know of several occasions when charging grizzlies have stopped in their tracks at the sound of one. This said, be aware that bears are curious and very smart. What most people interpret as a "charge" is often just curiosity. Once the bear determines "what you are," it will usually run away. An air horn alerts them.

Pepper Spray

Pepper spray (sometimes called "bear mace") contains 2 percent oleoresin capsaicin and derivatives—the flaming ingredients in red pepper. If properly used, it will stop nearly all bears all the time. Herrero observed that even a dangerous mother with cubs will run away from

Pepper spray is more effective on bears than guns! In one study of forty cases, 58 percent of humans who shot attacking bears received some injury. But only 8 percent of those who used pepper spray were harmed. Pepper spray *must* be available when you need it; the holster (left) is a *must!* The rubber band on the trigger provides "belt-and-suspenders" security.

Here's some pepper spray advice:

- The effect on the bear may be temporary, so leave immediately after discharging the pepper. Black bears (but not grizzlies) often develop a tolerance for the spray over time. A black bear that has been sprayed before may not be discouraged when sprayed again.

- Everyone in your group should use their spray simultaneously.

- Be sure that the wind is not blowing in your face when you spray!

- If possible, stand behind a tree when you spray. The tree will break the bear's impact or at least cause it to slow down. Fire the first blast when the bear is about 10 feet away.

- Try to spray the bear in the face when its mouth is open or it is inhaling.

- Don't practice with your pepper spray (or spray tents, canoes, or other objects with it) in hopes of repelling bears. The bears don't like to be sprayed with pepper, but they do like the taste of it.

- If you must field-test a can of pepper spray, wash it thoroughly with soap and water afterward and clean the nozzle with rubbing alcohol before you take it on a camping trip. The slightest pepper residue will attract bears. Better yet, buy a "practice can" (it doesn't contain pepper) to perfect your aim.

the spray more than 80 percent of the time. Herrero did not find a single case where spraying a bear with pepper enraged it and made it more aggressive.

The large, 1-pound can sprays up to 30 feet; pocket-size models go half as far and deliver less pepper. Get the largest can you can find! A belt holster with a fast release is essential. Bear mace won't do you any good if it's locked away in your pack or dangling from a belt clip you can't quickly unsnap.

Pepper spray is legal in Canada. Still, your spray may be confiscated if the customs official believes you have no need for it. Say you'll be camping in bear country and you should have no problem. Counter Assault and Pepper Power are the most popular brands. Get the largest size possible (at least 8 ounces/230 grams) so you'll have enough pepper for several shots. Concealable, personal-size pepper spray containers are illegal in Canada.

Guns or pepper spray? Dominic Domenici, a US Fish and Wildlife Service officer, believes that pepper spray is far more effective than guns. He says that in one study examining forty cases, 58 percent of humans who shot attacking bears in Wyoming and Montana (outside national parks) received some injury by the bears. But only 8 percent of those who used pepper spray were harmed.

P.S. "Bear mace" works even better on human attackers than on bears! This said, be aware that pepper spray is not 100 percent reliable. Studies suggest that it may not work against enraged animals or seriously starved ones that are determined to eat your food (or you!). And it may not discourage a drug-enraged human attacker who is bent on destruction.

Always remember:

- Never approach a fresh kill or cubs.

- Don't sleep in fishing clothes. Clean fish away from camp. Dispose of fish entrails in the water; wash slime off your boat; establish kitchens downwind of camps.

- Wear a hat or bandanna when cooking to reduce the accumulation (and smell) of grease in your hair. Freeze-dried foods are relatively odorless.

- Never feed a bear.

- If you see a bear in the distance but the bear doesn't see you, retreat quietly. Calling attention to yourself could mark you as a target.

Electric Bear Fence

I've spent thousands of nights in bear country and I've never had a serious problem. Still, sleeping out when bears are about is very frightening for some people. Perhaps the most restful solution is to surround your camp with an electric bear fence. They range in size from just big enough to surround a small tent to large enough to enclose a camp. A basic backpacking model will weigh about 3 pounds and emit about 6,000 volts when touched—enough to discourage the biggest bear. Prices start at about $250 for a "tent size" model. Small fences are generally powered by D-cell batteries. Larger units may use six- or twelve-volt batteries. There are even some solar-powered options. Type "electric bear fence" on your internet search engine and you'll be deluged with choices.

The "Bear Shock" Electric Fence from UDAP Industries (www.bearspray.com) really works! The model pictured here weighs less than four pounds and encloses a 27 x 27-foot area.
Mark Matheny

A Final Note

Desk-bound environmentalists would have you believe that all wild animals are harmless, while Rambo survivalists will suggest otherwise. Facts indicate that you are more at risk when crossing a four-lane highway than in a face-to-face encounter with a bear. Nonetheless, some critters, like some people, are plainly crazy and quite unpredictable. So beware of the small percentage of bears who don't share your live-and-let-live philosophy. Don't overreact to bear encounters; just follow the recommended guidelines. And be aware that you are much safer in seldom-traveled wilderness than in heavily used national parks where bears are used to the sight of people and the taste of their garbage.

For more information about bears, refer to the recommended reading list in appendix A.

Ax

The trend today is against the use of axes in the backcountry. The argument is that they are more often used to deface green trees and injure people than to produce firewood. In truth, it is not the tool that is dangerous, it is the person who wields it. Outdoor experts value a good sharp ax. They know it is much simpler to produce fire after a weeklong rain if a splitting tool of some sort is available.

What size ax? Old-time camping books suggest use of the full-length to three-quarter ax under the guise that these are safer than the short hand ax (hatchet). Hogwash! A properly used hand ax is the safest of all edged tools. It is lighter and more compact than a large ax, and when used in conjunction with a folding saw, it will produce all the camp wood you need with surprisingly little effort.

The author's favorite Gransfors axes, from top to bottom: small forest axe, wildlife hatchet, mini–belt hatchet.

In case you're wondering, my favorite axes are those built by Gransfors Bruk of Sweden. Every ax is hand- and hammer-forged on century-old machines and hardened to Rockwell 57C, which is harder than US axes and as hard as most good knives. Each completed ax (a work of art!) proudly bears the initials of its maker. If you cut your own firewood, consider the Gransfors splitting ax—it is superior to any US–made maul.

The 11-ounce Gransfors mini-hatchet is my favorite for solo camping. It will outcut most axes twice its size!

Also, check out the Council Tool US-made axes. This company has been making fine axes and fire-fighting tools since 1886. Their Wood-Craft Camp Carver, with 16" curved handle is exquisite!

Using an Ax

Here are the rules for safe, efficient use of the hand ax:

1. Saw wood to be split into 12-inch lengths (see the Saw section).

2. Use the hand ax as a *splitting wedge.* Do not chop with it! The folding saw performs all cutting functions.

3. Set the ax head lightly into the end grain of the wood. One person holds the tool while a friend pounds it through with a chunk of log. When splitting very thick logs (more than 6 inches), take multiple splittings off the edges.

4. *Safety concerns:* Hold the ax solidly with both hands. Allow the log hammer to do all the work.

To Produce Kindling

Kindling splits easiest from the end grain, a process that's made simpler and safer if you use a stick of wood to hold the upright in place.

Sharpening: You'll need a flat-mill file and a coarse (soft) natural or synthetic sharpening stone. A fine stone is required if you want a razor edge. I use the coarse stone dry (no lubricant), but I lubricate the fine hone with WD-40 or kerosene. Diamond stones should be lubricated with water. It is important to keep the hone scrupulously clean by frequently flushing its surface with light oil or water, as the case may be (don't mix them!), to remove grit. If the lubricant becomes cloudy, it's time to flush it clean. If you don't, the suspended filings will dull the edge.

Large-pore carborundum, aluminum oxide, and diamond hones are best used dry or lubricated with water. Thick cutting oils just gum up fine-grained Arkansas and Wachita stones. I lubricate these with WD-40 or kerosene. For more tips on sharpening stones, see the

Kindling splits easiest from the end grain, a process that's made simpler and safer if you use a stick of wood ("keeper stick") to hold the upright in place.

Use this method to safely split short logs with a hand ax. Hold ax handle firmly with *both* hands while a friend uses a log chunk to pound the head on through.

discussion about sharpening hones in the Knives section of this book.

Sharpening procedure:

1. Drive two pegs into the ground about 4 inches apart, or use a peg and log chunk as illustrated (Figure A-1). File perpendicular to the edge. A file guard (tin can lid with hole punched in center) placed over the rat-tail handle is recommended to prevent cutting fingers.

2. File one edge (one side of the blade) uniformly until a burr appears on the opposite edge. The burr is hard to see but easy to feel with a finger. Then file the burred edge until a burr develops on the other side of the blade (the side you first filed).

3. Then switch to the coarse stone. For greatest safety, hold the ax blade in the palm of one hand and use a circular motion of the stone. Hone each edge uniformly until all the burrs are gone.

4. Check for nicks: Slide a smooth wood or plastic stick *very lightly* along the sharpened edge—you will feel the slightest nick. If the edge feels butter smooth, you're done.

Figure A-1. Sharpening an ax

If you want a razor-fine edge—though not essential on a working ax—switch to the fine stone and hone the knife's edge perpendicular (no circular motion) to the stone's edge as is recommended for sharpening knives (see photo on page 106).

Care of the ax: Axes are forged from carbon steel so they must be kept clean, dry, and rust free. A small amount of gasoline or naphtha (Coleman fuel) will remove pitch and wood stains. Keep ax heads oiled or greased when not in use. The best rust preventative is RIG (Rust Inhibiting Grease) Universal, available from sports and gun shops. Edged tools coated with RIG may be stored for years without rusting.

Blueing the head: Most axes have painted heads to minimize rust. For ease of maintenance and beauty, grind off the paint, buff the head, and apply cold gun blue (available at most hardware and sports shops) to the bright metal. The ax head will develop a mildly rust-resistant blue-black sheen, which is instantly restored by dabbing on more gun blue.

Sheathing the ax: Sheaths that come with edged tools are usually too thin and flimsy for practical field service. Make your own as follows:

1. Obtain two pieces of ⅛-inch-thick sole leather from a leather company or your shoemaker.

2. Soak the leather in warm water until it is soft, then cut two matching pieces, as shown in the photo on the next page.

3. Contact-cement (I suggest Weldwood contact cement) a ¼-inch-wide strip of leather all around the edge. Then rivet on a buckle or Velcro security strap and contact-cement the sheath halves together. Rivet the edges of the sheath for

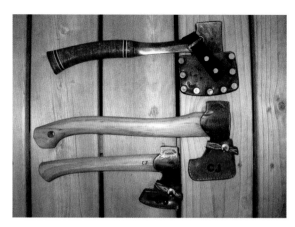

The heavy sole-leather sheaths shown here require less than 1 hour to make. Leather and rivets can be purchased by mail from Tandy Leather Company.

greatest security, or have your shoemaker sew it for you. Two-piece hammer drive rivets can be purchased from any leather-supply store. Hand axes are never carried on the belt so no belt loop is necessary.

Making a permanently bonded head: Camping books traditionally suggest that you occasionally soak the heads of wood-handled axes in water or oil to expand the handle eye so the head won't come loose. The "water treatment" is dreadfully temporary; oil works only marginally better. Here's a permanent solution:

1. Use a very blunt screwdriver or edge of a flat file as a wedge to drive the factory-installed wooden wedge tightly into the handle eye. You should be able to sink the factory wedge a full ¼ inch to ⅓ inch below the level of the steel ax head.

2. Drive a small steel wedge solidly into the heart of the sunken wooden wedge. The steel wedge will not go in all the way, but its head must be below the level of the steel ax head.

3. Fill the void (trench) with slow-cure or 5-minute epoxy. You now have a permanently bonded head that will never come loose.

The Case for the Full-Size Ax

For serious woodshed splitting, you can make a case for a full-size ax with a 3½-pound head and a 32- to 36-inch handle—but only if you don't have a splitting maul! Given the excellent saws and splitting mauls we have today, the big ax has pretty much outlived its usefulness.

If you want something lighter and smaller but with nearly as much power as a full-size ax, consider the three-quarter ax. This size ax is very useful for clearing trails and canoe portages.

"Chopping" Deadwood with the Big Ax

A large-frame bucksaw is far superior to any ax for cutting wood. But if you lose your saw or break the blade, you should know how to use an ax. Here's a safe, efficient way to chop dead, downed wood with a full-size ax.

1. Face the downed log and grasp the ax firmly at the pommel of the handle with one hand. Place the other hand just behind the head. Lift the ax hip-level high, then start your swing. The handle should slide through your "bit" hand (hand closest to the blade) as the blade comes down.

2. Chop three times on one side, then reverse hand positions and chop three times on the other side (Figure A-2). This should release the chip, the width of which should roughly equal the diameter of the log. Note that if you don't change hands when you reverse the blade angle, the bit will

Figure A-2. Change sides and hands every three strokes.

Figure A-3. Always chop limbs from the underside.

fly across your body—a dangerous and inefficient situation.

3. When you've cut halfway through the log, rotate it 180 degrees so the ax blade won't break through to the ground where it can nick and dull.

Splitting Logs

Do not set logs upright on the ground to split them—the ax may bury itself into the ground and strike a rock. Instead, chop out a level "splitting" platform and split the upright log

from the end grain. Some camping texts suggest that for safety's sake, you should split logs from the side, not the end. I disagree. If you can't hit the center of an upright log with an ax, you need practice or a more accurate friend!

Always chop limbs from the underside, as illustrated in Figure A-3.

Where to Store Your Ax

Keep your ax sheathed and in a pack when it's not being used. Never leave an ax stuck in a log—someone could trip over it! It's better to place the ax on its side, blade tucked under a heavy log or rock, as illustrated in Figure A-4.

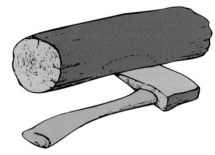

Figure A-4. The safest way to store an unsheathed ax is with the blade under a log.

B

Baking

Reflector ovens and Dutch ovens are traditional for backcountry baking. However, both require a good hot fire and/or glowing coals. Modern campers rely almost exclusively on stoves for all their cooking, so the oven should reflect this change in style.

Traditional Dutch ovens (left) and aluminum reflector ovens (right) produce mouthwatering breads. But they are heavy and bulky, and they require a good hot fire and/or glowing coals.
David Wescott

Commercial Ovens

A number of commercial ovens are designed for use with trail stoves. But all add bulk and weight to your kit—they're just one more thing to lug along.

Improvised Ovens

Here are some baking tools and ideas for those who want to go light.

The Gelatin-Mold Oven

You'll need a wide-ring aluminum gelatin mold and a cover of some sort (Figure B-1).

Figure B-1. The gelatin mold oven

1. Grease the mold and put your batter into the outside ring. Decrease the suggested amount of water by up to 25 percent for faster baking.

2. Bring the stove to its normal operating temperature, then reduce the heat to the lowest possible blue-flame setting. Center the gelatin mold over the burner head, top it with a high cover (necessary to allow sufficient room for the baked goods to rise), and relax. Cooking times are nearly identical to those suggested in the baking directions.

3. Cool the mold by setting it in a shallow pan of water for a few moments, then pop out your entree.

Tips for using the gelatin-mold oven:

- Wind reduces the efficiency of the gelatin mold, so use a good wind shield around your stove.

- Large-burner stoves like the Coleman Peak 1 and double-burner models may burn the edges of the bakestuff. An electric stove burner shield—available for a few dollars at most supermarkets—will eliminate this problem. Simply place the shield under the gelatin mold. The air space between the shield and mold bottom will prevent burning. The large-size burner shield will fit large-ring gelatin molds perfectly.

Other uses of the gelatin mold: Your gelatin mold also may be used as a steamer to rehydrate dried fruits and vegetables. Here's how:

1. Place dried fruit or beans in the gelatin mold ring with about two tablespoons of water.

2. Fill a stainless-steel Sierra cup with water and set it on the chimney of the mold.

3. Cover the mold and cup and turn the stove to medium high. Boiling water from the Sierra cup will vaporize and steam your fruit or vegetables to tenderness in a fraction of the time of simple soaking. It's the steam that does the trick.

You can also fire the gelatin mold with a small (2⅝-ounce) can of Sterno, or HEET (yellow can), a small tin can filled with rubbing alcohol. Don't use the large-size cans of Sterno—they put out too much heat. To ensure ample draft, use a pair of sticks to prop the ring about ½ inch above the Sterno. You must ventilate the high

cover with a matchstick or the Sterno (or alcohol) will go out.

You may also use the gelatin mold as a pot support on your stove. To heat a single cup of water on your trail stove, set a water-filled Sierra cup into the gelatin mold chimney. A cover will speed heating and save stove fuel.

Double-Pan Method of Baking

Use this method if you don't have a gelatin mold. You'll need two nesting skillets, a high cover, and a half-dozen small nails or stones.

1. Evenly scatter some nails or stones onto the surface of the large (bottom) frying pan. Don't use stones from a lakeshore or riverbank as the trapped moisture could cause those stones to explode when heated. Small sticks, or tiny balls rolled from aluminum foil, may be used in place of nails or stones (Figure B-2).

2. Place your bakestuff into the small frying pan and set it on top of the nails (the two pans must be separated by nails or stones to prevent the food's burning).

3. Cover the unit and place it on your stove. Use the lowest possible blue-flame setting.

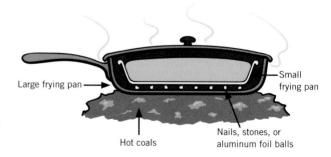

Figure B-2. The double-pan oven

Warning: Don't use this method with a thin aluminum skillet on the bottom—you'll burn a hole right through it!

Bannock (Camp Bread)

Bannock is bread that is traditionally baked before an open fire in a large straight-sided skillet. Bannock is fast and easy to make—no need for special ovens, aluminum foil, pot covers, or baking thermometers. Just grease the skillet, press in the dough, fry lightly for a minute or three, then prop the pan before a cheery blaze as illustrated in Figure B-3. No wondering "when it's done"—the beauty of bannock is that you watch it bake.

Bannock and bacon for breakfast. What could be better?
David Wescott

Figure B-3. When the bannock is solid, prop the frying pan before the fire at a 60-degree angle.

Ingredients: In the old days sourdough was the preferred ingredient. Now most campers use commercial mixes that are handier but less tasty. Here are three of my favorite recipes.

World's Best Bannock

On a recent canoe trip down the Rio Grande in Texas, my friend Rob Kesselring prepared what I think is the world's best traditional bannock. For several years Rob lived and worked in Canada at a Chipewyan community above the sixtieth parallel. He learned how to make bannock while winter camping with the natives. These are his instructions.

"No other camp food is as relished on a long trip as bannock. Commercial mixes can't compare," Rob said.

The ingredients are simple: white flour, lard, baking powder, and salt. You need a stout skillet and a big, blazing fire. Do not premix your ingredients. The premix will lose its lifting properties and could even explode. Bushcraft expert Mors Kochanski has documented cases of exploding bannocks that were made with bad baking powder.

For each bannock, you need a pile of flour the size of your fist, enough baking powder to cover the inside of your palm, and salt enough to balance on your thumbnail. Don't double the recipe—you risk burn on the outside, goo on the inside.

Procedure: Place the skillet directly on the fire. Spoon in a big dollop of lard. It should look like an iceberg on an inky sea. When the lard is melted and almost smoking, remove the skillet from the fire and pour 90 percent of the lard into a depression in the flour mixture. Next, add a splash of water and knead the dough ball until its consistency is uniform and just slightly elastic. *Tip:* The texture will be better if you cut in soft lard rather than melted.

Heat the skillet until it is smoking hot. Then remove it from the heat and spread the bannock out in the hot pan. Then, prop the skillet up facing the fire at a steep angle, with just enough back lean to keep the bannock in the pan. When the bannock turns golden brown, flip it over and cook the other side.

Wilderness expert Rob Kesselring prepares "fry-bread bannock" over an open fire in the Boundary Waters Canoe Area of Minnesota. Rob Kesselring

There are four don'ts:

1. *Don't* substitute whole wheat flour for white. Your bannock won't rise as high and it will taste like a cross between pie crust and Wheat Thins.

2. *Don't* substitute vegetable shortening for fresh, sweet hog lard. Smell the lard you buy; it should smell sweet, not sour.

3. *Don't* use a flimsy aluminum or steel fry pan. If this is what you have or if you're cooking on a trail stove, fry the bread, don't bake it before a fire. For frying, use less lard in the mixture and more in the pan. A dollop of dough about the size of a Ping-Pong ball and flattened like a burger is perfect. Many campers prefer the fried-bread treatment to traditional flame-baked.

4. *Don't* prepare your bannock before a wimpy fire. You need a big "hanging fire" (high burning, airy blaze) that reflects heat deep into the pan.

Bannock can be enhanced with raisins or wild berries. Cranberries are best. Raspberries and blueberries are hard to knead in without tainting the color. The traditional (and I think tastiest) way to eat bannock is with fresh lard and salt on top.

Easy Scratch Bannock

At the outset, let me make it perfectly clear that this recipe cannot compare to Rob Kesselring's "world's best" bannock. This "easy scratch" method is for those who travel light and are in a hurry.

In a plastic bag or a bowl, mix 2 cups of flour, 3 rounded teaspoons of baking powder,

1 heaping tablespoon of nonfat dry milk, and 1 teaspoon of salt.

To this, add 5 tablespoons of liquid margarine or canola oil and enough cold water to make a stiff dough. Work the dough just enough to mix the ingredients. If you knead too long, the bannock will be tough.

Now mix in 2 tablespoons of honey and/or a few spoonfuls of blueberry jam. Sprinkle cinnamon and sugar and/or brown sugar on top. Creatively lace the surface of the bannock with liquid margarine (optional). Bake as directed below.

Baking the bannock: Gently fry the bannock on very low heat (on a mix of hot ashes and coals) until it is firm—about 3 to 5 minutes. If you prop the bannock before the bottom is solid, the dough may slide out of the pan!

Prop the pan at a steep angle to the flames and relax. In about 20 minutes the bread will start turning golden brown. The bannock is done when a wood sliver comes out clean.

Tips: Don't make the batter too thick—½ inch thick is about right. Use a frying pan with relatively straight sides so the dough won't slide out when propped before the fire; avoid thin aluminum skillets, which may warp, and Teflon-coated ones, which may flake from the heat.

Serious Sourdough Bannock

Put about 2 cups of flour, 1 tablespoon sugar, and ½ cake of yeast into a plastic bucket with a loose-fitting lid. Add enough warm water to make a pancake-like batter. Let the mixture sit at room temperature about 3 days until it "sours."

Making the bannock: Remove about 1 cup of well-stirred liquid and place it in a mixing bowl. To keep the unused mix from oversouring, replace the amount of batter you take with an equal amount of fresh flour and water.

Add about ¼ teaspoon baking soda (the secret is in the soda—don't add too much!). Mix thoroughly. A chemical change will occur and the mixture will bubble up into a meringue-like fluff. Add a dash of salt, about a tablespoon of sugar to taste (don't add too much!), a little melted shortening, and enough flour to make a stiff dough. Make a stiff "working" dough for bread or rolls; thin it out for pancakes. Options are endless.

You can keep sourdough almost forever if you keep diluting it with fresh flour and water. The mix will oversour (possibly explode—or at best, ooze out of your bucket) if you don't "use it and dilute it" on a regular basis. Refrigerating the working mix stops the chemical reaction. Sourdough can be dried and stored and used to start a new mix.

Tips:

- Don't store sourdough in an aluminum pot: A chemical reaction will occur that will adversely affect the flavor. Stainless steel and stoneware are OK.

- Butter and margarine have better flavor than cooking oil.

- The most convenient way to carry sourdough on the trail is to mix ½ cup of starter with flour until you get a soft ball. Roll the ball in more flour and store it in a plastic bag half filled with flour. This should keep a week or more. (Thanks to Scott Power for this useful tip, which I discovered in his delightful book *Cooking the Sourdough Way: Tips, Stoves, and Recipes*. Scott—a superb wilderness chef—developed a wealth of scrumptious recipes that you'll want to try.)

Binoculars

Binoculars are worth bringing along on wilderness canoe trips. They enable you to quickly locate portage trails and campsites on complex lakes, and they are a wonderful tool for checking rapids. A monocular is not good enough; you need two-eye depth perception for interpreting river dangers.

Boots

Today's hiker chooses the lightest, most flexible footwear he or she can find. The trend began when we quit thumbing our noses at Native peoples—American Indians and Eskimos—who routinely traveled the most difficult terrain while wearing moccasins, sandals, or no shoes at all. The coup de grace was quietly administered when American and British mountaineers were outfooted by sandal-wearing Sherpas who casually carried loads far in excess of those toted by well-heeled climbers. Specialized lightweight running shoes set the trend; featherweight hiking boots logically followed suit.

Which Boots Are for You?

There are boots of all leather, leather and nylon, pure (synthetic) rubber, or leather and rubber combinations. There's also a diversity of unique winter wear. Here are the differences:

Combination leather and nylon boots are light, supple, comfortable, and most popular. They require almost no break-in. The best models are suitable for the most strenuous off-trail applications, with the exception of rock climbing or boulder hiking. Unfortunately, most of

these combo boots cannot be resoled when they wear out—a factor to consider if you'll subject them to heavy use.

Supple, *all-leather boots* that can be resoled (check them out, most can't) are the sturdiest, most reliable, and probably the best buy. All-leather boots will outlast leather/fabric combos by decades.

Gore-Tex liners: Some of the best boots (especially leather/fabric ones) come with liners of waterproof Gore-Tex. Though Gore-Tex liners perform admirably over the short haul, they may not be reliable in the long run. If the Gore-Tex liner in a fabric boot fails, you're

Chota mukluks, which the author prefers for canoeing, are no longer manufactured. NRS Boundary Boots are similar and excellent.

doomed to having wet feet—an instant displeasure the moment you walk through dew-moistened grass. And these boots are hot! Yes, Gore-Tex does "breathe" but not very well. If you flat move out when you hike, you won't like Gore-Tex boots at all. Traditional all-leather boots can be made acceptably water resistant by a judicious application of wax or grease, but fabric ones cannot.

Despite convincing advertising, Gore-Tex boots have not proven reliable enough for day-in, day-out use in wet country. And neither has any brand of all-leather boots. If you want truly waterproof footwear, follow the lead of lobster fishermen and Alaskan guides and select knee-high rubber barn boots or green "Wellies," as the British call them.

Also, check out the Chota and NRS line of waterproof neoprene boots. Regrettably, my once favorite Chota Quicklace Mukluks are no longer manufactured. I'm now hooked on knee-high NRS Boundary Boots which are similar, and excellent. They are my favorite for cold water wilderness canoeing. Hip-high Chota hippies work well for trips that mix hiking with over-the-knee wading.

Neoprene is a good insulator, so these boots also work well for active winter sports like snowshoeing. For occasional wet weather—stepping in and out of water—my vote goes to the leather/rubber Maine Hunting Shoe offered by L.L. Bean, which also comes in women's and children's sizes.

Knee-high Tingley rubber overshoes are the choice of many wilderness canoeists who must alternately paddle, portage, and wade in cold water. Tingleys are very flexible; they roll to fist size and their soft, nonaggressive rubber soles won't slip on wet rocks. These boots are actually better for rock hopping than most wet shoes that are built for the purpose. Lightweight Tingley boots are sold in stores that service construction workers and other outdoor professionals. They are inexpensive.

Wear wool socks inside canvas sneakers and Tingleys over the sneakers, and you're set for an arctic canoe expedition or a sloppy walk through a swamp. For transitional cold in near-freezing, sloppy conditions, substitute wool-felt snowmobile boot liners for the running

For occasional wet weather—stepping in and out of water—LL Bean Maine Hunting Shoes ("Bean Boots") are hard to beat.
Mike Rapatz

Tingley boots are flexible, waterproof, and inexpensive, and they won't slip on wet rocks. They are popular with construction workers and other outdoor professionals. Wear your tennis shoes inside the Tingleys. In cold weather substitute wool-felt snowmobile boot liners for the running shoes.
Heather Novaday Maier

shoes. Be sure to wear warm insoles inside (or under) the felt boot liners.

Tips:

- Wear two pairs of wool socks—lightweight liner and medium weight—inside your boots. Wear the lightweight liner inside out, so the abrasive seams (which can produce hot spots and subsequently blisters) will not touch your skin.

- Old-fashioned sneakers were made from cotton canvas that provided good ventilation. Modern tennies are mostly plastic, which gets dreadfully hot. Here's a cool tip from Rod Johnson, a world-class hiker/mountaineer and the owner of Midwest Mountaineering in Minneapolis: Rod says your feet will stay a lot cooler if you cut the hot foam tongue out of your trail shoes. It really works! And surprisingly, you don't feel the pressure of laces at all. This trick cools down everyday running shoes too.

Barefoot shoes: Modern hikers prefer lightweight, synthetic shoes (which are basically beefed-up sneakers) to old-fashioned leather boots. "Light hikers" are more comfortable than heavy boots and they do less damage to trails. But as the lightweight trend accelerates, some hikers are going to the dark side, by choosing "barefoot shoes," which are like wearing no shoes at all. Merrell began the trend with their Vibram FiveFingers shoes, which have individual toe pockets. Users say they provide a truer barefoot experience than similar shoes without toes.

Some years ago, Rod Johnson gave me a pair of his favorite shoes—Merrell Bare Access Trail Gloves. Rod is an under-sung wilderness expert who has hiked and kayaked all over the world, often going for weeks at a time with minimal gear. He wears Trail Gloves year-round, one pair barefoot in summer, another with socks in winter. The shoes are feather light—about 7 ounces each in my size nine. My feet feel like they're wearing nothing at all. I was skeptical about wearing them because for years I've battled a bad case of plantar fasciitis in both feet. Custom orthotics didn't help much; I thought my hiking days were over. When the problem recently (miraculously!) vanished, I was advised by my podiatrist to never go barefoot again, and to always wear supportive shoes!

Could the doctor be wrong? I wore the Merrells for a weekend—no problems. Then a full week and all was fine. I kept checking for signs of the old plantar fasciitis but there were none. My feet were never tired, bruised, or chafed. Normal shoes, even my beloved Crocs, now feel heavy and awkward. I'm discovering what African runners have known all along— that barefoot is best.

How to Break in New Boots

The traditional method: Wear boots an hour or two each day until they fit properly. This painful procedure takes about a week.

The preferred method: Fill each new boot full of lukewarm tap water. Allow the water to soak in for about 15 seconds, then pour it out. Now put on the boots (with the correct socks, of course) and walk them dry—takes about 3 hours and results in about 50 percent break-in. Wear the boots around the house for about an hour each day for a week following the water treatment, and they'll be sufficiently broken in for hiking. This procedure works better with leather boots than with those made from synthetic fabrics.

Care of Boots

Sponge dirt and grime off leather boots with saddle soap and water. Work up a good lather, then remove the suds with a damp sponge. Gentle sponging with plain soap and water is the best way to clean the fabric panels on leather/fabric boots.

Allow boots to dry thoroughly, away from heat, then apply an oil-based preservative like mink oil (with or without silicone) to oil-tanned leather. Apply a wax-based compound like Sno-Seal to chrome-tanned leather. Waxes do a much better job of waterproofing than oils and greases. Fortunately, waxes are compatible with oils and greases, if used sparingly. You can improve the weather resistance of oil-tanned boots considerably by topping the base oil (which should be well absorbed into the leather pores) with wax-based compounds.

To apply boot grease or wax: Melt the preservative (leave the tin in hot sunlight for a few minutes) and apply it to lightly warmed leather with your bare hands. Rub in thoroughly and allow boots to "sunbathe" until the excess preservative is absorbed. Repeat application of the product until it is no longer absorbed by the leather. A dry rag may be used to remove excess grease that remains after the second application.

To dry wet boots: Never put boots too near a fire (if you can't hold your hand near the flame for 30 seconds, it's too hot for your boots!) or in an oven to dry them. You can speed the drying of wet boots by stuffing them with fire-warmed pebbles placed inside socks.

Always carry some boot wax in a small poly bottle on all your outings. Apply it frequently in wet weather.

Removing mold from boots and leather gear: Boots and leather goods stored in damp areas (basements) are sure to mold. The best way to remove mold is with a 25 percent solution of vinegar, household ammonia, or oxygen bleach, which will go deep into the pores of the leather and kill fungal hyphae. Thoroughly rinse the treated leather with clear water and allow it to dry before you apply preservatives. Sunlight kills fungus too, so give your leather goods frequent airings outdoors.

To improve the warmth of boots: Install warm insoles. The best all-around choice is probably

⅜- to ½-inch-thick wool-felt snowmobile-boot insoles (80 percent wool, 20 percent polyester), but closed-cell neoprene or EVA (ethyl vinyl acetate) insoles are less compressible and warmer. However, closed-cell foam insoles may be too hot under some conditions. You should have at least two pairs of insoles for your winter boots. Change insoles every day.

Tip: Punch some holes in your synthetic insoles and your boots will be much cooler to wear.

Oversocks: If your boots are too small to accept warm insoles, try wearing thick wool socks over them. Of course, the sock bottoms will quickly wear through, but what is left will add considerable warmth.

Winter Boots

Military surplus rubber "Mickey Mouse" boots are among the warmest mass-produced boots you can buy. However, they are very uncomfortable for walking. Pure-white "bunny" boots—another surplus item—which are made from wool felt, are wonderfully warm and are great for hiking. Wear rubbers or Tingley boots over them in wet snow.

Canadian Sorel boots, or fabric-top snowmobile boots, are the preferred choice for one-day use but become damp after a good workout. The felt liners in these boots must be changed daily or frostbite may result.

Mukluks are roomy knee-high moccasins that are designed for snow. They have a canvas or soft leather outer shell and a wool or synthetic liner that is usually removable. Traditional Native American–style mukluks, like those made in Ely, Minnesota, by Patti Steger Holmberg, are by far the warmest, most comfortable, and breathtakingly beautiful

Traditional canvas mukluks like these by Steger, which are made in Minnesota, are the warmest, lightest, most breathable and comfortable of all winter boots. Left: Short (11-inch-high) all moose-hide mukluk. Right: Tall (18-inch-high) canvas top/moose-hide bottom mukluk. The soles of these boots are waterproof.

winter footwear you can buy. World-famous arctic explorer Will Steger swears by Steger mukluks, as do most sled dog racers and snowshoers. There are more than a dozen styles of Steger mukluks and moccasins.

Foot wraps: The late Gil Phillips, known by the Boy Scouts as the "foam man," perfected the use of low-cost open-cell polyurethane foam for clothing, sleeping bags, and footwear. Gil and his Scouts relied on foam "everything" for their subzero encampments. Gil's proven system is recommended by the Boy Scouts of America and is described in detail in the *Boy Scouts' Fieldbook* and in *Okpik: Cold Weather Camping,* which are available from Boy Scout suppliers. Here's the basic plan:

1. You'll need a loose-fitting canvas or nylon mukluk (military-surplus models are sometimes available) and two circular pieces of soft, 1-inch-thick open-cell polyurethane foam, like that used for pillow padding.

2. Fold the foam in half, then quarter it, as illustrated in Figure B-4. Pull aside an outside foam layer and put your foot inside with the single foam layer at your heel. Wrap the double layers of foam right and left around your foot and insert both foot and foam into the mukluk. On long trips dry and refold the foam liner every few days. Foam foot wraps are incredibly warm, even without socks.

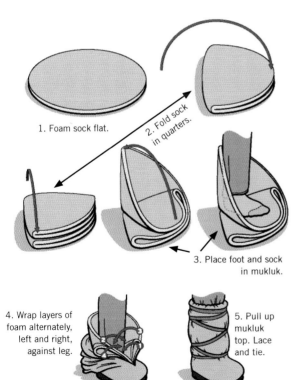

1. Foam sock flat.

2. Fold sock in quarters.

3. Place foot and sock in mukluk.

4. Wrap layers of foam alternately, left and right, against leg.

5. Pull up mukluk top. Lace and tie.

Figure B-4. Making a foot wrap

Tip: Two thin felt liners are warmer than one thick one. In 2003 I attended an arctic survival school in Spitsbergen, Norway (latitude 74 degrees north). Temperatures plunged to –30°F. Our winter survival instructor wore three ⅛-inch-thick wool-felt liners (nested one inside the other) and double felt insoles inside his knee-high mukluks. His feet were never cold, even after hours of standing around on glacial ice.

Tip: To dry damp wool-felt liners in below-freezing weather, allow them to freeze, then knock off the ice crystals. Place them inside (at the foot of) your sleeping bag when you retire. They should be dry enough to wear by morning.

Boots in Summary

- For relatively dry three-season use, traditional lightweight all-leather boots are best. Combination leather and fabric boots tend to be less waterproof but lighter, more comfortable, and cooler.

- For mixed (wet and dry) conditions, try leather top/rubber bottom shoepacs like the traditional L.L. Bean Maine Hunting Shoes. "Bean boots" are the most popular boots in the world. Millions of pairs have been sold . . . and resoled. These are a good choice for fall hiking and hunting in the wetland states.

- Neoprene NRS Boundary Boots and Tingley rubber boots, worn over sneakers, are good for boating; they provide good traction for rock hopping. Tingleys fit more loosely than pull-on rubber barn boots—they may come off your feet if you wear them in sticky mud. NRS Boundary Boots are warm enough for mild winter use.

- Mickey Mouse boots are best for standing around. Sorels or fabric-top snowmobile boots work well if the felt liners are changed every day.

- White bunny boots or felt-lined canvas mukluks (with warm insoles) are a good cold-weather combination for dry snow.

- Foam foot wraps really work, even in severe weather.

Bottles and Food Tubes

Various sizes and shapes of polyethylene bottles are commonly used by campers to store liquid and semiliquid foods like jam, peanut butter, pancake syrup, and cooking oil. Most of the plastic containers on supermarket shelves are too flimsy for strenuous camping trips; you need thick-walled, tough containers for serious backwoods use.

Nalgene bottles are the most reliable containers for foodstuffs. They were originally designed for packaging chemicals, so you know they're bombproof!

By far the most reliable containers for foodstuffs are Nalgene bottles. They were originally designed for packaging chemicals, so you know they're bombproof. Nalgene containers are positively leakproof and deservedly expensive. All the best camping stores carry them.

Free bottles (Figure B-5): Hospitals and clinics once threw out plastic "sterile water for irrigation" (SWIG) bottles after a single use. You could get a box full for the asking. SWIG bottles were tough as nails, didn't absorb odors, and had graduated markings and a ring for hanging. Now the medical community has largely switched to sterile plastic bladders, which are useless for camping. But some clinics still use these bottles so it's worth a check. **Note:** New 250ml, 500ml, and 1,000ml bottles are available on the internet from BoundTree Medical. Type "Sterile Water For Irrigation" into their search box. The 1,000ml Bottle is item #357139. These bottles are very inexpensive.

Almost every liquid—from soda to pancake syrup—now comes in plastic bottles. The bottles, but not the flip-up tops, are generally reliable. Either replace the tops with screw caps (available at wine stores) or melt the pop-up openings shut in the flame of your trail stove. Finally, don't overlook liter-sized plastic soda bottles.

Plastic food containers will retain odors after use. A thorough washing won't help much, but a mixture of baking soda and water will. Allow the soda-water solution to remain in the bottles for 2 weeks and odors will all but disappear.

Plastic food tubes, which are available at camping stores, resemble large toothpaste tubes. They are commonly used to hold jam, peanut butter, and other semiliquids. The tubes are filled from the open back end and are sealed

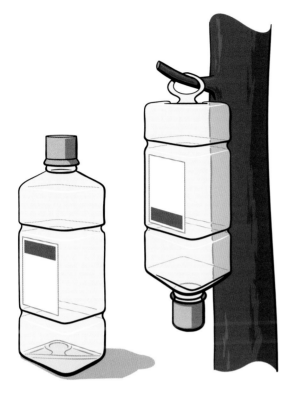

Figure B-5. Sterile water for irrigation bottles

Bugs are attracted to dark colors, especially navy blue and black. Note how the blackflies swarm on the blue wool pants but not on the yellow bag tucked into this man's belt.

with a marginally effective plastic clip. To use a food tube, unscrew the cap and squeeze the container (like a toothpaste tube). The idea sounds great but the product is unreliable, especially when the tubes are filled more than two-thirds full. Expert campers don't trust food tubes. I suggest you don't either.

Bugs—Mosquitoes, Flies, No-See-Ums, and Ticks

Colors and Biting Insects

Dark colors, especially navy blue and black, attract insects. Powder blue, yellow, mist green, white, and other light colors have a neutral or mild repelling effect. Avoid dark-blue rain suits (the most popular color)! Contrary to popular belief, red does not repel blackflies (almost nothing really repels them). Red is a fairly neutral color that neither repels nor attracts insects.

Know Your Enemies

Mosquitoes

They like to bite at dawn and dusk and just before or after a rain. They seem to like navy-blue colors more than do other insects. Air Force–blue wool pants and shirts are an abomination in the woods and are nearly impossible to wear on buggy days. Mosquitoes are mild-mannered compared to flies. Most repellents will keep them away.

Horseflies and Deerflies

Horseflies and deerflies are much larger than houseflies. They're most active at midday when the sun is up. They zoom in fast and take a quick bite, which may become infected if you don't clean it fast. Flies can bite through thin liner socks but not through thick wool ones.

Blackflies

In the northern United States and Canada, blackflies, which are about the size of rice grains, are the most dreaded pests. They're most active in the calm of dawn and dusk, and they breed in fast water—a reason why canoeists don't like to camp by rapids and falls. Big winds and temperatures below 40°F usually keep them away. Blackflies have tiny mouths so you may not feel their bite—but they leave a bloody wound that is easily infected and may swell to golf-ball size. The good news is that the worst-biting species hatch in spring and have only one generation. Adults live six to eight weeks. Most blackflies are gone by late June in the northern states and

Head nets are essential if you camp in blackfly country. Sue Harings, the author's wife, is geared up for a long portage on the buggy tundra. Hood River, Nunavut, Canada. Note "Bearbear," our stuffed toy mascot.

southern Canada. In the high arctic they hang around till the first fall frost.

Blackflies prefer the constricted areas around wrists, ankles, behind the ear, etc., and they hone in on eyes, ears, and nostrils. Only the most powerful—nearly pure Deet—repellents will discourage them, and then not much. Closely woven clothing, neck-to-toe long johns, head nets, bug jackets, and full "body armor"—like the Susie bug net, described on page 36)—are the best way to keep them at bay. Tuck your trousers into your boots or blouse them over the top with military blousing bands or elastic cords. Velcro tabs on shirt cuffs will seal your armor completely. If you don't want to get bitten in blackfly country, stay home! Nothing else really works.

Biting Midges (No-See-Ums)

They're called no-see-ums because they're so tiny they can fly through the holes in conventional mosquito netting. Their bite feels like the jab of a sharp needle. The pain goes away fast but the wound itches for some time. The tiny holes in no-see-um netting are hard to see through and they restrict ventilation. Tents that have no-see-um nets become intolerably hot on bright sunny days—when no-see-ums are about. Standard wide-mesh mosquito netting will keep no-see-ums at bay if you spray the net with repellent or permethrin.

Ticks

Watch out for deer ticks, which carry Lyme disease (see page 116), and the lone star tick, which is the host for Rocky Mountain spotted fever.

Removing an embedded tick:

1. Ticks must be on your body for a long time in order to bite. If you remove them within

6 hours, you're probably safe. A vigorous shower will remove most ticks before they dig in.

2. Don't pour gasoline, alcohol, or other chemicals over an embedded tick, and don't cover one with Vaseline or heat one with a match or cigarette: This could cause the tick to disgorge the contents of its stomach into you!

3. Do carefully scoop under the tick's body and slowly pull it from your skin. Blunt tweezers work OK if you're careful (don't twist the tweezers!). William Forgey, MD, author of *Wilderness Medicine: Beyond First Aid*, recommends the Sawyer Tick Plier (Figure B-6) for easy tick extraction.

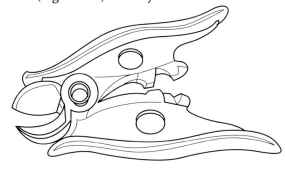

Figure B-6. Sawyer Tick Plier

4. Finally, wash the affected area with soap and water and apply an antiseptic and adhesive bandage.

Repellents and Insecticides: Your Best Hope Is Bug Dope!

Deet

The most effective repellents contain Deet—a chemical that contains N,N-diethyl-meta-toluamide. Generally, the more Deet a repellent has, the longer it works. However, too much Deet may burn sensitive skin and dissolve plastics—eyeglasses, Swiss Army knife handles, and plastic-coated fabrics. A bottle of Deet once leaked through a friend's trouser pocket. The repellent dissolved a huge swatch of his polypropylene underwear in a most embarrassing place!

No one knows for sure how much Deet is needed to keep bugs away. Everyone's body chemistry is different. However, my own experience in the Canadian bush suggests that 25 percent deet, *in a mixture with other ingredients*, will keep away most insects. The remainder of the repellent should be a soothing lotion or alcohol. Lotion is kinder to your skin and it evaporates more slowly than alcohol, so the repellent lasts much longer. Save pure Deet as a last resort for arctic rivers, where blackflies number in the billions and the lesser repellents you've tried don't work.

Caution: Children should never use pure Deet—it will burn their sensitive skin.

Repellents for dogs: Deet should not be used on animals. Instead, use biodegradable pyrethrums or permethrins. These are found in tick and flea spray, which you can get in hardware stores and western tack shops.

Permethrin

Permethrin is an insecticide. You put it on your clothes, not your skin. (Human skin metabolizes the chemical and renders it useless in a short time.) It's the best tick protection you can buy.

The agricultural-grade permethrin you get at garden shops will work, but it smells awful and it doesn't bond to fabrics. I like Sawyer's Premium Insect Repellent (it contains 0.5 percent permethrin), which is odorless, bonds well to fabrics, and lasts 6 weeks. Some clothing makers, notably ExOfficio (Buzz Off clothing) and L.L. Bean, offer clothes that are treated with permethrin—naturally, with EPA approval. The commercially treated garments contain a higher concentration of permethrin than you would normally apply yourself, so the treatment lasts longer and survives more washing cycles. Sawyer Products has an EPA-approved "military-style clothing treatment kit" that's similar to the one used by the military—you soak your clothes in the permethrin solution for 2 hours, then hang the clothes to dry. The treatment lasts through six washings.

The beauty of permethrin is that you apply it to your clothes, not your skin. And the treatment lasts a very long time. Spray your tent netting with permethrin and watch bugs die! Blackflies that are enclosed within a tent or netted tarp go nuts and crawl to the highest point, so dope these places too.

Natural Repellents

Big claims are made for "natural" insect repellents that don't contain Deet. Ingredients may include cedar oil, eucalyptus oil, tea tree oil, geranium oil, pure vanilla extract, rubbing alcohol, and spices like cinnamon, basil, thyme, garlic, catnip, spearmint, and more.

How well do these "natural" repellents work? For casual backyard use on mostly mild-mannered mosquitoes, they are adequate. But add blackflies—or hours of exposure—and you'll want Deet. Do Ben-Gay, Vicks VapoRub, and Skin So Soft lotion repel mosquitoes? Yes, but not very well and not for long. In an article entitled "Insect Repellents, Quick Ratings," *Consumer Reports* (July 2019) found that the effectiveness of a repellent largely depends on how much Deet it contains. Generally, more Deet is better. The table below compares some findings. The higher the score, the more effective the repellent.

Tip: If you're in the north woods and don't have bug dope, peel strips of bark from spruce trees and rub the inner bark on your skin. Naturally, this will damage the tree, so please strip bark only in an emergency. Or cover exposed areas with mud.

Build a Skin Barrier with Sunblock

Kurt Avery, president of Sawyer Products, suggests you rub sunblock deep into your skin, wait 10 minutes, then apply the insect repellent.

Product	Active Ingredient	Type	Effectiveness Score
Deep Woods Off Sportsmen	Deet 98%	pump	92
3M Ultrathon	Deet 34%	cream	72
Ben's 30 Wilderness Formula	Deet 30%	pump	67
Cutter Backwoods	Deet 25%	aerosol	70
Repel Sportsman Formula	Deet 20%	cream	55
Cutter All Family	Deet 7%	pump	32
Skin-so-soft Bug Guard Plus IR3535 Unscented Expedition	IR 3535	aerosol	24
Natrapel Plus	botanical	aerosol	4
bugAway Lymonessa	botanical	pump	1

The sunblock keeps your body from absorbing too much of the repellent. If possible, select one of the new "bonding base" sunblocks that penetrate deep into your skin. Film-based sunblocks—like the kind available everywhere—cover just the surface of your skin.

Head Nets and Bug Jackets

Head nets are essential for early-season trips in the northern United States and Canada. Nonmilitary styles that don't have a hoop around the face are best because they roll to fist size and fit in your pocket. You can make a head net in a few minutes. Just sew up a wide rectangle of mosquito net large enough to fit over your head and wide-brimmed hat. Make the net long enough to drape lazily on your shoulders. Don't sew an elastic band into the hem. Spray the hem with repellent and even blackflies will be confused. Spray the entire net if no-see-ums are about.

Head nets are best constructed of dark-colored standard-mesh mosquito net, both for good visibility and ventilation. It's difficult to see through a milk-colored no-see-um net. If you can't find a dark-colored head net, buy a light-colored one and darken the eye panel with black marker or spray paint.

Bug jackets armor your body against biting insects. Some styles rely on chemicals (Deet or permethrin) to keep bugs away; others block them with close-knit mesh. Chemically treated jackets are cooler to wear and they prevent bugs from landing—a plus when you're eating or drinking. I've spent a lot of time fighting bugs in the Canadian north, so I'm very picky about bug jackets. Here are my favorites:

Chemically treated (Deet) style: The US Military Surplus Insect Repellent Jacket is a

The US Army Insect Repellent Jacket shown here (and similar foreign military bug jackets) are occasionally available from military surplus outlets. Netted jackets aren't popular; you'll have to search the internet to find them. Netted jackets must be charged with a full bottle of Deet. Point Lake. Nunavut, Canada. Author at left.)

wide-mesh "cotton string" jacket. To activate, soak it in pure (100 percent) Deet overnight then hang it out to dry. Bugs won't land on the treated jacket.

With frequent everyday use, the treatment lasts about 2 weeks. It is easily recharged with Deet in the field. This jacket is cool, compact, and comfortable. You can buy full-strength Deet at most sport shops and treat the jacket yourself, or spray it with permethrin. Some foreign countries offer surplus military "string jackets" that are similar to the US military model. However, Deet-treated mesh jackets aren't very popular so you'll have to search the web to find them. Still, this type is my favorite because it is well-ventilated (cool) and the Deet repels every insect you are likely to encounter.

- *Chemical free:* The Original Bug Shirt (made in Canada) combines fine-mesh netting with ultralight, densely woven cotton or polyester microfiber. The zippered hood has an integral face mask so you don't need a head net (you have to unzip to eat). Cord-lock closures at the wrist and waist provide an impenetrable seal. The full-closure sleeves are long enough to tuck your hands inside while napping.

- *Make your own bug jacket:* Impregnate with peremethrin (use a spray can or soaker kit) any light-colored cotton or polyester long-sleeve shirt. Add a head net and you're set for battle.

Susie Bug Net

First, you apply Deet to all exposed skin. As more insects gather, you add a head net, then a Deet-impregnated bug jacket. Ultimately, you rant and swear, then in disgust retire to your insect-proof tent. Meanwhile, friends nearby enjoy a bug-free after-dinner brandy and a glorious sunset inside their "Susie bug net"—a personal-size bug armor designed by my wife, Sue Harings.

Materials needed: A piece of mosquito netting 12 feet long and 7 feet wide, plus enough ⅛-inch-diameter shock cord to span the hem. Don't use no-see-um net: It's not strong enough and you can't see through it. **Important:** Insect netting should be black; other colors reflect light into your eyes and cloud visibility. Try this experiment: Paint a portion of netting black with Magic Marker. Compare the two views. You'll be amazed!

Procedure: Fold the netting in half to produce a rectangular sheet that measures 6 feet by 7 feet. Sew up the two long sides, hem the bottom, and install the bungee cord in the hem. The finished net will weigh less than a pound and compress to football size.

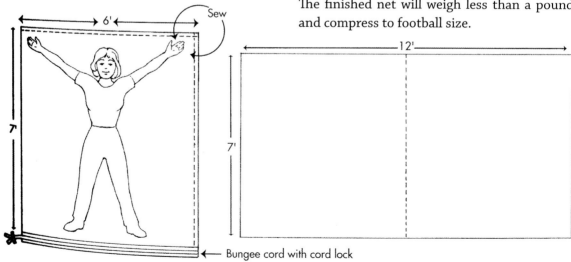

A Susie Bug net is easy to make. Or order one from Cooke Custom Sewing in Lino Lakes, Minnesota.

Here are some uses for your Susie bug net:

1. Eat inside it; there's room for two.

2. Sleep out under the stars. The net covers you from head to toe. Cinch the bungee cord tightly around the foot of your sleeping bag.

3. Use it as a portable outhouse when bugs are bad.

4. Bathe in it! Amble to the beach as a ghostly apparition in your Susie bug net. Wear your life vest and you'll float confidently inside your bug armor.

5. Lay the net over breads, cheese, and lunch meats to keep flies away.

6. Rig a tripod inside and you have a tiny bug-proof tepee in which to wash dishes, cook, and make repairs.

Roll and stuff your Susie bug net under a pack flap so it will be available at meals and river rest stops. If you don't want to make your own, the Susie bug net is available from Cooke Custom Sewing.

Some Final "Repelling" Tips

*   Bugs will avoid your face if you saturate a cowboy neckerchief with repellent and tie it loosely around your neck. Spray the underside of your hat brim too!

*   Some of the most effective first-aid products for bug bites contain aloe, a plant-derived ingredient that has been around for thousands of years. Aloe soothes inflammation, inhibits swelling, and keeps skin moist. It also soothes burns and kills bacteria and fungi. For the product to be effective, aloe should make up at least 80 percent of its formula.

*   Liquid or cream repellents are much more potent (a better buy) than sprays.

*   Household ammonia and water will cut the sting of mosquito bites. For bee, wasp, and hornet stings, apply a wet salt pack and allow it to dry. The salt will draw the pain away quickly.

*   Sew Velcro tabs to your shirt cuffs (Figure B-7) so you can seal off this area from blackflies and mosquitoes.

The author enjoys a bug-free lunch under his Susie bug net. Along the Caribou River, near Hudson Bay, Manitoba.

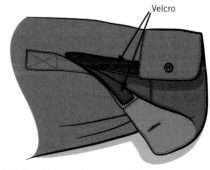

Figure B-7. Sew Velcro tabs to your shirt cuffs to keep bugs out.

Bush Living

Sharron Chatterton is a retired wilderness canoe guide, college instructor, and writer who lives a contemplative life in a lakeside cabin near Teslin, Yukon, Canada. Here she explains how the solitude and demands of bush living shape the personality of those who live and work in wild places.

—CJ

Sharron Chatterton relaxes on the beach in front of her cabin on Teslin Lake, Yukon, Canada.

The wilderness promotes traits that encourage survival. Surrounded by the unpredictable and beyond rescue, wilderness travelers safeguard unknown outcomes against disaster. Their goal is safe arrival to their destination, not arrival by some time or date. Some "great feats" are simply their cautious journeys.

Wilderness makes an individual self-reliant: able to function alone, to perform all tasks independently, and to know the adaptive capability of every tool. To the bush traveler, rescue is an urban myth—there are no buffers against irresponsibility! Wilderness dwellers accept what is, not what was or ought to be. They plan carefully and they don't take chances. Actions are purposeful; tasks are always completed. To use energy on valueless projects or to leave important work undone is unthinkable. There is too much to do to get bored.

Long periods spent in silence create an ease without talk, value for the understandings that flow without language, and a need for silence. Silence conserves energy, frees one's attention for more important work, and, lacking confrontation, creates gentleness. Simple wisdom breeds in silence.

Wilderness travelers become hyperalert and observant. The land exhibits what happened, is happening, and might happen next to the ears, eyes, nose, and skin. These sensors function in overdrive, constantly receiving information.

Some believe that wilderness living breeds antisocial behavior. In truth, the wilderness man or woman becomes asocial—he or she has a lingering love of society but little need for it. The wilderness, not the nation that manages it, evokes their allegiance. This alienation from political boundaries and reassociation with the natural world defines the "wilderness heart."

Survival is the hidden foundation of bush morality. It is what allows one to kill animals to eat, blaze trees to mark a return trail, or sidestep a slipper orchid. An experienced bush dweller learns never to interfere with another. To pass without offering help is a cardinal sin. To solicit help unnecessarily is another. Survival encourages cordiality among neighbors—you might have to depend upon one for help.

There are deeper effects of wilderness than those on human personality: There is a growing need to reduce belongings, to hunt and gather, and to be nomadic. Nature—not other humans—controls the routine. There is a growing intimacy with animals and with death. Consciousness passes old barriers and metaphysical experiences occur. Wilderness rearranges behavior, reconfigures mental constructs, and transforms the inner self forever.

Yet personality change is what we first perceive in committed wilderness travelers. We see it in epic soloists, long-distance trekkers, and in those who work in wild places—guides, researchers, and itinerant wanderers. In fact, all of us, even we who paddle a simple slough alone or walk a dog along the bluffs—even farmers, loggers, and deep-sea fishermen whose wilderness experiences we consistently deny—have personalities deeply marked by wilderness.

C

Camera

Waterproof protection: Most photographers rely on waterproof Pelican or Otter boxes to protect their cameras from rain or a boat capsize. These boxes are reliable if you take certain precautions (see Waterproof Bags and Boxes, page 196).

Regrettably, those wonderful military assault gas-mask bags are no longer available. They were constructed from rubberized canvas and were ideal camera containers. Vinyl copies aren't as rugged or waterproof. Waterproof "dry bags" that have roll-down closures or water-tight zippers are the current "soft bag" options.

Tip: Make a cylinder of closed-cell foam that will fit snugly inside your waterproof dry bag. Cut a circular bottom. Glue or duct-tape the pieces together. The foam will protect your camera from knocks and shield it from the sun.

Some boaters still use metal GI ammo boxes. But beware of damaged and rotten seals. The seals are easy to replace—if you can find them!

You can rig a quick waterproof "shoot-through" bag by placing your camera inside an *aLOKSAK* waterproof plastic bag (see page 196).

Canoe- and Boat-Rigging Tips

(See my books *Canoeing Wild Rivers* (Fifth Edition) and *Canoeing and Camping* for a wealth of detailed canoeing and canoe-rigging tips.)

Compass: For ease in navigating complex lakes, secure a wrist compass around the aft canoe thwart. This will enable you to simultaneously paddle and follow a plotted course.

Custom improvements: Thread loops of fabric shock cord through holes drilled in the canoe's

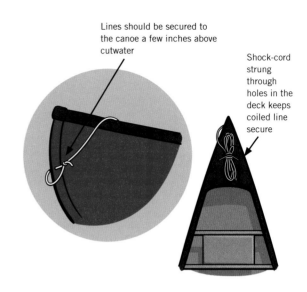

Lines should be secured to the canoe a few inches above cutwater

Shock-cord strung through holes in the deck keeps coiled line secure

Figure C-1. End lines, shock cords, and lining holes

thwarts and deck plates. End lines (painters) stored under the shock-cord loops will stay put in a capsize and on portages. Oddities can be secured under the thwart cords.

Fiberglass and Royalex canoes should have lining holes or rings installed a few inches above cutwater, not high on the deck as is the common practice. See Figure C-1.

Multiuse bailer: A 2-quart plastic water pitcher tied to a canoe thwart makes a handy bailer and is useful for mixing powdered drinks in camp.

Sponge: A large sponge is useful for mopping up paddle drips.

Canoe pockets you can portage: Where to store small items like eyeglasses, suntan lotion, and repellent is always a problem on canoe trips. Of course, you can store these small items in packsacks, but getting to them is a hassle. So why not install pockets in your canoe?

An early pioneer of canoe pockets was Verlen Kruger, whose 7,000-mile canoe trip from Montreal to the Bering Sea made canoeing history in 1971. Verlen simply attached plastic bicycle baskets to his canoe thwarts. The baskets provided a convenient—though not capsize-proof—place to store small items.

Thwart bags are the modern alternative to bicycle baskets. Most clip or Velcro to a canoe thwart. Unfortunately, few thwart-bag makers have given much thought as to what to do with these bags when it's time to portage.

You can turn any small fanny pack or nylon briefcase into a "portageable" thwart bag by simply sewing on buckles or Velcro tabs that will secure around a thwart. Add a detachable shoulder strap and you'll be set for the portage.

You can buy commercial thwart bags from Cooke Custom Sewing, Granite Gear, Frost River, and Duluth Pack.

Seat improvements: Drill holes in canoe and boat seats so they won't pool water when it rains. Glue (contact cement) closed-cell foam to the surface of canoe and boat seats to increase comfort and warmth. The foam will also add flotation to the craft.

Emergency repair kit: The only emergency repair kit you really need for a canoe or boat is a roll of 2-inch-wide duct tape. Duct tape sticks to anything. Use it for emergency repairs on all your camping gear.

Paint decks on aluminum canoes flat black to reduce glare.

For kneeling comfort when paddling, glue foam knee pads into your canoe. You can buy precut knee pads at canoe and kayak shops or just cut up a closed-cell foam sleeping pad. Weldwood contact cement is the most reliable adhesive and will work on any surface.

Tying canoes on cars: Best hitch for this is the power cinch. See the section Knots, Hitches, and Lashings on page 110.

Yoke: A yoke is essential if you plan to carry your canoe alone for even short distances. A curved hardwood yoke, with overstuffed foam-filled shoulder pads, is the most comfortable combination. Commercial yokes cost upward of $50 and are seldom very good. You can make a much better yoke than you can buy.

Finished pad

New England Yoke can be painful

Fabric

(Foam)

Bolts, not screws

Staple fabric to wood block

Drainage holes in bottom of pad

Wood clamps for quick removal–or bolt to gunwale

Figure C-2. A homemade yoke with drainage holes will take the sting out of a long carry.

—Sponge

The author attaches a removable yoke to his solo canoe. Note the big foam-filled yoke pads and the sponge secured under a shock-cord loop around the seat frame.

Make your yoke from white ash (preferred) and finish to the dimensions illustrated in Figure C-2. The completed yoke should have some flex, which will take the sting out of a rigorous carry. Use open-cell polyurethane foam (pillow padding) for the shoulder pads. Naugahyde or other heavy plastic upholstery material is the best covering fabric. Attach the yoke to the balance point of the canoe (some prefer a slightly tail-heavy arrangement) with bolts or wood clamps. The clamp-and-wing-nut setup is best if you have a solo canoe (the yoke location interferes with paddling) or plan to carry a third person in the canoe. You can easily remove the yoke to provide more room for your passenger.

Make a Belly Cover for Your Canoe

If you've ever paddled a canoe in icy wind-whipped rain, fought the waves of a big lake, or edged down huge rapids, you know the value of a canoe cover. My book *Canoeing Wild Rivers* (Fifth Edition) has detailed plans for making the Jacobson three-piece tandem cover, the Jacobson two-piece solo cover, and the split-center dogsled model designed by arctic canoeist Bob O'Hara. Commercial versions of this cover are available from Cooke Custom Sewing. Dan Cooke supplies a no-shrink Mylar template, which ensures a perfect fit on any canoe.

You don't need a full splash cover unless you're a whitewater fanatic or are canoeing the Canadian north. The one-piece "expandable belly" described below provides enough protection for all but the most severe conditions. If you can sew a straight stitch, you can make a belly cover in about 3 hours.

The belly section described below weighs about a pound and stuffs to football size. You can use it as a small sail or tablecloth or as a rain cover for packs and firewood.

Materials

Pattern: None! The canoe is your pattern.

A one-piece, expandable belly cover will keep out side-splash and cut wind by nearly 50 percent. Photo taken along the North Knife River near Hudson Bay. The canoe is a 17-foot PakBoat (folding canoe). This is an O'Hara, split center section—ideal for quick access and high loads.

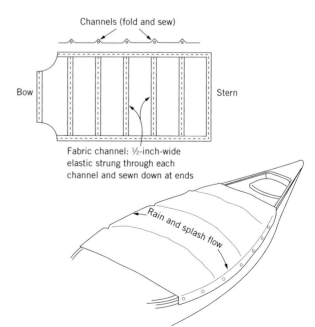

Figure C-3. Making a belly cover for your canoe

Snaps: Twenty-four brass snaps. Check them with a magnet to be sure they're not plated steel.

Waterproof nylon: A weight of 2.5 ounces per square yard is strong enough for friendly waterways; 4-ounce to 6-ounce stuff is best for the arctic barrens.

One-inch-wide seam tape or nylon webbing: About 20 feet.

Extras: 2-inch-wide Velcro, 1-inch-wide pajama elastic.

Procedure

1. Pop rivet snaps through the hull, 2 inches below the rails, 8 inches apart. Begin the snap line at the rear edge of the front seat and end it at the back thwart. Use an aluminum backup washer behind each rivet. You'll need about twelve snaps for each side of the canoe.

2. Cut a 60-inch-wide piece of fabric that reaches from the front edge of the bow seat to the rear thwart. Hem all sides, then sew seam tape to the inside hem. Next, fold over and sew the "water deflector channels," illustrated in Figure C-3. Thread pajama elastic through the channels and rear hem. Tighten the elastic slightly, and then sew down the ends.

3. Set snaps through the hem to match those on the canoe. Nylon stretches when wet and shrinks when dry, so don't pull the material too tightly.

You can modify the belly to accept a passenger by installing a quick-release skirt in the center.

Gel-Coat Repair and Maintenance Tricks

It's doubtful that you'll ever have to repair major damage to a well-built fiberglass or Kevlar canoe or boat. However, you may need to mend chipped gel coat on the bottom—it's easy, if you don't follow the manufacturer's directions. The recommended procedure calls for filling the break with color-matched liquid gel coat, then sanding and polishing to blend the repair.

Nothing could be more difficult or frustrating. Catalyzed liquid gel coat is runny; you must prop the boat at an awkward angle to level the flow, then build a well of masking tape to contain the resin. Then you have to nurse the slowly hardening liquid with a flat stick to keep it from overflowing the well.

Here's an easier way:

1. Remove the shards of damaged gel coat.

2. Mask the work area, then catalyze polyester or gray auto-body putty (use extra MEKP hardening agent to produce a "hot" mix) and work it into the break to overflowing. The putty is thick and won't run, so there's no need to prop the canoe or build a tape well. ***Caution:*** MEKP (methyl ethyl ketone peroxide) is toxic and can cause blindness. Wear safety goggles and rubber gloves! And mix everything in a well-ventilated area.

3. When the putty is firm (about 5 minutes), slice off the excess with your jackknife. Allow the remainder to cure for another half hour, then sand it level with progressive grits of sandpaper. Finish to silky smoothness with wet 400-grit sandpaper.

4. Spray-paint the patch with matching auto acrylic. When the paint has dried, buff it out with a mixture of paste wax and pumice. Or use a commercial fiberglass boat wax (it contains pumice), which you can get at any marina.

Your patch is now complete. The whole process takes about an hour.

To keep gel coat looking like new: Occasionally use a commercial hull cleaner (I've had good results with Star Brite) to remove scum lines and stains from fiberglass and Kevlar gel coat. Paste wax will brighten and protect the hull. Canoe retailers often wipe on a coat of Lemon Pledge before they display their fiberglass canoes and boats in the store.

Canteen

Only cheechakos and bona fide cowboys use traditional canteens these days. Expert campers rely on poly bottles to carry thirst quenchers. Plastic bottles are cheaper, lighter, and easier to pack than metal canteens.

Some backpackers and paddlers prefer the convenience of a self-contained hydration system, like the popular CamelBak, which you wear on your back (it has pack straps). Water is held inside a plastic bladder that is protected by a tough nylon cover. Water is delivered via a plastic tube that has a sophisticated no-leak mouthpiece. Hydration systems are great for people on the go, especially those who must have their hands free.

Plastic soda bottles make fine canteens, and they fit nicely into the side pockets of small hiking packs. Several companies make insulated (neoprene) covers for these bottles.

Tip: Fill your water bottle four-fifths full of water and freeze it to assure a supply of cold water during the next day's hike. In below-freezing weather carry your bottle upside down in your pack. This will prevent ice from forming in the mouthpiece.

A glass or stainless steel vacuum bottle assures a cold (or hot) drink throughout the day.

The traditional bota, or wine bladder, remains popular with skiers. It also makes a fine, easy-to-carry canteen for summer hiking.

Here's a good way to warm up your sleeping bag on a cold night: Pour boiling water into your canteen, roll the canteen in a towel or shirt, and take this homemade hot-water bottle to bed.

Do not put carbonated beverages or alcohol into aluminum cups or bottles. They will react with the aluminum!

The tough Mylar bag (bladder), which lines wine boxes, makes a great "giant" canteen (Figure C-4). Sew tough nylon around the

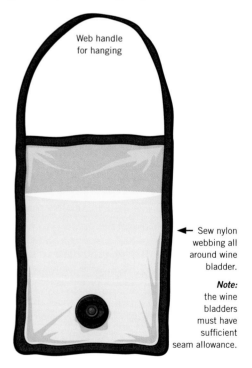

Web handle for hanging

← Sew nylon webbing all around wine bladder.

Note: the wine bladders must have sufficient seam allowance.

Figure C-4. Wine-bladder water bag

bladder so you can hang the unit from a tree and dispense liquid through the efficient rubber faucet-like spout. **Note:** The rubber spouts are easy to remove if you grasp the lip with a thumbnail and pull. No amount of twisting and forcing will break it loose.

MSR Dromedary bags are lightweight and super-tough. They come in three sizes: 4, 6 and 10 liters. The 3-in-1 cap allows fast fills and small sips. They have a tasteless BPA-free food-grade liner that can tolerate boiling water and freezing. Bags can be set flat or hung and used as a drinking water or wash station. When empty, the bags take up almost no space at all.

Four-liter model shown here.

Cartop Carriers (Canoe Racks)

Canoeists still mourn the passing of car rain gutters, which accepted all manner of clamp-on devices. No current system is as secure as racks that bolt directly to the drip eaves of the car. I'm convinced that the world's first closed cars had rain gutters because they were designed by canoeists for canoeists!

Regrettably, the days of the wonderful generic racks that attach to a car's drip eaves are over. With the exception of full-size vans and a few SUVs, all of today's vehicles have airplane-style doors that require specially fitted brackets. Thule and Yakima lead the way in gutterless designs and offer racks to fit nearly every car model.

Caution: The load brackets that come with gutterless carriers are built to fit the rooflines of specific vehicles. Do not jury-rig them to fit cars for which they are not designed!

Even if you don't plan to buy a second canoe, you may need to shuttle a friend's, so be sure to order double-length (80 inches) crossbars—the factory standard 48-inch carrier is too short to carry paired canoes. Be sure your cartop carrier has locking bars to prevent theft. Even then, many paddlers prefer to remove their expensive racks and store them inside their cars when they're on the river.

Never set canoes on hard, unpadded carriers—the gunnels are sure to be damaged. Here's how to protect your canoe, your car, and your peace of mind:

1. Sew or duct-tape scrap carpeting around the crossbars. This ancient low-tech method is still the best way to protect fine woodwork. Most "show" canoes ride on old-fashioned carpeted racks. Carpeting tells the canoe world you care about your canoe!

2. Yakima, Quick-N-Easy, and a few other companies use tubular aluminum conduit crossbars (Yakima covers theirs with plastic). Some canoeists armor the conduit with rubber heater hose—it slides on easily if you lubricate the rubber with brake fluid.

3. You can bolt L-shaped plastic gunnel brackets (an optional accessory) to the crossbars. The brackets provide a wide, protective bearing surface for the canoe's

gunnels and prevent the craft from shifting in wind—a safety advantage. If your canoe has wooden rails, you may want to glue closed-cell foam or scrap carpeting to the hard plastic faces of the brackets.

4. *Tip:* If you will carry your canoe on unpadded crossbars, do this: Buy 2 feet of 1-inch diameter, flexible clear plastic water pipe. Cut the pipe into four equal sections then cut one wall of each section lengthwise. Slip the cut pieces over the gunnels of your canoe, spaced to align with the crossbars. The plastic tubes will protect the rails from abrasion.

Be careful not to hit your head on the ends of oversize canoe racks when you get in and out of your car. To cushion the occasional blow, some canoeists replace the plastic caps on the ends of the crossbars with thick rubber furniture tips. Others tie short pieces of brightly colored surveying ribbon to the bar ends so they'll be more visible in dim light. One friend has impaled tennis balls on the ends of his canoe rack; another has tied small bells to the crossbars. The bells jingle in the slightest breeze—a reminder to be careful.

Tie-Down Procedures

Separately tie down each canoe you carry! Do it right and the canoe will remain rock solid even at illegal speeds. Here are the rules for safe travel:

1. Run *two* strong ropes or straps over the belly of the canoe and secure each to its respective crossbar. Do not string one long rope from crossbar to crossbar—it could loosen at highway speeds and the canoe could come off the car.

2. Attach *two* lines to the bow and two lines to the stern of each craft. Secure each line to eye bolts in the bumpers, to padded S hooks that ride in secure notches under the bumper, or to loops of webbing or Kevlar cord secured to bolts or fittings under the hood (Figure C-5)—the latter is the best plan for cars that have plastic bumpers. Pull the webbing up through the crack between the hood and fender when you need it. Don't wind ropes around bumpers; sharp bumper edges (even plastic ones) can cut or abrade them.

3. Don't use rubber tie-downs or elastic shock cords to secure canoes to cars! There should be a law against using these stretchy devices.

Straps or ropes? Many paddlers prefer heavy-duty straps to ropes for cartopping canoes. Straps are fast and easy to adjust and they stay tight in any weather. But straps may be stolen if you leave them on the cartop carrier while you're off paddling. Ropes are a low-theft

Figure C-5. For cars that don't have metal bumpers, attach tie-down lines to loops of nylon webbing or cord that are secured to a bracket or bolt under the hood.

item and can be left tied to the roof rack for a quick tie-down and getaway after the trip. **Caution:** Don't toss straps over the roof of your vehicle when you load your canoe—the metal buckles may take a chunk out of the canoe or car! Straps are best passed to a friend or—if they're long enough—walked around the car. Ropes are safe to throw. Straps are more reliable than ropes only if you don't know how to tie the right knots. Most serious canoeists I know prefer ropes to straps. **Exceptions:** when carrying a single canoe on a small, narrow car or a bunch of canoes on a trailer.

Concerns for Carrying Fragile and Paired Canoes or Multiple Canoes on a Double Rack

You can break the back of a fragile canoe if you secure its ends too tightly. For this reason, many canoeists prefer to tie only the bow. Racers never tie down the tail of their ultralight canoes!

Whenever you carry two canoes side by side on an overhead rack, always pad the inside of one of the canoes so the finish won't be galled if the two crafts shift sideways and touch.

If you carry two canoes on a double rack, place the lightest and most fragile canoe on the passenger side of the carrier. This will allow the sturdier and more rigidly tied craft on the driver's side to take the abuse of high winds generated by passing trucks.

Multiple boats: If you carry more than two boats on a rack built for two, layer them two or three abreast and separate each level with a pair of 2 x 4s. Each wooden 2 x 4 *must* be separately tied to the metal rack (to prevent shifting under load) as shown in the photo. I once observed a van with nine whitewater boats on top. They

Three securely cartopped canoes. Note that the wooden 2 x 4 crossbars are tied to the metal rack.

were stacked like cordwood and appeared quite secure.

Children (Tips for Camping with Kids)
Rain Gear

The best rain gear for young children is an inexpensive plastic poncho, a coated nylon windbreaker, and a sou'wester-style hat. Trim the poncho to fit with scissors. Waterproof the stitching of the coated jacket with seam sealant (every camp shop has it). Be sure to glue the seams on the sou'wester hat too.

Rationale: The youngster wears the coated wind shell under the poncho—it keeps arms

This little girl is set for water and sun. Note the rubber boots and broad-brimmed hat and the properly sized life jacket.
Steve Piragis

Camp Clothing and Sleeping Gear

Cotton clothing (except underwear) should be avoided except in the predictable heat of mid-July. Woolens may be too scratchy for some youngsters, so the logical solution is Orlon acrylic. Acrylic sweaters, gloves, and hats dry quickly after a wetting and retain their insulating properties when damp or soiled. Acrylic garments are also quite inexpensive; they are ideal for spring canoe and boat trips, for adults as well as kids.

Hats: Kids need three hats on a camping trip: a brimmed cap for sun, a warm stocking cap (wool or acrylic) for chilly days, and the traditional sou'wester for rain.

Sleeping gear: Kids do not need air mattresses or foam pads for comfort. Their young bones will happily conform to the most uneven ground!

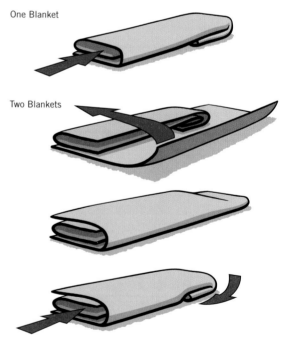

Figure C-6. For summer use, two blankets work as well as a sleeping bag. Here's how to fold them for maximum warmth.

dry and provides a secondary "drip" layer in prolonged rain. The sou'wester hat is worn over the poncho hood and is tied beneath the chin. Together, these garments provide serviceable and inexpensive protection from rain.

Emergency rain gear for kids (or adults) may be fashioned from a large leaf-and-lawn-size garbage bag. Cut head and arm holes, provide a sou'wester hat, and you'll stay reasonably dry.

Wet-weather footgear: Running shoes and galoshes, or any rubber boots sized large enough to fit over the sneakers, are all you need. When rains quit, the boots are removed and freedom of foot is instantly restored.

You must provide a foam pad (not an air mattress—these conduct cold!) if down sleeping bags are used. Body weight compresses the underside of a down bag to near-zero thickness, and chilling will result unless insulation is provided. The typical polyester sleeping bag provides sufficient insulation below so that, except in very cold weather, mattresses may be omitted.

Sleeping bags are unnecessary for typical summer camping. One or two light wool or fluffy acrylic blankets, folded as illustrated in Figure C-6, will provide plenty of warmth in temperatures to 45°F.

Increasing the warmth of a sleeping bag: The warmth of a sleeping bag is partly related to the amount of space the body has to heat. By reducing dead-air space, you'll increase warmth. Figure C-7 shows an easy way to reduce the dimensions, and add warmth, to the typical station-wagon-sized sleeping bag. A flannel "draft collar" sewn to the top of a sleeping bag will increase warmth considerably.

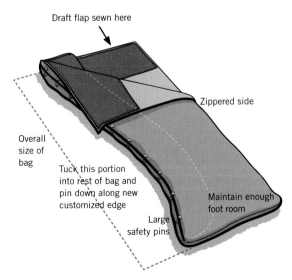

Draft flap sewn here

Zippered side

Overall size of bag

Tuck this portion into rest of bag and pin down along new customized edge

Maintain enough foot room

Large safety pins

Figure C-7. Customize a sleeping bag for children.

Insects (see Bugs—Mosquitoes, Flies, No-See-Ums, and Ticks, page 31): A head net and a Susie bug net are wise investments if you'll be camping in buggy country. Choose mild, cream-based repellents rather than more powerful chemicals, which may burn sensitive young skin.

Toys: Kids will want to bring a favorite doll or teddy bear. Be sure to provide a "raincoat" (plastic bag) for the toy, so it won't be ruined in foul weather.

Clothing
How to Tell the Real Thing from Designer Wear!

With today's "outdoor look," you'd think it would be easy to locate suitable clothing for backcountry camping. Hardly! Only a handful of manufacturers currently offer attire that is truly functional. The vast majority of clothing makers are simply producing stylish garments that parrot the outdoor look.

Clothes that are designed for generic outdoor sports will work for serious camping, but there are concessions. Here are some things to consider:

- *Tight, trim fit:* Outdoor clothing should be cut large enough to permit unrestricted movement of arms and legs, even when extra clothing is worn beneath. Shirt and jacket sleeves should be generously sized, even to the point of billowing. Buy one size larger than you normally wear at home.

- *Pants with integral belts:* You can't secure sheath knives and multitools around your waist.

- *Confining hoods:* Designer hoods are slim, trim, and stow away into fashionable collars. Wilderness hoods are large enough to fit over a brimmed hat. Hood zippers continue to the nose.

- *Pocket overkill:* Designer wear features more pockets than you can possibly use, suggesting utility but driving up tailoring costs. Really now, when was the last time you used more than two pockets in your parka or raincoat?

- *Pants with zippered legs:* Legs can't be easily shortened; the zippers clog with debris; zipper failure is just a matter of time.

- *Pants with elastic at the ankles* restrict ventilation and may be uncomfortable when tucked into boots.

- *Any garment that has tiny zippers:* They fail fast!

- *Wind jackets that are "water-repellent":* Water-repellent coatings reduce breathability—exactly what you don't want when working hard! **Note:** Gore-Tex garments are not breathable enough for active wear.

- *Garments that don't seal at the throat.* A gap here encourages an icy wind!

- *Fancy re-thread cord-locks:* They're time-consuming to tighten and loosen. Speedy adjustments are important when you're hiking hard or paddling into a wind.

- *Noisy Gore-Tex garments:* The sound of stiff, crinkling fabric is annoying.

- *Navy blue clothing* attracts mosquitoes more than any other color.

- *Velcro on the sides of wide-brimmed hats:* When the wind blows hard, the brim blows up and sticks to the Velcro. Snaps are better.

- *Cord-lock waist on rain pants:* When the pants get wet, they become heavy and sag—a single cord-lock may not be enough to hold them up. Double cord-locks or an integral belt is better.

- *Non-bonded fabric liners in rain jackets and pants:* If they get wet they may stretch and hang down below the hem and absorb water. Bonded liners are best.

- *Rain pants with elastic closures at the ankles.* They restrict ventilation. Primitive man learned long ago that water doesn't flow uphill.

- *Armpit zippers on raincoats* are fine for hikers whose arms hang down when they walk. Canoeists and kayakers raise their arms when they paddle and water flows over the sleeve zippers! Waterproof armpit zippers solve this problem, but they're expensive and bulky.

The least expensive and most versatile trousers for camping are military surplus 65/35 poly/cotton rip-stop fatigues (BDUs). For cold-weather use, surplus wool trousers are the norm. Trouser legs should hang straight (no cuffs) so they won't trap the environment as you walk through it. **Caution:** Avoid pure nylon pants if you will sit close to a campfire. Wool pants or those with some cotton content are safer around open flames.

Wool or synthetic? Despite the ballyhoo over synthetic fabrics like polypropylene, fleece, and chemically treated polyesters, good wool

Sue Harings, the author's wife, is dressed for a cold day on the Canadian tundra. She is wearing a sou'wester-style hat, two wool neck warmers, full merino wool long underwear and mittens, polyester field pants, and knee-high green wellie boots. These are definitely not "designer" clothes!

still performs as well as or better in cold, damp weather. In practice, the human body is less sensitive than the machines used to prove manufacturers' claims of superiority.

I tried a variety of natural and synthetic fabrics when I attended the winter work and survival school in Spitsbergen, Norway. Wool was rated the warmest fabric of them all! And there was no guesswork to the ratings because students were wired with sensors whose data were later fed into a computer. Skin temperatures don't lie! When it comes to longevity, good wool outlasts them all.

Still, synthetics have their place—as wind stoppers, dry liners, comfy fleece outergarments, and underwear for those who can't stand wool (even soft merino wool) next to their skin.

Buy what you can afford, but don't be swept off your feet by exotic claims for space-age fabrics. Except in the heat of summer, only cotton in pure form is unsuitable for camping.

Summer wind parka: Your most useful garment on a camping trip is a simple, porous, nylon or cotton-polyester wind shell. Emphasize "simple" and "porous." You don't need a fancy hood that turns with your head, armpit zippers, or a microfiber liner. You do need a hood that will fit over your wide-brim hat, a zipper that runs almost to your nose (and seals your throat), excellent ventilation, and a large enough size to fit over your fleece jacket or wool sweater. Your wind shell should roll to fist size and weigh almost nothing.

Inexpensive, breathable wind jackets used to be widely available at discount stores. Now, they all have a "durable water repellent (DWR)" finish that repels light rain but seriously reduces breathability. To test: Pour a small amount of water on the garment. If the water beads and runs off, it has a DWR coating. And no amount of washing will get all of it out! Bicycle and cross-country ski shops commonly carry porous (no DWR) wind shells, though most don't have protective hoods. Piragis Northwoods Co. in Ely, MN has a completely breathable no-DWR hooded wind anorak, which I highly recommend. I'm proud to say I had a hand in its design.

Why no bells and whistles on a wind parka? Because they add weight and bulk and provide little real utility. Forget coated fabrics and

A porous (no **DWR** water-repellent finish!) wind shell, like this Piragis Northwoods Co. wind anorak, adds warmth without weight. San Juan River, Utah.

Winter wind parka: Same rules as for the summer parka, with these exceptions:

- Tightly woven cotton or cotton-polyester is softer and more flexible than nylon in extremely cold temperatures.

- Size should be knee length and one size larger than your usual summer parka.

- An anorak style provides more freedom of movement than a full-zip model—and the constantly connected anorak zipper is less likely to jam. For extreme subzero temperatures, choose buttons, snaps, or Velcro over zippers. A winter parka must have a protective beard flap behind the zipper.

- A fur-trimmed hood (coyote fur doesn't frost up and it's not too pricey) is essential in bitter cold and blowing wind.

- Gore-Tex can be dangerous in bitter cold temperatures (especially if you are very active) because its tiny pores can't eliminate perspiration as fast as it's produced. Condensation builds and produces a sauna inside. When you remove the Gore-Tex jacket, the trapped moisture freezes and the fabric becomes stiff as a board. Under some conditions the garment may even freeze on you! High porosity is essential in active cold-weather clothing! **Note:** Treating a porous cotton or nylon windbreaker with a water repellent like Scotchguard will reduce its porosity and its ability to move moisture.

Gore-Tex—they are not breathable (porous) enough for active wear. You may put on and take off your wind shell dozens of times a day as you adjust your comfort system. If your jacket is too bulky to stuff into a pack pocket or to loop around your waist, you'll wish you'd left it at home!

Blue jeans are a particularly bad choice and have accounted for several deaths due to hypothermia. Even in the heat of summer, I would never wear blue jeans for camping.

Long underwear: I've tried many brands. These are my current favorites:

- Icebreaker: Stylish underwear and outerwear woven from silky soft pure merino wool. Beautiful, functional, and wonderfully warm. The flat-finished weave is less likely to catch on brush and unravel. I just love the merino T-shirt and boxer shorts!

- Klar Ullfrotté: Underlayer, midlayer, and outer-layer garments woven from two-thirds pure merino wool and one-third polyamide (for strength and elasticity). First choice of the Scandinavian military and widely used by police departments and rescue personnel the world over, Klar Ullfrotté may be the warmest long underwear on the planet. Their balaclava and two-layer mittens are awesome! The downside is that these garments are not stylish (they come in just two colors—blue and olive green) and the tiny interior woven loops that make them so warm can catch on vegetation and "string out." You must wear a protective wind shell over them. Few stores carry Klar Ullfrotté garments. You'll need to search the web to find them.

- Smartwool: Everyone knows about Smartwool socks. But their merino T-shirts and long johns are terrific too.

- Thermax: This nonallergenic DuPont fabric insulates well, even when wet. It breathes in hot weather, feels nice against the skin, and it doesn't smell—even when it goes unwashed for days. My wife, Sue Harings, who is very conscious of odors, insisted that I recommend Thermax and its relative Thermistat by name. Available from Cabela's.

- Body-Sensors by Terramar: Knitted from hollow-core polyester fibers with activated carbon and embedded nano-silver. The carbon absorbs odors; the silver kills bacteria. There are three thicknesses—warm, warmer, and warmest. The silky-soft, coal-black fabric doesn't smell like a dirty sweat sock as the days go by.

- Socks: Merino wool socks are the most comfortable way to go in any weather. Wool has a much wider temperature-comfort range than synthetics, which means you'll be warmer when it's cold and cooler when it's warm. Smartwool, Icebreaker, and Klar Ullfrotté merino wool socks are excellent. Crescent sock company's new merino FITS socks are extraordinary!

Tip: Pack a small nylon sack inside your clothes bag or pack to serve as a laundry bag to keep dirty clothing separate from clean items.

Care and Cleaning of Clothing

Woolens may be dry-cleaned or washed by hand or machine (gentle cycle only). The best method is to hand-wash—a 3-minute soak in a mild detergent (Woolite, Ivory Snow, or any mild dishwashing detergent), then hand-rinse and spin-dry in a machine.

Spun-dry woolens are best dried flat or hung on wooden hangers, out of direct sunlight.

Woolen outergarments should be washed in cold or lukewarm water to prevent shrinkage and prolong the life of the fibers. But cold water may not destroy the bacteria and body odor that accumulates in garments worn next to the skin. Klar Ullfrotté recommends that you wash their woolens in 60°C (140°F) water, which will kill many microorganisms. Most good woolens are conditioned and preshrunk in very hot water during the manufacturing process. The manufacturer's label will tell you what you need to know. An advantage of wool is that it will withstand higher washing temperatures than most synthetics. And when it comes to longevity, wool outlasts them all.

Note: Synthetic garments lose some thermal efficiency with each wash cycle. Wool, on the other hand, *gains* thermal efficiency each time it's washed. Maximum warmth comes after about five wash cycles.

To alter the fit of wool garments: Everyone knows that woolens shrink when exposed to hot water and rough handling. However, shrunken garments can also be restored to a semblance of their original shape by rewashing, stretching, and slow drying. These unique characteristics of wool will enable you to get a custom fit from military surplus and garage-sale items.

For example, the sleeves on most shirts are too long for me, so I shrink them by washing them (just the sleeves) in very hot water. The shirt is then spun dry in a hot clothes dryer. Careful monitoring of the drying process produces the exact sleeve length I want. When sleeves have shrunk, they'll hold their size for the lifetime of the garment. This procedure is not unique. For years, lobster fishermen have boiled their wool mittens to make them warmer and more resistant to wind. This is the same principle used in the manufacture of world-famous Dachstein mittens and sweaters. Wool hats, gloves—anything—can be made more wind- and waterproof by "boiling."

Polypropylene garments cannot be dry-cleaned. The solvent will dissolve the plastic fibers. Hand- or machine-wash in cold water and air-dry. Polypropylene melts at very low temperatures, so don't ever place these garments in a hot clothes dryer or too near a fire.

Polypropylene accumulates body oils and smells quite ripe after a few days afield. Embedded grime also reduces the thermal efficiency of the fibers, so wash these garments frequently. Because of their tendency to retain odors, hunters are switching from polypropylene underwear back to conventional fabrics. Deer can probably smell a sweaty polypro undershirt a mile away when the wind is right! *Gore-Tex* must be washed frequently to maintain waterproofness.

Procedure:
Machine wash Gore-Tex garments in warm water with a small amount of liquid detergent. Do *not* use powder detergents, fabric softeners, or bleach. Better yet, use one of the efficient, complete-rinsing Gore-Tex cleansers sold at camping shops.

- Rinse the garment twice to make sure it's free of detergent.

- Hang or tumble dry on a warm, gentle cycle—see garment care instructions to see the preferred method.

- When the garment is dry, increase dryer heat to medium and dry for an additional 20 minutes. This will revive the DWR treatment that makes water bead—

important because air and moisture won't pass through water-clogged Gore-Tex pores.

- *Warm-iron alternative:* If you don't have a clothes dryer or care instructions that say "hang to dry," use a clothes iron set on warm/no steam to revive the DWR finish. Place a towel between the iron and garment to prevent scorching.

Coated fabrics (rain gear) must never be dry-cleaned or machine-washed. Hand-wash them in warm water with any good detergent. Rinse and air-dry.

Be sure coated fabrics are bone dry before you store them. The stitching and nylon won't rot but the polyurethane coatings will. Certain microorganisms attack polyurethane coatings, which will cause separation (peeling) of the chemical from the fabric.

How to Dry Clothing When There's No Wind and the Sun's Not Shining

Method 1. Wring as much water from the fabric as you can. Then tightly roll the clothes in a cotton towel, or better yet, an absorbent synthetic chamois or PackTowl. Set the rolled towel aside for a few minutes. Next, heat some rocks in the fire or in a covered pan on your stove. Remove the damp clothes from their towel wrapping and roll the heated rocks inside the clothes. Small articles of clothing—like socks and underwear—will usually be dry enough to wear in about an hour. Old-time woodsmen commonly placed hot rocks in their wet socks to dry them.

Method 2. Wring out the water and roll in a towel, as above. When you prepare supper on your trail stove, place a pair of socks or a thin article of folded clothing on top of the cover of your cooking pot. Heat from your cooking pot will help dry your clothes. Sounds weird but it works really well!

Method 3. String a parachute-cord ridge line inside your tent and pin (use diaper pins) your damp (towel-wrung) clothes to the line. Clothes should hang straight, not be folded over the cord. Secure a candle lantern to the ridge line (it must not touch your clothes or tent!). Close the tent. Your things will be much drier in an hour. Even without a candle lantern, your clothes will dry some if you simply allow them to hang all night.

Note: Normal tent temperatures average about 10°F warmer than the outside temperature. A candle lantern may add another 10 to 15°F. **Warning:** Do not leave a burning candle in a tent unattended!

None of these methods produces perfect results. The best plan is to use all three. *Tip:* Use diaper pins, not commercial clothespins, to secure items to a clothesline. If you pin through the line, items will stay put in the strongest of winds.

Color Can Save Your Life!

Blending with nature is part of what wilderness camping is all about—and for many, this means dressing the part. The rule—widely encouraged by federal authorities—is to avoid bright colors that take the "wild" out of wilderness. Go instead with gentle green, olive drab, and autumn brown.

This is fine if you're on a beaten path where campsites dot the trail. Color the tents blaze orange and suddenly you're in Camelot! Yes, bright colors can diminish the outdoor experience.

But they can also be a safety factor, as these examples illustrate:

Cree River, Saskatchewan, canoe trip: A forest fire prevented us from reaching our take-out spot. We camped instead on an island 5 miles upstream. The sky was smoky yellow, visibility was hardly better than none at all. We had little hope that our bush plane would find us in the morning.

At 7:45 a.m. we heard the roar of an engine, and seconds later a single Otter swooped out of the sky and chugged to our doorstep.

"It was that checkerboard tarp that caught my eye," said the pilot.

Gull River, Ontario: I lost the trail partway through an undefined and unrefined portage. So, I set down my grass-green canoe to scout the way. I found the trail shortly, but it took an hour to locate my boat. Right then, I vowed I would never own another "camouflage" canoe!

A tundra tarp saved my marriage! On August 12, 1992, Sue Harings and I were married at Wilberforce Falls along Canada's Hood River. The wedding was nearly aborted 10 days earlier, when I discovered that I had left the "wedding pack" (a white Duluth pack that contained Susie's ermine-trimmed wedding dress and all the wedding treats) at the float plane dock in Yellowknife, NWT, 400 air miles away.

Brightly colored equipment can save the day, possibly even your life! This multicolor Cooke Custom Sewing tarp saved my marriage! The story is in my flagship book, *Canoeing Wild Rivers* (Fifth Edition). Location: Wilberforce Falls, Hood River, a few miles from the Arctic Ocean, Nunavut, Canada. Note the wedding presents in the foreground.

When Susie learned the pack was missing, she wanted to postpone the wedding. Really!

But flying out behind us (headed for a different river) was Canada's famed canoe man, Michael Peake. Mike put the pack aboard a twin Otter bound for Cambridge Bay, and asked the pilots to "find Cliff."

They did—the co-pilot pushed the pack out the door at an altitude of 300 feet! It fell like a missile (no harm done) and the wedding was on again! Neither pilot saw our five overturned red canoes or our five red and yellow tents which were clustered together. It was our Cooke Custom Sewing multicolor rain tarp that saved the day! The full story is in my book *Canoeing Wild Rivers* (Fifth Edition).

Moral: Patchwork color pattern beats one solid color.

Color your packs "visible." I tie streamers of yellow plastic surveying ribbon to those that aren't.

Compass

The most practical and reliable field compass is the orienteering type. This style features a built-in protractor, which allows you to compute bearings without orienting the map to north, and a liquid-dampened needle that stops in 3 seconds. Detailed instructions come with all orienteering compasses. However, you should know how to determine declination.

Declination is the angular difference between geographic or true north and the direction the compass needle points. As you can see from the standard declination diagram in Figure C-8, the difference can be quite large, especially if you live in the far East or West. Declination values are constantly changing. Values (to the nearest fraction of a degree) are

The orienteering compass allows you to determine a bearing off a map without orienting the map to north. This is a Suunto MC-2.

given in the legend of all topographic maps. Or you can access them—for anyplace in the world—from these websites:

United States: NOAA Magnetic Declination Field Calculator (https://www.ngdc.noaa.gov/geomag/calculators/mobileDeclination.shtml#WMM)

Canada: Magnetic Declination Calculator (https://www.geomag.nrcan.gc.ca/calc/mdcal-en.php)

To adjust your compass for declination, apply the rhyme: Declination east, compass least, or declination west, compass best.

Example: You are traveling in California where the declination, as given in the diagram (and your topo map sheet), is 16 degrees east. You have computed a true map heading to an objective, using the protractor function of your orienteering compass. Your true map heading is due east, or 90 degrees. Adjust this figure for declination by applying the "east is least"

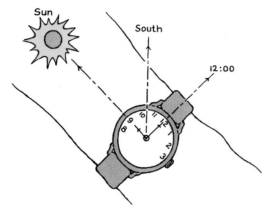

Your watch as a compass. You can use a digital watch if you mentally impose a round watch dial over the digital face.

(subtract) rhyme: Simply subtract 16 degrees from 90 degrees and travel on a magnetic heading of 74 degrees.

Conversely, the declination would be added (west is best) to your map bearing if you lived in New York, east of the zero (agonic) declination line.

Note: It makes no difference in which cardinal direction you are traveling on your map sheet. The declination in your area holds constant for the entire map sheet (usually), and there is seldom more than a few degrees of difference from one area of a state to another. Once you have determined your area declination, you need only remember the rhyme to apply it to any true direction computed from your map.

One degree of compass error equals approximately 92 feet per mile of ground error, so you must consider declination when traveling in

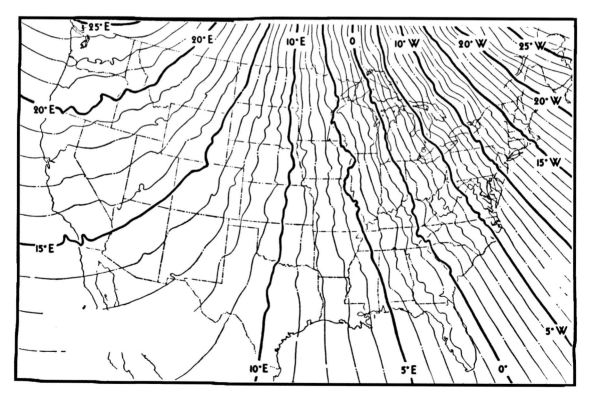

Figure C-8. Standard declination diagram
National Geophysical Data Center, www.ngdc.noaa.gov/geomag/declination.shtml

regions substantially distant from the agonic line.

A detailed discussion of the compass and navigational techniques is found in my book *Basic Illustrated: Map and Compass.*

Your watch as a compass: You'll need a conventional dial watch for this procedure (a digital watch can be used if you mentally impose a round watch dial over the digital face).

Hold the watch level and rotate it until the hour hand points to the sun. Halfway between the hour hand and the 12 on the watch dial is due south. This procedure is reasonably accurate provided your watch is correctly set for the right time zone . . . and you are north of the equator.

Your compass as a watch: The sun will be at these approximate bearings at these approximate times:

East	6 a.m.
Southeast	9 a.m.
South	noon
Southwest	3 p.m.
West	6 p.m.

Compass or GPS? Now that just about everyone owns a Global Positioning System (GPS) unit, you can toss away your magnetic compass. Right? Hardly! You must understand how to use a compass in order to effectively use a GPS unit. See the GPS section beginning on page 98. A GPS complements a compass, it doesn't replace it!

Contact Cement

This is the best adhesive to use for gluing fabrics and/or porous items. Useful applications include patching holes in canvas tents and bags, gluing foam knee pads into canoes, repairing holes and tears in nylon fabrics, etc. Weldwood contact cement, in my experience, is the most reliable.

Cooking and Food Ideas (see also Baking)
Cookware

Prepackaged Trail King cook sets are a waste of money. Pot sizes are usually awkward and the frying pans are awful. Experienced campers usually assemble their own cookware, buying only those items they need.

Pots may be aluminum, stainless steel, or porcelain-lined steel. The concern that cooking in aluminum may cause Alzheimer's disease has been dismissed, and in any case is hardly a concern considering the minimal use received by camp cookware. Choose low-sided broad pots rather than high narrow ones. A low center of gravity is important if you're cooking on a less-than-rock-stable trail stove. For a crew of eight, you'll need three nesting pots, the largest of which is twenty-four cups.

You'll find better cookware at kitchen-supply and discount stores than at camping shops. What works at home works afield, provided it has a tight-fitting cover and is sized to nest with the rest of your pots and pans. Wire bail handles are necessary only if you do all your cooking on an open fire. One long pot handle or two protruding metal "ears" per pot are adequate if you have insulated pot holders, gloves, bandannas, or pliers.

Engrave lines on the inside of the pot sides at two-cup intervals and scratch the total capacity (e.g., sixteen cups) just below the rim. This will eliminate guesswork and the need for measuring cups at mealtime.

Skillets: The "camping" skillets I've seen are either too thin, too small, or the handles are

Figure C-9. A quickly removable spring-wire handle works on all pans and pots.

A tea kettle heats faster and is less tippy than a coffee pot, and you can pour with one hand.

weak or awkward to use. I prefer to purchase a high-grade Teflon-lined skillet (10- or 12-inch diameter) at my local discount store and cut off the Bakelite handle with a hacksaw. Then I make a universal-style, quickly removable handle from 0.187-inch-diameter spring wire (see Figure C-9). The mounting bracket on the skillet is made from hardware-store aluminum flat stock. Two brass bolts secure the bracket to the pan. I also outfit my large "spaghetti" pot with a rigid wire handle (Figure C-9), so I'll have better control when I drain liquid. When a pan wears out, I unbolt the bracket and transfer it to a new pan—no need to make a new one.

Store your cookset in a nylon bag.

Teakettle: A teakettle heats faster and is less tippy than a coffee pot and you can pour with one hand. An eight-cup kettle is about right for four; a twenty-cup model is better for groups of

eight or more. Teapots are ordinarily left on the fire as a major supply of boiling water, so consider an oversize (twenty-cup) kettle, even for small groups. A large teapot will speed heating of dishwater and save stove fuel.

On a long hike you may want to stop for tea—so always pack your teakettle (in a fabric bag) at the top of your pack where you can get it quickly.

Utensils: Experienced campers carry only an insulated metal or plastic cup, a metal spoon, and a sturdy plastic bowl. The individual belt knife or pocketknife performs all cutting chores. Forks—useful for vehicle camping—are a luxury. It's best to have identical, colored nesting bowls. Keep bowls in a fabric bag, stored inside your smallest cook pot. To prevent the spread of illness, each person should always use the same bowl.

You'll need these cooking utensils:

Pancake turner

Rubber spatula for scraping uneaten food from pots and bowls

Aluminum pliers or "pot grabber" (I prefer the official Boy Scout model)

Wooden stirring spoon

Tongs (metal, plastic, or wood)

Small wire whip or fork for reconstituting instant mixes

Salt, pepper, and other spices.

Sharp knife with a blade long enough to reach to the bottom of the peanut butter jar. An extra knife is always welcome in the kitchen.

Tip: Be sure your cup has a plastic snap-on lid that will keep coffee hot and heat-seeking insects out. Make a leash for your lid: Drill a small hole through an edge of the mug lid and tie a piece of heavy fishing line through the hole. Tie the other end of the line to the mug handle (see photo).

Your cup should have a snap-on lid to keep bugs out—and a leash so you won't lose the lid. Note the snap on the handle for attachment to a pack. A carabiner works as well.

A fabric utensil roll hung from a tight rope strung between two trees keeps spices handy and off the ground. Note the spoon-size coffee strainer and removable steel pot handles in the bottom row.

A fabric utensil roll (see photo) is used to store tools and spices. Set snaps or Velcro tabs at the top as illustrated so you can hang the roll from a tight line, out of contact with wet ground. If you string a tight rope under your rain tarp (see Tarps [Rain Flies], page 164) and hang your utensil roll from it, everything will remain dry in the rain.

Commercial utensil rolls, patterned after my design, can be purchased from Duluth Pack or Frost River.

Blacken your pot bottoms: Pots that are used on open fires get quite black outside. Some experts suggest that you coat the exposed surfaces with liquid soap or shaving cream so the carbon black will clean easily. The result is an awful mess for the dishwashing crew. I leave pots black (they cook faster and more evenly) and keep them inside a plastic-lined nylon sack between uses.

Aluma Black, a chemical used to blacken aluminum gun sights and mounts, works wonders on pot bottoms. Just daub the chemical on the pot, allow it to dry, and a rich blue-black color will result. Aluma Black is available from most gun shops. It is inexpensive. The product also can be used to darken the decks and rails of aluminum canoes and fishing boats.

Drying dishes: Pack a half-dozen sheets of paper toweling for each meal. The toweling is convenient for drying cookware, cleaning the stove, and the like.

Food Ideas

For a gourmet treat, drop chunks of raw fish into boiling soup and cook for a maximum of 5 minutes. It sounds terrible but tastes superb and is the logical solution to preparing fish when vegetable oil or stove fuel is in short supply.

Making popcorn: If you're tired of trying to season popcorn in a pot that's too small, try this: Carry some large grocery sacks on your next campout. As you complete each batch of popcorn, pour it into the paper bag (don't use a plastic bag—hot popcorn will melt right through it). Season the popcorn and shake the bag to mix. When the popcorn's gone, burn the bag . . . or fold and store it in a plastic bag for future use.

Making biscuits and cakes: Mix batter in a plastic ziplock bag. Add the water, knead the bag with your hands until the consistency of the mix is correct, then punch a hole in the bag bottom and force the gooey mess into your awaiting oven. Burn the plastic bag. No mess or fuss.

Quick'n' easy trail suppers can be prepared by adding any or all of these items to boiling soup mix: instant rice, dry noodles, elbow macaroni,

Bisquick dumplings (use a plastic bag to mix), or Potato Buds.

Pita (Mediterranean pocket bread) is another alternative to trail crackers. Pita contains preservatives (bagels often do not) and will remain fresh and tasty for at least 2 weeks in typical summer weather. One pita bread per person is substantial lunch fare when combined with the usual noontime extras.

Tortillas contain preservatives and last as long as pitas. Add beans, cheese, hamburger, etc., and you have a complete meal.

Cheese in soup? You bet! Sprinkle dried Parmesan cheese on soup for a gourmet treat. Chunks of cheese (any kind) add spark, flavor, and calories to trail spaghetti and chili.

A Thermos bottle is a practical accessory. Boiling water poured into a vacuum bottle that is not used for beverages may provide the nucleus for hot dishwater later. Saves running the stove (using precious gas) to heat dishwater.

Prepackaging saves time! Prepack everything you need to prepare a given meal in a ziplock plastic bag. Everything should be premeasured and mixed so that you don't have to fuss on the trail. For added simplicity, I traditionally pack my plastic-bagged breakfasts in green nylon bags, my lunches in blue, and my suppers in red. This saves considerable groping at mealtimes and provides abrasion resistance for the tear-prone zipper bags inside. Adhesive-tape labels or cardboard tags identify the specific contents of each nylon bag.

A few last tips:

- Place fresh vegetables, crackers, cookies, and other breakables in your teakettle to keep them from being crushed on a strenuous backpacking or canoe trip.

- A stainless-steel Sierra cup is a lousy drinking cup but it is a great ladle for soup and stew.

- An empty cardboard juice or milk carton makes a handy "safe" for crushable foods like cookies and eggs. Use the wax-coated carton to mix powdered soft drinks and as an emergency fire starter on a rainy day.

- Dried foods are generally bland unless they're heavily spiced. I carry salt, red and black pepper, oregano, basil, garlic powder, thyme, and rosemary.

- Farm-fresh eggs will keep for weeks without refrigeration! Small- and medium-size eggs have thicker shells than large eggs, so they're less apt to break on a hiking or canoe trip. You can check the freshness of eggs by floating them in a bowl of water. The deeper they sink, the fresher they are. Discard any eggs that float to the top. Pack a dozen eggs in *two* cardboard (not Styrofoam) egg cartons. Tape shut the twin cartons and seal them in a plastic bag. Set the sealed carton at the top of your pack. I've used this method for years on long canoe trips and I can't recall when I've had a broken egg.

Some Breakfast Favorites
Bacon/Cheese McPita/McTortilla

Option 1: Fry and set aside two thin slices of Canadian bacon per person. Scramble or fry one egg per person and set it aside. Now, lightly fry an open-face Mediterranean pocket bread (pita) or a tortilla in a teaspoon of cooking oil.

When the bottom of the pita or tortilla is brown (20 seconds), flip the bread over and lay thinly sliced cheese on top. Pile on the bacon and egg, add a dash of your favorite salsa (optional), and immediately toss a dash of cold water into the sizzling skillet. Cover and steam for 15 seconds then serve immediately. In 1 minute you'll have a wholesome, delicious sandwich.

Option 2: Same as above, but omit the egg.

Option 3: Cut pita bread in half and fill the pockets with any fresh thin-sliced or grated cheese. Generously sprinkle garlic powder and oregano (optional) over the cheese. Fry each pita half in a well-oiled, covered skillet for about 20 seconds. As soon as you flip the pita, add a dash of cold water—and cover—to steam the cheese.

Tortillas are less filling than pitas but they have a more delicate, toasty flavor. Cook each tortilla flat in a well-oiled skillet for about 10 seconds, then flip it over and add cheese and garlic powder to the toasted side. Immediately roll the tortilla into a burrito shape, add cold water to steam, then cover and simmer for 20 seconds.

Cinnamon Tortillas, Stewed Fruit, and Canadian Bacon

Make a tortilla burrito as described above, but substitute margarine, cinnamon, and white or brown sugar for the cheese and garlic. Tastes just like a cinnamon roll!

Boiled dehydrated apples and brown sugar, with a side of Canadian bacon, round out this perfect meal.

Note: Freshly baked pita bread and tortillas will keep at least 2 weeks without refrigeration if they are well sealed when you leave home.

Peanut butter on pancakes? Sounds awful but tastes divine. The peanut butter melts into the hotcakes and provides a rich taste.

To make good-tasting boiled camp coffee: Bring water to a boil, then remove the pot from heat. Add 1 heaping tablespoon of ground coffee per cup, plus an extra tablespoon for the pot. Stir coffee into the water, put on a lid, and set the pot aside for 5 minutes to allow the grounds to settle. Do not boil pot-brewed camp coffee; you'll destroy the delicate flavor and introduce a muddy metallic taste. *Tip:* Pour the settled coffee through a spoon-sized mesh-strainer and you'll enjoy a totally ground-free brew.

For classy coffee, add cinnamon or almond extract and you'll draw raves from everyone. A quarter teaspoon of almond extract or powdered cinnamon per eight cups of coffee is about right.

To make delicious camp mocha, use one packet of hot chocolate mix per cup. Fill cup with fresh-brewed coffee and top with some mini-marshmallows. Teenagers love this drink!

Hot pancakes for a big crew: Mix pancake syrup and margarine or butter in a small pot and heat—keeps pancakes hot when they are prepared in advance for a large group.

Lunch

Lunch should be easy. If you can't unwrap it, slice it, spread it, or open a can, forget it. On a severe day you might boil some water for tea or soup, otherwise a cold lunch saves time. My lunches are similar and include cheese, pita bread, sausage that needs no refrigeration, peanut butter, jam, something salty (nuts, pretzels, etc.), something sweet (Snickers bars are the universal favorite), and occasionally, Hudson Bay Bread (everyone's favorite!).

Hudson Bay Bread

Hudson Bay Bread has been the traditional lunch fare in youth camps from Maine to Minnesota and throughout Canada. Charles L. Sommers Canoe Base, in Ely, Minnesota, has been serving it to Boy Scouts since 1960. It is rumored that the base got the recipe from the Minnesota Outward Bound School near Ely. Hudson Bay Bread is a hands-down favorite on strenuous trips, but it may be too rich (it contains about a million calories!) for snacking at home. It's really more of a moist granola bar than a bread. There are many variations. This is the "official" recipe, to which I add chocolate chips (a must!). The following recipe makes a 10-day lunch supply for a hungry crew of four. Eat it alone or top with peanut butter and/or jam.

Ingredients

> 3 cups soft margarine or butter
>
> 4 cups white sugar
>
> ⅓ cup light Karo corn syrup
>
> ⅔ cup honey
>
> 2 tsp maple flavoring (Mapleine)
>
> 19 cups (yes, 19!) finely ground rolled oats (not instant oats!)
>
> 1½ cups sliced almonds
>
> 1 cup chocolate chips

Cream together the above ingredients. Gradually add the sliced almonds and chocolate chips and rolled oats. Some cooks add shredded coconut and raisins.

Preparation
Press into a greased cake pan about ¼ to ⅛ inch thick. Bake at 325°F for about 20 minutes, until golden brown. Don't overcook! Press down on the "bread" with a spatula (to

prevent crumbling) before you cut and remove the squares from the pan. "Teen serving size" (twice what most adults will tolerate) measures about 3½ inches square. Wrap each square in plastic wrap. Shelf life is a full summer or more. Unused bars freeze well and keep till next year.

Swift Suppers

Here are some things to consider as you plan your suppers:

- Most freeze-dried and dehydrated entrees consist of three parts—pasta or rice; freeze-dried chicken, beef, or shrimp; and spices. Remember this, and you can mix and match a variety of foods to suit your tastes.

- The meat is the most expensive part of any dried meal. One-quarter pound of freeze-dried hamburger (essential to make spaghetti, stroganoff, or chili) costs three times as much as a Big Mac! Chicken and shrimp are even pricier.

However, you can easily dry these meats yourself in an inexpensive home dehydrator. Several excellent vacuum-sealing machines are available. I've had good luck with a powerful home unit called the FoodSaver by Tilia. *For example, here's how to dehydrate hamburger:*

1. Fry the hamburger, drain the grease, then pour boiling water through the meat to remove as much fat as possible.

2. Line each dehydrator tray with three sheets of absorbent paper toweling and spread the hamburger out on the trays. Allow no more than 1 pound (¼-inch thickness) of hamburger per tray.

3. Turn the dehydrator to high (140°F) and wait 24 hours. Vacuum-seal (best) the dried hamburger or double-bag it in ziplock bags. Use a drinking straw to remove as much air as possible from the ziplock bags. Vacuum-sealed, dehydrated hamburger will keep about a year at room temperature; carefully zipper-bagged meat should last a month. As a safety precaution, keep dehydrated meats frozen until just before your camping trip. Use dehydrated hamburger in spaghetti, chili, soups, and stews.

Hamburger/Cheese Vegetable Soup

Add 1 pound (about ¾ cup) of dried hamburger to instant vegetable soup. Toss in a heavy handful of wide egg noodles or instant rice and add some dried mushrooms and a few slices of cheese. A dash of red pepper and garlic powder complete the recipe.

Spaghetti and Chili

To prepare spaghetti, you'll need dehydrated hamburger, pasta, spices, and tomato paste. Chili requires dehydrated beans, which are easily made by drying canned beans: Dump the canned beans (after pouring off the liquid) on the dehydrator tray and turn the heat to high. The beans will be dried and ready to pack in about 8 hours.

To make spaghetti sauce, line the dehydrator trays with plastic cling wrap and spread any commercial sauce evenly on the trays. In 12 hours you'll have a thin, rubbery mass that resembles a fruit roll-up. Peel the dried sauce off the plastic wrap, roll it up, and freeze it. Later, break chunks into a plastic poly bottle. Add water to the chunks to rehydrate the sauce.

If you don't want to mess with making your own sauce, order tomato powder at your local co-op. Add a little water to the powder and you'll have paste; add more water for sauce or soup.

Pita Pizza

This is everyone's favorite meal!

Ingredients: One or two pieces of pita bread per person, dried tomato powder, fresh mozzarella cheese (hard, fresh cheese keeps nearly a month if it's vacuum sealed), oregano, garlic powder, salt, cayenne pepper. Add any or all of the following: dried pepperoni, summer sausage, hard salami, Canadian bacon, fresh onion, green pepper, dried or canned mushrooms.

Procedure:

1. Slice and fry the meat and drain off the grease on paper toweling. Thickly dice the vegetables and mushrooms, fry them in olive oil, then drain off the grease and set the veggies aside.

This delicious steam-fried pizza, which cooks in less than a minute, is everyone's favorite. Note the insulated cover (see Cozies, page XX) on the frying pan lid—a must to retain heat and steam-melt the cheese. Naan and pita bread make excellent pizza crust and keep fresh for about a week.

2. To make the pizza sauce, pour ½ cup of tomato powder into a bowl and add water to make a thick paste. Sprinkle in two parts dried basil, one part oregano, heavy dash of garlic powder, salt, and cayenne. Half a teaspoon of anchovy paste kicks up the flavor. Heat 3 tablespoons of olive oil, then add the sauce mixture and gently simmer for a few minutes.

3. Fry an open-faced pita at low heat in a well-olive-oiled, covered skillet. When the bottom of the pita is brown (about 20 seconds), flip over the pita and thickly spread on tomato sauce, cheese, meat, and precooked vegetables to taste. Immediately add a dash of water (to steam melt the cheese) and cover the pan. Allow the pizza to cook at very low heat for half a minute, or until the cheese has melted.

Add Fresh Vegetables to Your One-Pot Meals!

Fresh onions, tomatoes, and green peppers will keep about 5 days on a camping trip, if they are properly packed.

Place onions in a cotton or paper bag. Stow the bag inside a rigid container.

Here's how to prepare and pack green peppers and tomatoes:

1. Wash the vegetables, then float them in a sink full of drinking water that has been treated with about ⅛ cup (the amount isn't critical) of chlorine bleach. Allow the vegetables to soak for several minutes in the treated water before you dry and pack them away. The bleach will kill the surface bacteria that promotes spoilage. A similar procedure is used in some of America's finest restaurants to keep vegetables fresh.

2. Separately wrap each vegetable in clean paper toweling. Pack the towel-wrapped veggies in a paper or cotton sack and set the sack inside a teakettle or other crushproof container. Do not wrap vegetables in nonporous plastic!

Tip: When you're ready to cook, wash in fresh water only the portion of vegetable you need. Do not wash the entire vegetable! Doing so will introduce water-borne bacteria, which may accelerate spoilage.

Two Slick Cooking Tips

1. As mentioned, a dash of cold water in a hot, covered skillet will quickly steam-cook foods. You can also use this method to restore the freshness of week-old bagels, pita bread, and tortillas. Simply "steam grill" the bread in a covered skillet for a few seconds.

2. If you insist on carrying loaves of bread, here's an old woodsman's trick that guarantees perfect toast: Distribute a heavy pinch of table salt on the surface of a hot, dry (no grease!) skillet. Set a slice of bread on the salt. Do not cover! When the bottom of the bread is toasted to a golden brown, flip the bread over and toast the other side. The salt won't burn or stick to the bread or skillet.

How to Prepare Freeze-Dried Foods So They Always Taste Good

Freeze-dried foods are fickle. Prepare them according to directions one day and they're great. Repeat the procedure another time and . . . ugh!

Take heart. Here's a foolproof cooking method that works regardless of the weather, the zodiac, or a cranky stove.

Step 1: Read the cooking directions but don't take them too seriously. What works at home on the range often fails on a flat rock in a nor'wester.

Step 2: Separate the component parts of the food. Generally, there are three parts—a meat portion; a noodle, rice, or vegetable portion; and a spice packet. (See the first example under "Why Some Meals Fail," below, for the specifics of preparing cook-in-the-bag meals.)

Typical directions say: *Add contents of all packets to X cups of boiling water. Reduce heat, simmer 15 to 20 minutes or until noodles [or whatever] are tender.*

Step 3: Put 20 percent more water in your cooking pot than the directions call for. Add the meat, vegetables, and spice packet, along with your favorite spices, to the cold water. Cover the pot and bring to a boil.

Step 4: When the water is at a rolling boil, add the noodles or rice packet. Boil for 30 seconds, stirring constantly.

Step 5. Remove the pot from heat; cover, then set it on an insulated pad (closed-cell foam). Cover the pot with an insulated cozy (see Cozies, page 70.) and allow the food to self-cook for about 20 minutes.

Step 6: Eat and enjoy. All portions of the meal are thoroughly cooked and the taste has been fully developed.

Why Some Meals Fail

You haven't cooked the meat long enough. Half-cooked reconstituted meat spoils the whole stew. Except in very warm weather, cook-in-the-bag foods just don't get done enough. It's best to place the cooking bag in a covered pot of near-boiling water for 10 minutes. Add about 10 percent more water to the cooking bag than the directions call for.

You burned the pasta! This is easy to do on a one-burner trail stove, especially if you plop the contents of all food packets into the boiling water simultaneously. If your stove's turned on high, you may burn the meal quicker than you can say "Turn the heat down, Jack!"

Insufficient water. Remember, you can always boil out too much water, but there's not much you can do with a stew that's so thick it's burned and glued to the pot bottom.

Not enough spices. Don't underestimate the value of spices when preparing freeze-dried foods. Most quick-cook products are unacceptably bland unless they're well spiced.

Spoilage. Dehydrated foods come packed in plastic and have a shelf life of about 1 year. This is because plastic is not a complete water barrier. Freeze-dried foods come packaged in aluminum foil, which is an absolute vapor barrier. Consequently, these products have an unlimited shelf life.

This should tell you something about end-of-season food sales. Don't buy dehydrated foods in September if you plan to use them the following July. Your autumn "bargain" may turn out to be summer indigestion.

It's important to realize that many products contain both freeze-dried and dehydrated components (for example, spaghetti with freeze-dried meatballs). While the foil-wrapped meatballs won't spoil, the plastic-wrapped spaghetti and spices might. Only foods that are completely sealed in foil are immune to spoilage. Unfortunately, you almost never see these products offered at sale prices.

Introduction of bacteria and/or water vapor during repackaging. Don't handle dried foods or expose them to air any longer than necessary when you repackage them. This will reduce the chance of bacteria and water vapor getting into the food.

Tip: Slice meat and cheese with a knife that's been dipped in boiling water. This will reduce transfer of bacteria into the food.

Cold-Weather Cooking Tips

Stoves used on snow must be set on a support or they'll melt the snow beneath and quietly sink out of sight. Fires built in snow must also have suitable support.

Don't set stoves on pieces of closed-cell foam (so the fuel tank will retain heat . . . and pressure) as is recommended by some authorities. A hot stove will melt the foam and stick solidly to it. Instead, place a piece of plywood, Masonite, or tile on top of the foam and set your pot on this.

Pot covers are essential for winter cooking. Open pots lose too much heat; in subzero temperatures, water may not reach boiling unless it is placed in a covered pot. Metal pot covers get extremely hot. I rivet a nylon loop on top that I can safely grab with my hand.

Snow provides a natural windscreen. Dig in your stove so it's completely protected from the wind. Subzero temps and a good wind will lengthen cooking times considerably.

Insulate your water bottles so they won't freeze: Carry water bottles in an inside parka pocket so they won't freeze. In camp, store them upside down in the snow. The frozen interface will then be at the bottle's bottom and you'll be able to pour the liquid from the capped end. Snow is a marvelous insulator: Water bottles stored overnight this way will be "pourable" come morning.

Light for the kitchen: Winter nights come early; often there is insufficient light to cook by. You'll want a powerful headlamp with a series of LEDs. Lithium batteries are essential when it's bitterly cold. *Tip:* To preserve your night vision, use the red light setting.

Securing drinking water in winter may require that you bore through the ice of a frozen lake. For this, an ice chisel is better than the traditional cumbersome auger. Fit a short length of threaded pipe to the tail of the chisel so you can screw on a pole to provide weight when chopping. Don't use a hand ax for chiseling—it is awkward and dangerous.

How to wash dishes in subfreezing temperatures: Heavy rubber gloves will protect hands from the cold. Dishwater should be near boiling. A copper sponge or 3M nylon pad is all you need to remove food particles from pots and bowls. Detergents aren't necessary, as there is no bacterial growth in subfreezing temperatures. In fact, dishes need not be washed at all. Some authorities recommend that you clean dishes with snow—a particularly inefficient practice. Boiling water and rubber gloves work much better!

Foods that don't work well in winter: Frozen cheese looks and tastes like candle tallow. Peanut butter and jelly are sure to be frozen; there is no way to keep these items thawed unless you carry them in your pockets.

Gasoline is dangerous in cold weather! Gasoline, naphtha (Coleman fuel), and kerosene freeze at very low temperatures. If these fuels contact exposed skin in subzero temperatures, instant frostbite will result. Always wear rubber gloves when fueling stoves in cold weather. (See Stoves, page 153, for a thorough discussion of safety and troubleshooting procedures.)

Cord and Cord Locks (see also Knots, Hitches, and Lashings)

The best camp utility cord is ⅛-inch-diameter nylon parachute cord. Nylon cord should be "hot cut" (use a butane lighter) rather than sliced, so its core and sheath won't separate.

Singe (melt) the ends of nylon and polypropylene cord and rope to prevent unraveling. Nobody whips the ends of ropes anymore.

Nylon cord locks are small, spring-loaded nylon clamps used to secure the cords of sleeping bags, parka hoods, and stuff sacks. Every camping shop carries a good supply of them for the do-it-yourselfer who wants to add versatility to his or her camping outfit. A less expensive solution that works as well is to purchase nylon hose clamps from scientific supply houses. You can buy a dozen rubber hose (tubing) clamps for the price of one cord lock.

Figure C-10. Secure your stuff sack with a quick-release loop.

You don't need cord locks to secure the thongs of nylon stuff sacks if you learn the simple knot illustrated in Figure C-10.

Now comes the hard part—threading the pair of ⅛-inch-diameter nylon parachute cords through the tiny cord-lock hole. One cord goes through easily; the second dies a slow death in midpush. Ultimately frustration reigns and the "good idea" is disgustedly thrown into a drawer for use later.

Here's an easy way to thread the paired cords through the cord-lock hole: Place the tips of the cords side by side, one tip ⅛ inch below the other. Then tape the two tightly together. Press open the cord-lock button, and voilà, the cords go through instantly—simple and fast.

Cozies

It's a cold, blustery day and you're anxious for a hot meal. You boil water on your gasoline stove, then place spaghetti noodles in your largest pot, stirring constantly so the noodles won't burn. You know that if you stop stirring and cover the pot, the pasta will boil faster. However, it may also burn and stick to the pot bottom. But if you continue to stir the uncovered food, heat will escape into the air and the spaghetti will take much longer to cook. What to do?

1. Bring the water to a rolling boil and add the uncooked spaghetti. Turn down the heat to medium and stir until all the noodles are absorbed into the water.

2. Turn off the stove. Cover the pot and set it on a closed-cell foam pad.

3. Immediately cover the pot with an insulated tea cozy or a sweater or jacket (not nylon—it melts!). Pile additional clothes on top to keep the heat in.

4. Entertain yourself for 20 minutes while the spaghetti slow cooks in its own heat. "Cozy cooking" saves time, stove fuel, and a burned pot bottom! Use this process when you make rice, soup, or hot cereal.

Tip: Make insulated cozies to fit all your pots. I prefer a two-piece model (top hat and pot band) like the one illustrated in Figure C-11, because it's more versatile and energy efficient than a one-piece model. The encircling band keeps the pot from losing heat to a cold wind when you remove the cover to stir your food. This saves considerable cooking time and fuel on cold, blustery days. Fitted cozies are essential for winter camping, camping trips above the tree line, and whenever you must cook a lot of food for a large group. A skillet-cover cozy keeps heat in when you steam-cook pita pizza, bagels, and tortilla burritos.

Cozies speed cooking, save stove fuel, and keep food hot long enough for seconds. Note the insulated cozy band (made from ironing board material) on this pot. The noninsulated (bare metal) zone near the pot bottom keeps flame away from the cozy. When the food boils, Cliff will remove the pot from the heat and set it on the closed-cell foam square at left. Then, he'll add the pot cover, with its insulated cozy. The food will self-cook from retained heat and be ready to serve in 20 minutes.

I also make a fitted cozy for my teakettle. The spout pokes through a slit that's controlled by a Velcro tab. Fresh coffee will stay hot for about an hour in a cozy-covered kettle if you place the kettle on an insulated foam pad or fabric pot holder.

Cozy fabrics: Nylon or acrylics catch fire or melt! Cotton and wool work well. Insulated ironing board material is satisfactory. An old welding blanket is the best material of all because it won't melt or catch fire.

When I want to go ultralight, I use the "go light cozy" pictured. It's just a piece of closed-cell foam with cutouts for the pot handle. It speeds cooking and doubles as a hot pad—insulates the pot from the cold ground—when the food is done.

This lightweight foam, "go light" cozy-cover cuts cooking time and saves stove fuel. When the food has cooked, remove the foam piece and set it on the ground. Put the pot on top. The foam will insulate the hot pot from the cold ground.

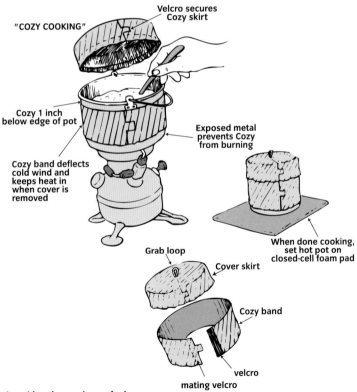

"COZY COOKING"

Velcro secures Cozy skirt

Cozy 1 inch below edge of pot

Cozy band deflects cold wind and keeps heat in when cover is removed

Exposed metal prevents Cozy from burning

When done cooking, set hot pot on closed-cell foam pad

Grab loop

Cover skirt

Cozy band

velcro

mating velcro

Figure C-11. Cozies speed cooking time and save fuel.

D

Dental Floss

Dental floss is the toughest "thread" you can buy. I use it to mend tears in packs, tarps, and other heavy-duty camping items. *Tip:* You'll need a heavy-duty sewing needle with a large eye to accommodate the thick dental floss.

If you crack a canoe seat, thwart yoke, or tool handle, try this: Apply instant epoxy to the crack, then tightly and evenly wrap the crack with dental floss. Spread instant epoxy over the wrap and allow it to dry. Your repair will never let go!

Dental Tool

A pointed dental tool (Figure D-1) is useful to remove a stubborn gasket from your trail stove, clean a fuel jet, or pick out a spring. Dentists throw out these tools when they get dull. Ask your dentist to save some for you!

Figure D-1. A dental tool is handy for nitpicking chores.
© Licensed by Shutterstock.com

Desert Camping

Desert camping is like any other kind of camping, with these exceptions:

1. The *water* in desert rivers is usually too silty to drink. Hence, you must either carry your own drinking water or use alum to settle the silt (see Alum, page 3) and afterwards purify it with a filter or chemicals.

Water from the Green River in Utah has been settled using the alum system. You can see the clear water on top and the sediment below. The clear water is being run through a filter/purifier to make it safe to drink.

2. In many federally managed areas, you must *contain all campfires* in a government-approved "fire pan," defined as "a durable, metal fire pan at least 12-inches x 12-inches wide, with at least a 1.5-inch lip around its outer edge and sufficient to contain fire and remains. The pan must be elevated off the ground to prevent scorching. If the fire pan does not have legs to elevate, place rocks underneath the pan." Ash must be packed out. In some areas you are allowed to throw cold ash into the river (check with federal authorities). A typical fire pan may weigh 10 pounds or

more! A much lighter and more compact fire pan can be made by combining a Littlbug stove with a steel automotive oil drain pan or other steel pan that meets the mandated dimensions. Prop the pan on some rocks and you meet the "elevation" requirement. A small steel garbage can lid can also double as a fire pan. The value of the Littlbug stove for desert use is that it produces a small footprint fire that won't overload the fire pan. And the stove uses much less wood than an open fire. **Note:** Littlbug offers a compact, 7.4-ounce stainless-steel "Fire Bowl" that effectively contains embers. The Fire Bowl works great but it is too small to meet federal fire-pan specifications.

Traditional fire pans are heavy and bulky. The Littlbug stove meets federal requirements if you use it with any steel pan (automotive oil pan) that measures 12 inches or more in diameter and has a 1.5-inch-high lip. When cranked up, the Littlbug provides quite a flame!

3. *Dust (fine sand):* Ever watch a cowboy movie and notice how the horses kick up dust with every step they take? Much of desert camping is like that—fine sand everywhere and in everything. Keeping your tent closed up tight helps, but not enough. You quickly learn to keep things in their stuff sacks until you absolutely need them.

Tip: Zippers really take a beating in the desert. If sand clogs your tent zippers, you'll need water and a brush to get it out. Zippers will run smoothly almost forever if they are occasionally cleaned and lubricated. I use a toothbrush and water to remove debris, followed by a dedicated zipper cleaner-lubricant like McNett Zip Care. You can also lube zips with WD-40 (I've used it successfully for decades), petroleum jelly, Chapstick, candle and crayon wax, and graphite (pencil).

Separated zipper? Function can usually be restored by slightly compressing (with a pliers) each side of the slider. Do not over-tighten! Doing so may cause the slider to jam permanently.

4. *Temperature extremes:* Days are hot, nights are cold. When we canoed the Rio Grande in January 2011, average morning (wake-up) temperatures ranged from 15 to 25°F. By midafternoon it had warmed to 78°F! I was glad I brought a 15°F, three-season down sleeping bag!

5. *Rains* are usually light and short if not nonexistent. Most nights you can get by without putting a rain fly on your tent.

6. *Things that scratch or sting and bite:* Shake out your boots in the morning before you

It doesn't rain much in the desert so you can often get by without a waterproof tent fly.

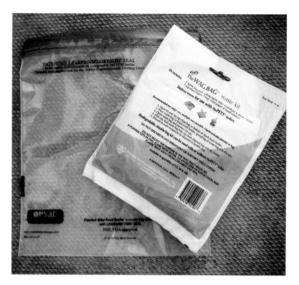

The Wag Bag waste kit (right), when used with an OPSAK odor-proof barrier bag (left) *and* a waterproof stuff sack (dry bag) keeps odors at bay.

put them on. They may contain creepy crawlers that sting or bite. It sounds attractive to wear shorts in the desert, but you may change your mind the first time you hike off-trail and encounter prickly vegetation. Everything is "sharp" in the desert!

7. *Human waste* must, in many places, be packed out. There are a number of approved toilet systems but few are very compact or work well for very long. The *Cleanwaste Wag Bag kit* is a compact, convenient short-term solution. It consists of a zip-close plastic bag and mesh holder, a gelling agent, odor neutralizer and decay catalyst, toilet paper, and hand sanitizer. It works fine for about 3 days, then the odor becomes unbearable. The odor can be stifled longer if you pack the used Wag Bag in an OPSAK (patented odor-proof-barrier bag), available from LOKSAK. The

The Biffy Bag earns high marks for odor neutralization.

Biffy Bag combines waste solidification powder and toilet paper with a cleverly designed plastic bag and an air-tight Mylar foil pouch, that is said to be 4,000 times more odor-proof than a standard garbage bag! I've used Biffy Bags on desert trips for as long as 8 days and they earned high marks. The manufacturer says that used bags placed in the hot desert sun remained odor-free for more than a week. That's impressive!

Diapers and Diaper Pins

Cloth diapers (if you can find them!) make excellent camp towels. They're lightweight, compact, and absorbent.

Diaper pins are much more rugged and visible in dim light than other safety pins. Uses are endless: They can serve as clothespins—pin through the line and wet clothes won't slide together—and as an emergency replacement pin for eyeglasses. Use them to secure pockets in packs and clothes when zippers fail, pin money and credit cards inside pockets, attach a whistle to a life jacket, hang a flashlight from a tent, etc. A dozen diaper pins are not too many to bring along on a camping trip.

Duct Tape/Repair Tape

Duct tape is the most useful repair item you can have. The hard-to-find olive drab "army" tape sticks better than the common gray tape found in hardware stores. 3M brand silver duct tape is the best. Gorilla tape is better than any duct tape.

Tear-Aid: These super-strong patches stay tight when applied. There are two types, A and B. B sticks only to vinyl and vinyl-coated fabrics; A adheres to everything else. These patches never let go! Once, while canoeing a rapid in Canada, my Royalex canoe struck a sharp rock which caused a leak. I put ashore, dried the break and cleaned it with an alcohol wipe, then I applied two type B patches (Royalex has a vinyl outer skin), one over the other. They held tight for the duration of the trip—130 miles. Later at home, I tried to remove the patches in order to effect a permanent repair. They wouldn't come loose. I had to grind them off!

Be sure to include some nylon filament (strapping) tape in your repair kit: It beats duct tape for mending broken canoe paddles, boat seats, and tool handles. *Tip:* Remove tape from its bulky roll and rewind it on a short pencil. Now you can "write about what you fix." Everything should be multipurpose on a camping trip!

E

Ethics in the Wilderness

This section is about the imperfect science of sanitation and ethical camping procedures. It is no longer acceptable to build beds of green pine boughs (or dead ones, for that matter), lash log furniture, trench tents, hack green trees, and otherwise disturb the natural environment to suit our whims. There's just too little wilderness and too many of us. If we are to preserve the remaining backcountry for future generations, then each of us must adopt a solemn "I care" attitude. We must unfailingly practice ethical use of our natural resources, and we must teach—indeed, preach—ethics to all who will listen. And for those who turn the other ear, there must be laws . . . and penalties. The alternative is regulation upon regulation and a lessened quality of experience for everyone. Here are the recommended land- and water-use procedures:

Disposal of human and food wastes: Bury these wastes in mineral soil (if possible) 2 to 6 inches deep, well away from water. The upper 12 inches of soil contain the majority of decomposer organisms and so ensure the fastest rate of decay.

Toilet paper should be burned. Unburned tissue may take a season or more to degrade. Human waste will be gone in a matter of days if the weather is warm. When camping on the granite rock of the Canadian Shield, or

Take only pictures, leave only footprints.

anywhere soil cover is at a premium, simply follow the recommended procedure for shallow burial and cover the waste with whatever soil cover is available.

Caution: Do not burn toilet paper unless you have a water bottle and can put your fire dead out! A number of forest fires have been caused by burning toilet paper.

Please do not leave leftover food around camp "for the animals." This will upset their ecology and make them dependent on humans—not to mention the aggravation they'll bestow on campers who will later occupy the site.

Fish entrails: It is illegal in most states to throw fish entrails into a lake or river, and for good reason. Bacteria consume the viscera and multiply, which raises germ levels to possibly dangerous proportions. Bacteria also use vast amounts of oxygen, which in turn robs fish and aquatic organisms of this essential element. Since food scraps react similarly, they too should never be tossed into a body of water.

Bury fish remains as you would food wastes—well away from water and your campsite. If you are camping in a remote area where seagulls are common, you may leave viscera on a large rock—well away from human habitation—for the gulls. This procedure is not acceptable on heavily used lakes!

When not to bury fish remains: Don't bury fish remains if you are camping in the heart of bear country. The rotting viscera will attract bears to you! Alaskan and Canadian guides prefer to toss fish remains well out into the lake or river, where they will be consumed by predator species. This procedure is recommended only for remote areas where bears are a problem. Popular parks have their own regulations.

Cans and bottles should always be packed out of the wilderness. Tin cans should be burned out and crushed flat with the back of an ax or your boot, then packed out. The typical steel can requires about 75 years to decompose completely; aluminum cans may need 500 years! A glass bottle could last a million years in the environment. We do not bury cans and bottles today. *Pack them out!*

Your garbage detail will be easier if you make a strong nylon bag, with drawstring, for this purpose.

Dishwashing: Dishes should never be washed in a waterway. Food scraps encourage bacterial growth, and even biodegradable detergents kill essential microorganisms. Dishes should be washed on land and in a large cooking pot. Dishwater is best disposed of on mineral soil, 100 feet from a lake or river.

Swimming is fine, but bathing in waterways is not. If you use soap to wash your hair and body, please rinse on the shore (with a bucket of water), well away from the water's edge.

Biodegradable products: It's fashionable today to extol the virtues of biodegradable products over those that do not break down by bacterial action. Certainly, you should choose biodegradable detergents, tissues, and toilet paper whenever possible. Be aware, however, that even the best biodegradable products depend upon bacteria, moisture, and time for decomposition. And this means increased germ counts, lowered levels of oxygen, and visual pollution for some time. There's no such thing as a free ride!

Bough beds: Cutting evergreen branches to make bough beds is illegal, immoral, and damaging to the trees. An air mattress or foam pad works better. The use of dead evergreen boughs or mosses should also be discouraged, as this material provides a surface cover that blots out sunlight and consequently kills vegetation below. Campsites should always be left as natural as possible so that nature can effectively do its thing.

Cutting green trees is, of course, illegal and damaging. Since green wood burns poorly, there's no sense cutting it for firewood. You'll find plenty of good dead firewood in the backcountry if you look for it (see Fire Making, page 81).

Graffiti: It's always shocking to see initials and names carved or painted on trees and rocks in the backcountry. But it does happen, even in the most remote wilderness. The cause is certainly ignorance and insensitivity, neither of which can be tolerated by those of us who know and care.

Noise: Most people take to the backcountry to experience peace and quiet. Loud, people-made disturbances are obviously unwelcome and, in state and national parks, usually illegal. Please keep stereos at home or use a personal radio or mp3 player with headphones.

Color: Some campers are offended by brightly colored camping gear and clothing. Consequently, the trend is toward gentle earth tones—greens, browns, and grays. However, there's no denying the safety (and photographic) advantages of brightly colored tents, canoes, and clothing in remote areas. Despite much hoopla, the color issue is exaggerated. There are more pressing environmental concerns in the backcountry.

Lugged hiking boots: Chunky-soled mountain boots churn up much more soil than nonaggressive footwear and are therefore discouraged in popular hiking areas. Primitive people got along quite nicely without Vibram lugs and you will too, not to mention the freedom of foot you'll enjoy by selecting lighter, more flexible shoes. Nonetheless, the damage that results from use of Rambo-style boots is probably overrated. Like color, there are more pressing concerns. See the Boots entry.

Fire site: Fire sites should always be left as natural as possible. In military terms, everything that's not growing or nailed down should be removed from the premises. Every scrap of paper and every shred of aluminum foil, down to the tiniest speck, should be picked out and hauled home. Ideally, there should be no partially burned wood left in the grate—absolutely everything should be consumed by flame before you pass on.

It is permissible, but no longer traditional (or even desirable), to leave cut firewood for those who will later occupy the site. Some modern campers consider the sight of a woodpile an affront, something that detracts from the wildness of the area. So cut only the wood you need and put your fire dead out—check it with your hands to be sure it is dead out—before you leave.

Education: Unfortunately, there are not yet enough of us who care and who will carry the

Axes don't damage trees; thoughtless people do!

banner for ethical land use. We must spread the word as gospel, but quietly, sensibly, and in a nonintimidating way, with full realization that you can always get more bears with honey than with guns. Studies show that the majority of campers mean well even though they often do what is improper. Most abuse occurs out of ignorance. The majority of people will willingly follow your lead if properly taught.

Selective Environmentalism

I taught environmental science at a Minnesota middle school for many years. I deeply believe that we are stewards of the earth and it's our job to take care of it and to pass a caring attitude on to the next generation.

This said, I take issue with "selective environmentalism." Here are some examples:

Save Trees: Use a Trail Stove Instead of a Campfire!

There are, of course, sensitive environments where you shouldn't make a campfire, and federal and state authorities have defined them all. But *properly maintained* campfires seldom harm heavily treed ecosystems. Indeed, burning fallen wood may benefit tree reproduction by removing dead wood which builds up on the forest floor and compacts the "litter layer."

There's also the concern that campfires produce carbon dioxide, which causes global warming. Yes, but so does driving 800 miles to reach a favorite wilderness area. Do the math: 800 miles at say, 25 mpg, equals 32 gallons of gas burned; 32 gallons X 6.3 pounds (weight per gallon of gas) equals 202 pounds of emitted hydrocarbons. Compare this with the weight of dead, downed wood you'll burn in your campfire.

Wash Dishes 150 Feet from Water

Federal authorities recommend that you go 150 feet from water to wash dishes (and everything else). One hundred and fifty feet is a very long way. Indeed, the typical novice camper who goes that far into the woods may get lost and not find his/her way back to camp! Fifty feet is a reasonable distance as long as you use common sense and don't pour waste water on ground that slopes toward the water.

Leave Your Ax at Home!

Show up with an ax on a wilderness trip and you can expect some unkind looks. But axes don't damage living trees; people do! The best way to protect the environment is to educate, not legislate. In Minnesota's Boundary Waters Canoe Area, hand saws damage more trees than axes!

Don't Burn Empty Plastic Food Bags in Your Campfire; It Creates Poisonous Hydrocarbons

When you compute the amount of hydrocarbons burned by just one jet plane flying from LA to New York, burning a few plastic bags in your campfire is the tiniest eye of small potatoes. If you're tripping in big bear country, the tiny (odorous) food particles that remain inside empty plastic food bags may attract bears to you! If you must carry out exhausted plastic food bags in bear country, thoroughly wash out the bags before you commit them to your pack. Otherwise, burn them!

Don't Cut Live Vegetation!

Generally yes, but there are exceptions. Here are two of them:

1. The last 3 miles of the MacFarlane River (Saskatchewan) are characterized by impassable falls and rapids. The river is very remote; hardly anyone ever canoes it, hence, portages are not marked or maintained. The seldom used portage was choked with trees—there was no way to get canoes across. Good thing we had two full-framed saws and two axes: we had to cut scores of trees to clear the 3-mile trail! Naturally, this practice would be unacceptable in well-traveled places. But this was northern Canada and as remote as it gets. The point is that what is acceptable behavior in one environment may be detrimental in another. Popular US trails are cleared by federal authorities; remote Canadian ones are not! "Zero tolerance" is always a bad idea!

2. Steel River, Ontario: A long dead tree leaned precariously over the best tent spot in camp. A good wind could send it crashing down on us. So we cut down that tree and sawed it up for firewood. Yes, this was probably illegal, but it may have saved our lives.

Federal authorities have a responsibility for human safety when they designate an area as a "campsite." If there are dead leaning trees that hang over prime tent spots, the feds should cut them down! "Political correctness" is too high a price to pay for human life.

F

Fabric Softener

An auto mechanic who loves camping recommends placing sheets of fabric softener inside sleeping bags and packs and in vehicles that will be stored in country garages where vermin can get in. The fabric softener repels bugs and rodents and keeps things smelling fresh. It really works!

Fire Making

Anyone can start a fire on a bone-dry day or when they're armed with dry newspaper, kerosene, or charcoal lighter. But let the day deteriorate to persistent rain, and where there's smoke there won't be fire! Here's how to make and maintain fire when foul weather comes to stay:

Tools

You'll need a sharp knife, hand ax, and a saw. (Folding saws are highly recommended.) Contrary to the ravings of some "authorities," it is nearly impossible to make fire in prolonged rain without all these tools.

Finding Wood

In an evergreen forest: Collect several handfuls of the dead lower branches of evergreen trees. Wood should range in size from pencil-lead thickness to no bigger than your little finger, and it should break with a crisp, audible snap. If you don't hear the positive "snap," the wood is too wet, in which case look for a downed, dead tree as discussed below.

If the wood is suitably dry, it will burst into a bright flame the moment a match is applied. Use a small candle to provide sustained heat to

Resin blisters on the bark of balsam fir trees contain a highly volatile resin that you can use to light your campfire.

The resin burns brightly when ignited.

your tinder ball if the bark of the wood is wet. From this point on, it's simply a matter of adding more wood and protecting the developing blaze from rain. (See "To maintain fire in a driving rain" later in this section.)

Look for resin blisters on the outside bark of balsam fir trees. Break a few blisters with a sharp stick and collect the highly volatile resin. Use the resin as a "chemical fire starter" to propel your tinder to flame.

Locate a dead, downed tree and saw off a portion that does not touch the ground. Grounded wood rots quickly and is apt to be unsound. Especially search for deadfalls that overhang a sunlit clearing or waterway. These are almost certain to be rot free, as sunlight kills microorganisms that cause decay.

If you cannot find a dead, downed tree to saw up, look for any floating log. If the log floats, the center is dry. Splittings taken from the heart will burn.

When you have completed your first saw cut through the deadfall, check the center of the cut log with your hand. Is it bone dry? It should be. Even a monthlong rain will seldom soak through a 6-inch log!

Next comes the "smell test." Smell the cut end of the log. Damp or rotten wood will smell moist and musty. If there is no odor, saw the deadfall into 12-inch sections, then split each chunk with your hand ax by the methods described on pages 14 and 15. It should require only a few minutes to reduce each log chunk to ½-inch-diameter kindling by this procedure.

Cut wafer-thin tinder from a few splittings with your knife. The key to producing long, thin shavings rather than little squiggly ones is to use a sawing rather than a whittling action. Even a small, dull knife will produce nice shavings if you persistently saw the blade back and forth.

The photo below shows a much more powerful way to cut long, thin shavings. Simply reverse the knife edge and smartly pull the knife and stick apart, as illustrated. Before you "pull," be sure the stick is located under the knife (not above it) and the sharp edge has a good bite on the wood.

Another knife trick is illustrated in the next photo. You can easily split kindling up to 2 inches thick with this method. ***Important:*** You need a sheath knife or lock-blade folding knife

Use this method to split wood with a fixed-blade knife. Simply hammer the blade through the end grain with a thick piece of wood.

A powerful way to cut thin shavings. Hold the knife firmly against your body (don't move it!), then pull the wood smartly through the blade. You'll have a pile of shavings in a matter of seconds.

for this procedure. A pressure-spring folder could close on your hand when you pound. Even the strongest lock-blade folder, however, will eventually be damaged by continued pounding on the spine. Get a sheath knife if you adopt this procedure.

Tip: Stumps and roots are rich in volatile resins. Conifers, especially, have so much pitch that they will burn on their own for hours—a reason why fires in evergreen forests are so devastating. If you can find an old broken-down stump, save some of the fatwood for starting fires.

Fire-Building Procedures

First, prepare piles of wood of varying thickness. Thickness should range from pencil-lead thin shavings to as thick as your thumb.

Next, build a well-ventilated platform fire following the steps below:

Step 1: Establish a fire base of 1-inch-diameter sticks as pictured. *The tinderbox should be no larger than the lid of a soup can!* Place three pencil-thin support sticks at right angles to the fire base.

Step 2: Meticulously stack wafer-thin shavings on top of the three sticks of kindling to a height of about 1 inch. Place the shavings so that plenty of air can get between them. Smoke is nature's way of saying you're smothering the flame!

Next, put two ½-inch-diameter support sticks at right angles to the fire base. These act as a "bridge" to support the heavier kindling you'll add over the tinder in step 3.

Step 3: Now pile on fine-split kindling above the tinderbox (across the bridge)

Prepare piles of wood of varying thickness. Thickness should range from pencil-lead-thin shavings to as thick as your thumb.

Soup can lid

Step 1. Set three parallel sticks across a log bridge. The fire base should be *no larger than the lid of a soup can* (shown here).

Step 2. Stack wafer-thin shavings on top of the kindling to a height of about 1 inch.

Bridge stick

Add two support ("bridge") sticks.

Bridge stick

Step 3. Pile fine-split kindling above the tinderbox (across the bridge). Your fire is now ready to light.

Light the fire, then immediately hand-feed fine shavings one at a time into the developing flame.

to lock the tinder in place. Again, leave space between the splittings so your fire can breathe. The photo here shows the fire "ready to light."

Your fire is now ready to light. Apply flame directly below the tinder (shavings). A small candle will furnish the sustained heat necessary to ignite damp wood.

Light the fire and immediately hand-feed shavings (not kindling) one at a time into the

developing flame. Don't heap kindling on until you have a bright, reliable blaze. The bright, smoke-free flame of the fire in the photo is due to the free flow of air (chimney effect) from below.

Fire-Starting Tips

Carry strike-anywhere matches in addition to a butane lighter and candle. Keep matches in a plastic jar with a cotton wad on top. A spent 16-gauge shot shell nested inside a 12-gauge case makes a tough watertight match safe. Some campers waterproof matches by painting on nail polish, but this causes match heads to deteriorate. A waterproof match case is a better idea. Or, forget matches and just carry a few butane lighters. *Tip:* A few puffs of air (blow on the spark wheel) will dry out a wet butane lighter.

An effective method of drying matches is to draw them briskly through your hair. Don't use your clothes as they are too abrasive.

Mautz Fire Ribbon, a semiliquid fire-starting paste, is available at most camp stores. Just squeeze it on like toothpaste. You can make your own fire starters by soaking miniature "logs" of rolled newspaper in paraffin.

Cotton balls dipped in Vaseline make wonderful fire starters!

Emergency fire-making kits: You'll need a flattened cardboard milk or juice carton, a handful of wood shavings (cedar is best), some splittings of scrap wood, Fire Ribbon, and a small candle. Store everything in a ziplock bag. When emergency strikes, rip up the milk carton, splash tinder with Fire Ribbon, and light your match. Materials will burn reliably for at least 5 minutes—enough time for you to search the woods for additional fuel.

Witch's broom is a blue-gray lichen that grows on the branches of some evergreen trees. It is extremely flammable when dry.

Paper is hydrophilic (loves water). It absorbs moisture on damp days. Don't depend on paper to start your fires!

(In an emergency, you can always burn money!)

One or two *sticks robbed from a beaver's house* make good kindling and tinder. Beaver wood has been de-barked so it is apt to be rot free. For the sake of the beaver, please take only one or two sticks, and then only in an emergency.

Emergency igniters: You can't beat a butane lighter and dry matches! The chemically impregnated magnesium rods sold as survival tools will ignite dry tinder but are next to worthless when things are damp. And magnifying glasses must be very large (at least 2 inches in diameter) to reliably ignite tinder.

Steel wool makes excellent emergency tinder.

Flour (any kind) will burst into potent flames if sprinkled lightly over a blaze.

Cooking oil (vegetable oil) will enrich a flame only if the fire is already very hot. Brazil nuts, potato chips, and corn chips burn brightly. Try trick birthday candles—the kind you can't blow out—to ignite damp wood. Some campers store a few popsicle sticks inside their stove fuel (gasoline or kerosene) bottles. The fuel-saturated sticks make powerful fire starters.

Make a tubular fire blower, shown in Figure F-1. You'll need a 6-inch-long piece of narrow-diameter copper or aluminum tubing and 18 inches of plastic or rubber Bunsen-burner hose. Most hardware stores have these materials.

Use your blower to nurse a fickle flame and whenever wood is too thick or damp to burn well. The concentrated air turbocharges hot coals and turns them into willing flames.

An unused rain jacket or small square of plastic will provide all the overhead protection

Figure F-1. Tubular fire blower

you need to start a fire in a driving rain. So will an overturned canoe, propped up by paddles shoved through the seat braces.

To maintain fire in a driving rain: Build a loose "log cabin" around your fire with whatever wood is available. Construct a two-tier flat "roof" for your cabin from newly cut kindling and fuel. The roof will deflect rain and the fire below will dry out the lower level of wood and bring it to flame. If you maintain a two-tier roof, you'll have a continuous supply of dry wood no matter how much it rains. **Note:** Since you're robbing the fire of oxygen, expect smoke . . . lots of it!

Banking the fire to preserve fuel: Use this procedure when you have a good hot fire but little wood to maintain it. Bank your fire by setting small logs, parallel to one another, across the top. The rule of thumb for a smoke-free flame is to allow a radius width between parallel pieces of wood. Thus, a pair of 2-inch-thick logs should be separated by a full inch to ensure adequate ventilation. Banking will reduce this distance to a mere (though identifiable) slit, which will naturally diminish use of oxygen and slow combustion. You should also eliminate any breeze coming into the fire. A large flat rock or a tier of logs will work fine.

Extinguishing the fire: Throwing water on a fire is not good enough. You must ascertain it is out by checking the once-fiery bed with your hands. If water is in short supply, use the "sprinkle/stir" method outlined below.

Sprinkle a handful of water on the flames with your hands. Continue to sprinkle until the fire has gone out.

Stir the fire with a stick and sprinkle some more. Repeat as needed until the fire is *dead out!*

First-Aid Kit and Procedures

The following recommendations are from the pen of my friend William Forgey, MD, the guru of wilderness medicine.

Dr. Forgey is a member of the Board of Trustees of the International Association for Medical Assistance to Travelers (IAMAT), a Fellow of the Explorers Club, and a Fellow of the Academy of Wilderness Medicine. A former captain, Infantry, in the US Army, he had over 30 months active duty in Vietnam prior to leaving the service and attending medical school at Indiana University. He was awarded the Bronze Star and Army Commendation Medal for his service in Vietnam. He is a past president of the Wilderness Medical Society.

Dr. Forgey has authored more than a dozen popular outdoor titles. His flagship book, Wilderness Medicine: Beyond First Aid, *is the ultimate medical resource for those who venture afield. His latest book,* The Prepper's Medical Handbook, *details how to provide medical care when you can't rely on anyone but yourself.*

—CJ

Dr. William Forgey

When facing a medical emergency in a wilderness location, it would be ideal to have a medical kit with exactly the right ingredients and the knowledge of how to use them. Well, let's face it, it probably ain't going to happen that way. Medical kits can be bulky, heavy, expensive, and hard to obtain. And even physicians can feel inadequately trained when faced with unfamiliar emergencies, especially in remote areas. So what to do?

When choosing items for an emergency or survival kit, I always apply the chocolate rule. I look at the item I'm thinking of including and compare it to a piece of chocolate of equal size. I look at one, then the other, thinking all the time, "which would I rather have in the bush with me?" Generally chocolate will win.

So it's obvious that even as a physician, I do not want to lug in a heavy medical kit, especially if I must choose between carrying it and something really useful and preferably edible. My solution to this dilemma is to make up a medical kit with multifunctional and cross-therapeutic components.

A multifunctional component is an item that has more than one use. Cross-therapeutic components mean that several different items in the kit can be used to treat the same problem. Such a kit has few components that generally handle many problems and because of their versatility, the kit does not exhaust easily.

Non-Rx Medical Kit

Brand names have been used to simplify spelling and product recognition or to minimize potential confusion between similar-sounding and variations in generic names between American, Canadian, and British sources.

❂ Alternative improvisation. Alternatives to these various medications are mentioned in

Topical Bandaging Module

Quantity	Item
10 pkg	Spyroflex 2½" x 2½" wound dressings (or carry 2 for each person)
2 pkg	Spenco 2nd Skin Burn Dressing Kits (or carry 1 for 2 people)
15 pkg	Nu Gauze, high absorbent, sterile, 2-ply, 3½" x 3½", pkg/2
25	Coverlet bandage strips, 1½" x 3½"
1	tape, waterproof, 1½" x 15½"
1	Sam Splint, 36½"
1	elastic bandage, 3½"
1	elastic bandage, 4½"
1	max-strength triple-antibiotic ointment with pramoxine, 1-oz tube
1	Hibiclens surgical scrub, 4-oz bottle
1	tetrahydrozoline ophthalmic drops, 0.05%, 15-ml bottle
1	hydrocortisone cream, 1%, 1-oz tube
1	clotrimazole cream, 2%, ½-oz tube
1	Cavit dental filling paste
2 pairs	examination gloves
1	irrigation syringe
1	overpack container for above

the treatment discussions for injuries and illnesses. Alternatives to various medical supplies are discussed below.

Spyroflex 2½" x 2½" Wound Dressings

Made by PolyMedica Industries, Spyroflex is a multiuse bandaging system that replaces wound-closure strips and coverings. It accelerates blood clotting, holds lacerations closed, protects the wound from the outside, treats abraded skin as well as leaking and dry wounds, and is an excellent cover for first- and second-degree burns. Most importantly, it establishes a local environment that speeds up wound healing. The dressing is a "smart" dressing that absorbs and evaporates the correct amount of vapor to produce the proper healing condition. This dressing can be left in place for up to 10 days, thus decreasing the need for large quantities of bulky dressings.

➕ Cellophane and duct tape: Cellophane, plastic food wrappers, or plastic sheeting of any kind makes an excellent wound covering. Held down with tape of any type, a cellophane dressing is nonadherent, seepage leaks from the unsealed edges, the wound can be observed, and the increased and appropriate moisture level of the dressing increases the rate of wound healing.

Spenco 2nd Skin

Truly a major advance in field medicine, this inert hydrogel consists of 96 percent water and 4 percent polyethylene oxide. It is used on wet, weeping wounds to absorb fluids and protect the injury. This is a perfect prevention or cure for friction blisters. It revolutionized the field treatment of first-, second-, and third-degree burns, as it can be applied to all three as a covering and for pain relief. This item should be in every medical kit. The ideal covering pad is the Spenco Adhesive Knit Bandage. If used in treating blisters, remove only the outer covering of cellophane from the 2nd Skin, cover with the Knit Bandage, and occasionally dampen with clean water to maintain the hydrogel's hydration. It will last a lot longer this way when in short supply.

Nu Gauze Pads

Johnson & Johnson has developed a gauze that is two-ply yet absorbs nearly 50 percent more fluid than conventional twelve-ply gauze pads. This may not seem important until a rapidly bleeding wound needs care. For years J&J has made a "Nu Gauze" strip packing dressing; however, the Nu Gauze Pads are a completely different material. They are a wonderful advance in gauze design.

➕ You can tear up cotton T-shirts or other clothing or bandannas for bandages. These cloths can be boiled and then air dried for reuse if necessary. Boil for 10 minutes.

Coverlet Bandage Strips

A Beiersdorf product, these common 1 x 3-inch bandage strips are the best made of their kind. They stick even when wet, will last through days of hard use, and stretch for compression on a wound and conform for better application.

➕ The ubiquitous duct tape or climbing tape can be used for closures. By folding the edges in slightly lengthwise in the middle, you can make a version of a butterfly closure. This allows the wound to breathe.

Hemostatic Dressings

Hemostatic dressings are bandages that rapidly cause clotting when blood gets in contact with them.

There are now five hemostatic dressings approved by the military. Since the addition of Combat Gauze (ZMedica LLC, Wallingford, CT, USA; www.quikclot.com) in April 2008 to the Tactical Combat Casualty Care (TCCC) Guidelines, based on the recent battlefield success, Celox Gauze (Medtrade Products Ltd., Crewe, UK; www.celoxmedical.com) and

ChitoGauze (HemCon Medical Technologies, Portland, OR, USA; http://www.tricolbio medical.com) have been added. To use, place into the wound on top of the bleeding vessel, and not on top of other bandage material. Direct pressure must be applied continuously for a minimum of 5 minutes or per the manufacturer's recommendation.

X-Stat has an applicator syringe with little pellets of expanding gauze that shoot into a deeper wound—but these require surgical removal and are not appropriate on a long voyage unless surgical assistance can be obtained within hours.

Junctional tourniquets are new devices designed to stop bleeding in groin or armpit deep vessel damage and require special training for use.

○ Gauze dampened with epinephrine or nasal decongestant can help decrease oozing blood.

Control of blood loss is a priority. This makes the "tourniquet first" approach appropriate if blood loss cannot be controlled by direct pressure on an extremity wound. The military initially approved two commercial strap and windlass-style tourniquets: the Combat Action Tourniquet (CAT) and the Special Operations Forces Tactical Tourniquet Wide (SOFTT-W), which are specially constructed to give a true 1- and ½-inch circumference without pinching when tightened using the windlass.

Due to the interest in "Stop the Bleed" programs caused in the United States by active shooter incidents, the American Red Cross is also comarketing the SOFT-T tourniquet. A number of additional tourniquets have been approved by the Tactical Casualty Combat Care folks. Their latest approved list may be found at www.deployedmedicine.com. Deployed Medicine is part of an ongoing research and development activity sponsored by the Defense Health Agency in partnership with the Joint Trauma System and Committee on Tactical Combat Casualty Care.

Waterproof Tape

This is a tough tape that can be used for splinting or bandage application. There are no brand advantages that I can determine. A 1-inch x 15½-foot roll on a metal spool is a usable size.

○ Duct tape, climbing tape.

Sam Splint

A Sam Splint is a padded, malleable splint that provides enough comfort to be used as a neck collar. It is adequately rigid to splint any extremity and universal so that only one of these needs be carried for all splinting needs. This item replaces ladder splints and the like. I never recommended the inclusion of splints in wilderness medical kits until this product was developed. It weighs less than 5 ounces.

○ Malleable splints can frequently be made from stays found in internal backpack frames. Other stiff materials can be used, such as strips of Ensolite foam pads or inflatable pads, held in place with tape or torn cloth.

Elastic Bandage

2-inch, 3-inch, and 6-inch: Obtain good-quality bandages that stretch without narrowing and that provide firm, consistent compression.

○ Elastic bandages can be replaced with almost any cloth that is firmly wrapped in place. The most stretchy form of cloth usually available is a cotton T-shirt.

Maximum-Strength Triple-Antibiotic
Ointment with Pramoxine, 1-oz tube

Each gram of this ointment contains bacitracin 500 units, neomycin sulfate 3.5 mg, polymyxin B sulfate 10,000 units, and an anesthetic pramoxine hydrochloride 10 mg. It is used as a topical antibiotic in the prevention and treatment of minor infections of abrasions and burns. This formulation also is an anesthetic that numbs the skin. A light coat should be applied twice daily. Neomycin can cause skin rash and itching in some people. If this develops, discontinue use and apply the hydrocortisone cream to counter this effect.

✪ Honey or granulated sugar placed on wounds is painless and kills germs by dehydrating them. A strong sugar solution draws the fluid from the bacteria, but human cells are able to actively avoid the dehydration process and are not injured with this technique.

Hibiclens Surgical Scrub

This Stuart product (chlorhexidine gluconate 4 percent) far surpasses hexachlorophene and povidone-iodine scrub in its antiseptic action. The onset and duration of its action is much more impressive than either of those two products.

✪ Many surgical scrubs are available without prescription and are ideal for wilderness use, but they can all be replaced with potable (drinkable) water irrigation. Remember, "the solution to pollution is dilution."

Tetrahydrozoline Ophthalmic Drops 0.05
percent, 15-ml bottle

These eye drops are used for allergy relief, to remove redness, and to alleviate discomfort from smoke, eye strain, and the like. They will not cure infection or disguise the existence of a foreign body. Place one or two drops in each eye every 6 hours.

✪ Rinse eyes with clean water. A wet, cold compress relieves eye itch and pain.

Hydrocortisone Cream 1 percent, 1-oz tube

This non-Rx steroid cream treats allergic skin rashes, such as those from poison ivy. A cream is ideal for treating weeping lesions, as opposed to dry scaly ones, but will work on either. For best results, cover with an occlusive dressing (plastic cover) overnight.

✪ Blistery rashes can be soothed and the leaking fluid dried by applying a cloth made wet with concentrated salt solution.

Clotrimazole Cream, 2 percent, ½-oz tube

This is one of the most effective antifungal preparations available for foot, groin, or other body fungal infections. Brand names are Lotrimin and Mycelex (vaginal cream). The vaginal cream in a 2-ounce tube is less expensive and works well on the skin surface, as well as vaginally.

✪ Dry, itchy lesions of any type respond to a soothing coating of cooking oil.

Cavit Dental Filling Paste

Cavit can be used for the temporary filling of cavities and repair of broken bridge work. Without being able to drill out the underlying decay, the cavity will need to be seen as soon as possible by a dentist for proper care or an abscess may form.

✪ Use oil of cloves to line the cavity for pain relief. A mixture of zinc-oxide powder (not the ointment) and oil of cloves, made up as a thick paste, can also be used as a temporary filling. Mouth sores can be numbed by applying

Benadryl (diphenhydramine) powder to the surface. Make a salt solution rinse if there's food stuck in the gum line.

Protective Gloves
Due to concerns with blood-borne pathogens (hepatitis B and C and HIV), it is prudent to carry protective gloves for first-aid use. These can be nonsterile (they are readily sterilized by boiling or treating with antiseptics). Vinyl gloves will last much longer in a kit than latex gloves, but the best are nitrile gloves.

✪ Use an empty food bag or waterproof stuff sack as a glove, or wrap your hand in the most waterproof material available.

Irrigation Syringe
The syringe is required for forceful irrigation of wounds. The best would have a protective spray shield, such as the Zero-Wet shield; otherwise, wear glasses to protect your eyes from splash contamination.

✪ The solution to pollution is dilution. Forceful irrigation is the best method for cleaning a wound and diluting the germ count enough so that the body's immune system can kill the remaining germs. Without a syringe, augment the volume of water that you are pouring on the wound with a brisk scrubbing action using a soft, clean cloth.

Non-Rx Oral Medication Kit
Percogesic Tablets
Use Percogesic tablets to relieve pain, fever, and muscle spasm. Each tablet contains 325 mg of acetaminophen and 12.5 mg of diphenhydramine citrates ideal for injuries of joints and muscles, as well as aches from infections. Diphenhydramine is also a decongestant. It also induces drowsiness and can be used as a sleeping aid or to calm a hysterical person. These indications are not included on the packaging information. Dosage is generally two tablets every 4 hours as needed. One of the most useful non-Rx drugs obtainable.

Ibuprofen Tablets 200 mg
Brand names for ibuprofen include Advil and Nuprin. It relieves pain, fever, menstrual cramps, and inflammation. Overuse syndromes such as bursitis and tendonitis are common in wilderness-related activities and this is an ideal treatment. The non-Rx dosage is two tablets four times a day. Ibuprofen should be taken with food to prevent stomach irritation or heartburn. The Rx dosage is four tablets taken four times daily, a dose that may be necessary for severe inflammation.

Diphenhydramine Capsules 25 mg
The brand name is Benadryl; many variations are sold containing other ingredients in addition to the diphenhydramine. For antihistamine action, these capsules can be taken one or two every 6 hours. To use as a powerful cough suppresser, the dose is one capsule every 6 hours. For muscle spasm relief, one or two capsules at bedtime alone or in combination with two ibuprofen 200-mg tablets are recommended. For nausea or motion sickness, take one capsule every 6 hours as needed. The Percogesic included in this module also contains diphenhydramine.

Bisacodyl 5 mg
This laxative works on the large bowel to form a soft stool within 6 to 10 hours. Use one tablet as needed.

Non-Rx Oral Medication Module

Quantity	Item
24	Percogesic tablets (pain, fever, muscle spasm, sleep aid, anxiety, congestion)
24	ibuprofen 200-mg tablets (pain, fever, bursitis, tendonitis, menstrual cramps)
24	diphenhydramine 25-mg capsules (antihistamine, anti-anxiety, cough, muscle cramps, nausea, and motion-sickness prevention)
10	bisacodyl 5-mg tablets (constipation)
12	loperamide 2-mg tablets (diarrhea)
24	cimetidine 200-mg tablets (heartburn, certain allergic reactions)
1	overpack container for above

Loperamide 2 mg

An antidiarrheal with the brand name of Imodium. Dosage for persons 12 or older is two tablets after the first loose bowel movement followed by one tablet after each subsequent loose bowel movement, but no more than four tablets a day for no more than 2 days. The prescription use of this medication is usually two tablets immediately and two with each loose stool up to a maximum of eight per day. Follow the package instructions for children's dosages.

Cimetidine 200 mg

The brand name is Tagamet. This medication suppresses acid formation. It may be used to treat certain allergic reactions. The non-Rx dosage is two tablets four times daily. Prescription use goes as high as four tablets four times daily for acid suppression. Stronger formulations of medications are available to treat stomach heartburn and reflux symptoms such as the PPI class of compounds including OTC omeprazole (Prilosec) and lansoprazole (Prevacid). If you have severe problems with these conditions, substitute them for cimetidine.

I have not included any prescription medications in the medical kit recommendations because you can generally manage all problems that you will encounter with the items listed above. For expeditions into very remote areas, it would be a good idea to add a few prescription items such as a powerful pain medication, antibiotic, and an eye anesthetic agent.

The best *pain medication* would be nasal inhaled Stadol (butorphanol). The drug is five times stronger than morphine on a milligram-per-milligram basis. One spray up a nostril should relieve the pain of a major broken bone. If not, spray the other nostril about 15 minutes later. If you spray too much medication into the patient's nose, it will run down his throat into his stomach and be deactivated by stomach acid.

A good all-purpose *antibiotic* to carry is Zithromax Tri-pack. This antibiotic is great for treating traveler's diarrhea and many upper respiratory infections.

An *eye anesthetic agent,* such as tetracaine ophthalmic drops, allows you to more easily examine an injured eye and remove a foreign body by flicking it out of the eye with the edge of a bandana. It also can provide instant pain relief to spark burns and branch lash-back injuries.

Be aware that these compounds delay healing and their use must be restricted. They usually need to be refrigerated, which is certainly a drawback for wilderness use. A few weeks in a pack will not be a problem, but this medication needs to be discarded after the trip.

It is no secret that wilderness first-aid skills require improvisation and basic knowledge of wound care and illness management. Ideally you will be able to take a course in wilderness first aid or even a wilderness-first-responder class. The reader is also referred to Dr. Forgey's book *Wilderness Medicine: Beyond First Aid*, which describes a more intensive first-aid kit and, more important, how to diagnose and treat injuries and illnesses in remote areas.

First-Aid Tips for Common Problems
Fishhook Removal (String-Pull Method)
A hook in the cheek will kill the planned trip. You must be able to treat this injury if you have anglers along. A hook through the skin is one of the most common wilderness injuries.

Treatment: The common advice is to work the embedded barb through the skin, cut it off, and extract the hook. But this won't work if the hook is embedded to the curve. You may have to back the hook out partially and reset the angle so the tip will clear the skin rather than work deeper into it. In any case, you'll have a messy situation with lots of pain.

Here's a painless way to extract the hook (Figure F-2):

1. Loop light cord or heavy fishing line around the curve of the hook.

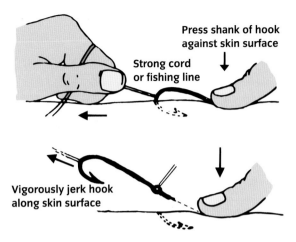

Figure F-2. String-pull method of removing a fishhook

2. Push the eye of the hook firmly against the surface of the skin.

3. While holding the shank down, firmly jerk the cord.

Dislocated Shoulder
A dislocated shoulder is one of the most common and painful ailments. Relocation is easy if you use the Stimson method illustrated in Figure F-3.

Procedure: Place the victim face down on a flat, elevated platform, like a rock face or an overturned boat. Place an approximate 10-pound weight inside a fabric stuff sack and tie the sack to the wrist of the fully extended arm with a soft handkerchief or padded belt. As the muscles tire, the victim will relax and the shoulder will relocate. The method is foolproof.

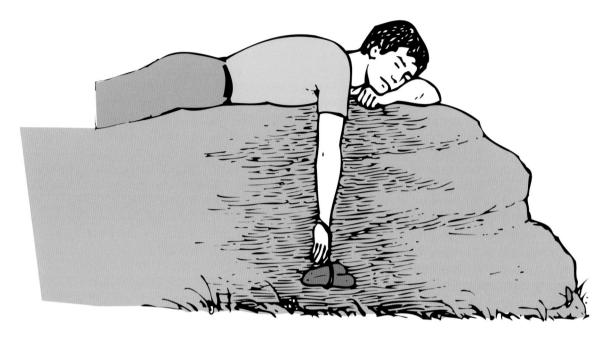

Figure F-3. Stimson method

Other Neat First-Aid Tips

Don't use freshwater from a lake or river to flush wounds. Surface waters contain microorganisms that can cause infection. Wounds should always be cleaned with boiled or chemically treated water.

Earaches are often related to a change in the pH (acid-base balance) of the ear canal. A recommended field cure is to flush the ear with diluted vinegar (acetic acid), which lowers the pH. No vinegar? Try urine (uric acid). It works!

Warning: Don't assume you can handle all emergencies with the few items and skills suggested here. When serious injury threatens, your best bet is to evacuate the victim immediately. The items and methods outlined in this book are not a substitute for the skills of a competent physician and the controlled environment of a hospital.

Flashlights and Camp Lighting Devices

Any light used for camping should be waterproof and have a lanyard ring so it can be hung in a tent. It should also have a positive rotary switch that won't accidentally turn on in your pack.

Headlamp or flashlight? Headlamps have all but replaced hand-held lights for camping, and for good reason: They are lightweight, powerful and, most important, "hands-free." Top models provide red-green color options (red doesn't reduce night vision) and emergency strobe signaling. Inexpensive, basic models are smaller, lighter and marginally less bright than full-featured units. If you're budget-buying, here's the place to save!

LED flashlights: LEDs have almost completely replaced incandescent bulbs, and for good reasons. They don't burn out and the LED bulbs are much tougher than incandescent bulbs. But all LEDs are not the same. Some are much brighter than others—they are graded like diamonds, and the brightest ones demand a premium price. You get exactly what you pay for.

LEDs are very efficient so their run times are much longer than bulbs—but not as ridiculously long (like hundreds of hours!) as some flashlight companies profess. Yes, LEDs do produce barely discernible light for a great many hours, but this light is usually too dim to be useful. Remember this before you leave extra batteries at home!

Tactical lights: In 2004 I had a dicey bear encounter along a river in Saskatchewan. The sky was dark gray when this bad boy came into camp. We tried to shoo him away, but he was persistent. One man activated his Surefire tactical light, which put out 120 lumens of light (that's about eight times brighter than a double D-cell flashlight). Seconds later the bruin was gone.

Tactical lights are so bright they will momentarily blind an attacker. I ordered a Surefire light as soon as I got home!

Bulb and battery basics:

- Other things being equal, the bigger the battery, the longer it will last.

- Alkaline batteries cost much more than zinc-carbon batteries but last about five times longer. Lithium batteries last longest (up to 10 years!) and are more reliable in cold weather, but they're expensive. Anne Bancroft was the first woman to travel across the ice to both the North and South Poles. She carried an MSR headlamp and a small Tekna flashlight that she wore on a string around her neck. Both lamps were

powered by lithium batteries—essential in the −70°F cold.

- Zinc-carbon batteries can be recharged and used in any flashlight, but the charge won't last as long as it will with expensive nickel-cadmium (NiCd) batteries.

- Gas-filled bulbs are much brighter and more expensive than vacuum bulbs, but they don't last as long. Generally, the brighter a bulb, the faster it will burn out.

Candle lanterns are more cutesy than functional. Batteries burn for about the same length of time as quality candles of similar weight, and artificial light is much brighter than open flame. Nonetheless, candle lanterns are fun toys, and they add some warmth to a tent on chilly nights. They are best at home for winter camping, where every BTU of heat is appreciated.

Mantle lanterns: The mini-size Coleman Peak 1 lantern puts out nearly as much light (for half the size and weight) as its traditional big brother. Mantle lanterns are considered essential equipment for auto camping but are viewed as gauche by the self-propelled camping crowd. However, they are strong enough to withstand the abuse of rugged canoe or horse-packing trips if you pad the globes and pack them well. The new mantles are much stronger than those of decades ago.

Caution: Never inhale the fumes from a newly lit (previously unburned) mantle. The gases released are highly poisonous!

If your gasoline lantern or trail stove won't generate pressure, the leather pump gasket may be too dry (needs oil). Most of the new pump gaskets are synthetic; the traditional leather ones work better. Some leather stool washers (check the plumbing section of your hardware store) fit some lanterns and stoves perfectly.

Don't fill a gasoline lantern or trail stove more than three-fourths full. You need air space to generate pressure.

Solar-Charged Camping Lights

There are a number of solar-charged camping lights and most are very good. But my favorite is the 4.4-ounce inflatable MPOWERD Original Luci Light. Its 10 LEDs put out 65 lumens of light (that's a lot!) at full charge. It deflates to the size of a thick pancake (it works deflated) and consumes almost no pack space at all.

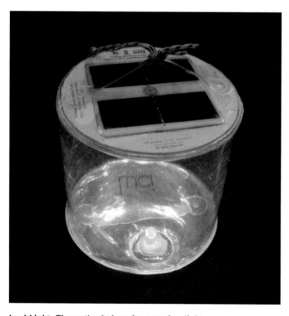

Luci Light. The author's favorite camping light.

Forest Fires

As a forester in Oregon many years ago, I fought several good-size forest fires. And I have been canoeing when the woods were ablaze all around me. Here's what to do if you're camping and see a forest fire heading your way:

Camping in an area where forest fires are active is both a chilling and thrilling experience. Along the Seal River, Manitoba.

- Fires often move in a predictable direction, so try to outflank a blaze by moving perpendicular to its path. Try to stay on or near water. If you're on a lake and the fire has reached you, move to the opposite shore and stay near the water's edge. If the shoreline is burning all around, get into the center of the lake and stay there. Wet down your clothes and hat. Remove all nylon and polypropylene clothing—these synthetics produce terrible burns!

- **Note:** Intense heat can turn the water in wet clothes to steam, which will burn

Camping in a recent burn is a dirty experience. Carbon black gets on everything. Along the Porcupine River, Saskatchewan.

you badly. Wet down your clothes only if there's a nearby water source where you can cool off.

- If sparks are flying and you have a boat, capsize the boat in the middle of the lake and get under it for protection. The craft will act as a spark shield. The large air bubble trapped inside the craft will enable you to breathe and speak normally.

- An intense ground fire generates its own winds, which may reach speeds over 100 miles per hour. If this happens, you may be in big trouble whatever you do. Generally, you'll survive even very large fires if you're at least 100 yards from a burning shoreline.

- Fires die down at night and flare up with the morning winds. So rest during the day and travel from evening through dawn. And remember, heat rises—the closer you are to the ground, the less smoky the air.

- Winds generally drive fires uphill. Seek out a valley to rest or camp.

- Fires may jump half a mile or more— don't think you are safe just because you're near a large body of water.

Camping in a recently burned area is a messy experience. The good news is that there is a lot of bone-dry wood and plenty of space to pitch tents. The bad news is that carbon black marks everything.

Frisbee

A giant Frisbee is more than a toy. Here are some practical uses: pot cover, serving platter for food, cutting board, camp seat, windbreak for your stove, tool for fanning a reluctant fire, containment tray for tools.

G

GPS (Global Positioning System)

The hottest navigational device is the handheld GPS (Global Positioning System) receiver. With a GPS unit, you can determine an accurate position anywhere on Earth in a matter of minutes. Or you can enter a set of coordinates of a place you want to go and the GPS receiver will provide a compass bearing and distance that will be updated by satellite information as you progress. Press a button and you get a speed readout and an estimated time of arrival.

Without a map, GPS can be used to track your location. Enter your starting position into the unit and save it as a waypoint. Establish other waypoints as you proceed, then, like Hansel and Gretel, follow your electronic bread crumbs home. GPS accuracy is generally 3 meters or less!

You must know how to read and interpret topographic maps in order to master GPS technology. You must also have—and know how to use—an accurate compass. The one built into a GPS has limited capabilities. Be aware that all handheld GPS units operate on small batteries that could fail when you need them most. Most of the new hand-held GPS units are waterproof so you can safely use them in the rain. Submersion in water for a very long time is another matter.

It is not wise to leave a GPS unit on for continuous positioning unless you have battery recharging capabilities or an unlimited supply of batteries. Lithium batteries are a smart choice, even in summer, when you don't need reliable cold-weather performance. The most useful GPS feature is its ability to verify

Learning to use a GPS unit is like mastering a computer. If you don't use it, you'll lose it! Note the UTM coordinates in the upper right window. If you plot the numbers on a topographic map they will indicate (within a few meters) where you are on the road. See UTM Coordinates, page 119, for details.

your location on a map—possible only if your map has a reference system to which your GPS unit can relate. Not all maps have appropriate reference lines. Those that do include all US and Canadian topographic maps that are marked with degrees of latitude and longitude. Canadian maps and US military maps also provide decimal-based Universal Transverse Mercator (UTM) coordinates, which are much easier to use than latitude/longitude. Any GPS receiver can be set to read lat/lon or UTM coordinates, as you prefer. (See page 119.)

Maps that don't have a coordinate system to which the GPS can relate include nearly all public road maps, most state and national park hiking and boating maps, and special-purpose recreational maps like those drawn for the Boundary Waters Canoe Area of Minnesota. If you use one of these special-purpose maps, you'll also need to carry a GPS-compatible topographic map.

The bottom line is that your map must have integral GPS coordinates or you won't be able to plot the fix your GPS unit calculates! Topographic maps are hard to find in most towns, but you can order them from the government sources listed in the Maps and Map Tricks section, page 118.

If your GPS has a built-in base map (most new models do), why not use it and leave your paper map at home? A GPS can break, become water-logged, run out of battery power, or just fail to find a fix. The latter is especially true in canyon country, deep forest, and anyplace where the instrument can't see the sky. Also, the screen is too small to provide a comparative view of the ground around you. Panning in and out every time you want to see what lies ahead is frustrating.

Sharing Your Location

Text your GPS coordinates to friends and family. They can use them to locate your position on the Google Earth world map. They'll see a picture that is similar to the SPOT photo on page 136.

Some things to consider when choosing a GPS unit:

- Learning how to use GPS is like mastering a computer; if you don't use it, you'll lose it! The best plan is to buy a unit that will mount in your car. Get a dashboard mount and a cigarette-lighter plug-in so you can practice setting waypoints, save track data, and master other operations without running down batteries. You won't become proficient if you use your GPS receiver just a few times a year!

- Large GPS units are generally more user-friendly than small ones. Miniature GPS receivers often have awkwardly placed controls, and their tiny antennas don't access satellites as fast or reliably as bigger antennas.

- Not all "waterproof" GPS units have waterproof battery compartments.

- Every GPS should have a simulator mode so you can learn the intricacies of operation more quickly.

Things you don't need in a GPS unit:

Electronic compass: An electronic compass is no more accurate (most are less accurate!) than a good needle compass. Unlike a needle compass, an electronic compass must be recalibrated every time you change batteries or move very far from its previously calibrated location. To recalibrate, you rotate the instrument (usually twice) 360 degrees—full circle. The compass must be held dead level during rotation. Sound bizarre? It is! If you go out of calibration range and forget to recalibrate, you're lost! Running by e-compass also consumes some battery power. Needle compasses "point for free."

Barometer: A barometer must be frequently recalibrated to provide accurate air-pressure readings. Yes, you will get a relative readout without calibration, which is useful to determine weather trends. But you can probably buy a watch with this feature for less money than what it will cost you in a GPS unit.

Thermometer: Electronic thermometers are slow to register readings. They're just one more thing to drain battery power. And they won't provide accurate readings if you hold the GPS in your hand.

Color display. The old black-and-white GPS screens, which were easily read in all types of light, are gone. In their place are multicolor displays which may be difficult to see in bright sunlight or unusual lighting. Not all GPS makers do color equally well. Best try the unit in varying light before you buy!

H

Hammocks for Camping

Hammocks are very practical for camping—that is, if you don't mind the curved sleeping position. When I was a kid, I used a military-surplus jungle hammock for all my camping. It had a waterproof roof and bug netting. Today, several companies make similar-style hammocks that are suitable for camping. The bad news is that gear storage is limited to the rain-protected patch provided by the small overhead fly. And of course, you must have two strategically placed trees for rigging. In rainy regions the best plan is to nix the factory rain fly and instead pitch a large nylon tarp over the hammock, then use this space for dressing and gear storage.

Hand Cream and Lip Balm

Moisturizers are among the most important—and forgotten—items on a camping trip. I double up on tubes and keep them in different places in my pack. Healing Badger Balm is the best hand cream I've found. It acts like an extra pair of gloves and reduces wind chapping. Its olive oil and aloe formula doesn't sting cracked skin. You can even eat this stuff!

Honey and Sugar—Good Medicine for Wounds

Honey will sweeten your tea and heal your wounds. It is slightly acidic so it effectively kills microorganisms. The University of South Florida in Tampa used honey on patients who were undergoing abdominal surgery. Doctors there found that the honey was more effective than some expensive antibiotics! If honey works well, sugar works better. Why? Because bacteria require moisture to survive, and sugar has none!

Dr. Avshalom Mizrahi, a microbiology professor at Hebrew University in Israel, discovered that honey is also good medicine for treating burns and ulcers. Medical reports show that people who took 2 to 3 ounces of honey each day over several months cured their ulcers.

Eagle's Nest Outfitters (ENO) hammock pitched under a rain tarp. This setup is secure and it provides a protected place for gear. Boundary Waters Canoe Area, Minnesota.

Hypothermia

Hypothermia (commonly called "exposure sickness") is the most common and dangerous of outdoor ailments. No one is immune to its icy grip. You can suffer hypothermia while climbing a mountain in Tibet or biking across Chicago. Dozens of people die from it each year.

Hypothermia occurs when body temperature drops below about 95°F. As blood is rushed to the vital organs, chilling spreads throughout the body. This is accompanied by clumsiness, slurred speech, and loss of judgment. Coma and death may result within a few hours if body temperature is not raised.

Hypothermics usually cannot identify their problem. They will maintain (often until death!) that they are "OK." You must observe symptoms, diagnose correctly, and treat quickly. Your friend's life may depend on it.

Check these symptoms:

- Slurred speech, stiffness in limbs (difficulty walking), an irrational view of reality. Victim acts irresponsibly—loses hat, mittens, or other equipment along the trail. Loss of short-term memory.

- Victim can't walk a straight line.

- Victim was shivering before and now shivering has stopped. ***Note:*** Mild shivering is nature's way of rewarming the body. It does not indicate hypothermia. Hypothermia begins with violent shivering. Be aware, however, that some people—especially those who are overtired—do not exhibit a shivering reflex. So do not rely on shivering to ascertain hypothermia!

Treatment:

1. Provide shelter at once! Any place out of the wind and wet is good.

2. Replace wet clothing with dry. Be sure the victim's head and neck are covered with warm clothing (hat, scarf, etc.).

3. Apply moderate, even heat. If a fire is available, use it. If there are several people in your party, have them loosely "hug" the victim to keep him or her as warm as possible.

   If the victim can swallow, hot soup (or water) will rewarm spirits and insides. Do not administer stimulants like alcohol, coffee, or tea.

   For serious cases (where the victim is unable to walk, suffers amnesia, etc.) administer the "sandwich" treatment. This consists of stripping the victim's clothes and sandwiching him or her between two nonhypothermics. Cover the threesome with sleeping bags and clothing. Be sure to insulate everyone from the cold ground (use a foam trail pad, additional clothing, leaves, grass, branches, etc.).

   Hypothermics must be handled gently: Roughhousing may initiate a heart attack!

4. Hypothermia drains both body and spirit. Considerable rest is warranted after the danger subsides.

K

Knives

The primary use for any camp knife is preparing foods. You'll slice vegetables, meat, and cheese; spread jam and peanut butter; and cut your supper steak. Rambo survivalists will insist on a stiff-backed sheath knife with a blade at least 6 inches long, while more gentle souls will argue the merits of a penknife. Between the two extremes are scores of expert campers who will agree that at least one knife in the camping party should have these two characteristics:

1. Enough length (4 to 5 inches) to slice meat and cheese and to reach deep into the peanut butter can without getting gunked up.

2. A thin, flat-ground blade for effortless slicing.

Nearly all knives sold for outdoor use have blades that are too thick. One-eighth of an inch across the spine is the maximum thickness permissible for a utility knife, no matter how

The primary use for a camp knife is preparing foods. A thin blade is essential, no matter how delicate the edge. Try slicing a tomato with the typical thick-bladed hunting knife and you'll see why!

delicate the edge. Try slicing a tomato with the typical thick-bladed hunting knife and you'll see why!

Your favorite kitchen knife would probably be perfect for camp use if it had a bit less length, more backbone, and better steel. In fact, the most popular knives on the frontier were the famous Green River models, which were nothing more than solidly built kitchen knives.

The primary camp knife may be a fixed blade or folding model. You'll pay much more for a good folder than for a sheath knife of similar length.

If your taste runs to folding knives, select a model with a 3- to 4-inch-long thin, preferably flat-ground blade. Lock-blade knives are safer than those with traditional pressure springs, and their blades can be opened single-handedly while you are wearing mittens. However, lock blades tend to loosen with time as the lock mechanism wears. Pressure-spring folders usually stay tight much longer.

If you've read between the lines, you'll conclude that you need two knives for camping: a thin-ground, kitchen-style model for preparing foods and a substantial multipurpose folder of some sort. I carry a sheath knife with a 4⅓-inch blade and a multipurpose Leatherman tool. There's also a Swiss Army knife hidden in my pack. The nail file and scissors are very useful.

Stainless or carbon steel? Stainless is much more difficult and expensive to work than carbon steel. It's also harder to sharpen, especially to the supersharp shaving edge I prefer. My experience suggests that most people—particularly those who are not expert at sharpening knives—will be happier with a high-grade carbon-steel blade than a stainless one. Granted, carbon steel rusts, but so does a fine

ARE BIG BLADES BEST FOR THE BUSH?

Many writers have attempted to define the perfect "bush knife"—that is, the best one to carry on a wilderness trip where help is an airplane ride away. Advice has been as wide (or narrow) as the author's experience, and a variety of blades—from Swiss Army knives and multitools, to huge hackers—have been recommended. Invariably, the nod has gone to big knives that are better for cutting through airplane doors than for doing camp chores. Are big blades really best for the bush? I think not. And neither do the experts. Consider this advice from the past:

> "The thick, chisel-edged belt knives which are generally sold are of little value in the wilderness. Get your belt knife too thin rather than too thick."
>
> —Calvin Rutstrum, *The New Way of the Wilderness*

> "The 'bowies and hunting knives' usually kept on sale, are thick, clumsy affairs, with a sort of ridge along the middle of the blade, murderous-looking but of little use."
>
> —Nessmuk (George Washington Sears), from *Woodcraft and Camping*, 1920

> "I like a small, light sheath knife. It is always open and 'get-at-able.' My knife is of the right size (4.5 inch blade), the right shape, and the proper thinness."
>
> —Horace Kephart, *Camping and Woodcraft*, 1917

> "Do not choose a knife with a large blade; we do not want to hack, but to carve. This is best achieved with a blade 8–12 cm (3–5 inches) long. It should have an edge on only one side; avoid blades that are very round . . . avoid serrated blades . . . I have found a fine flat bevel grind to be the most efficient for bushcraft."
>
> —Ray Mears, *Bushcraft*, 2002

Survival guru Mors Korchanski's preference for inexpensive Swedish Mora knives is well-known.

In summary, here's what the experts—old and new—want in a bush knife:

- A thin (no thicker than ⅛ inch at the spine), pointed blade, 3–5 inches long. When I was a Boy Scout in the 1950s—when every kid carried a knife—there was a saying: "The bigger the knife, the greener the kid!"
- Flat-ground (uniformly tapered) blades work best for slicing meat and vegetables and for spreading jam and peanut butter. Beveled blades have the edge for splitting wood but are awkward for fine work.
- Blade sharpened on one edge only. The flat spine can be used with a wooden baton to split kindling. *Caution:* Do *not* pound the spine of a folding knife—any folding knife! At best, the blade will eventually loosen; at worse, it may close in your hand!
- No serrations along the edge! I don't know a single camping expert who likes serrated blades! Serrated blades excel at just two things: cutting rope and slicing Thanksgiving turkey!
- Full tang construction for strength.

On a typical wilderness camping trip, daily cutting chores may include cutting and splitting thigh-thick logs to campfire size; whittling wafer-thin tinder; filleting fish; slicing lunch meat, cheese, vegetables, and bread; spreading peanut butter and jam; cutting cord, tape, and gauze; prying out a splinter.

How can one knife do it all?

It can't. That's why the experts bring several blades.

The author's favorite camp knives. All except the two Victorinox models are carbon (not stainless) steel. Top to bottom: Grohmann #1 flat-ground, carbon Camper; Idaho Knife Works "Cliff" knife; Gerber Shorty (no longer manufactured); Victorinox "Forschner" #40614; Old Hickory paring knife/ garage sale item (blade has been gun-blued); Victorinox lock-blade "Forester"; Mora carbon steel knife. All of these knives will do good work in the wilderness.

This is a left-handed version of the Spyderco army model (non-serrated). If you want a folding knife, this one is excellent!

ax or gun. If you're serious about the outdoors, you'll take joy in maintaining your knife. **Note:** If you need to make fire with flint and steel, a carbon-steel blade will produce sparks. Most stainless-steel blades won't.

Steel hardness: The Rockwell (Rc) test is the standard by which the hardness of steel is measured. The higher the number, the harder the steel. Generally, hard steels take and retain a better edge than soft steels. There's a limit, of course—steel that is too hard may be too brittle for knives. There's a common agreement that a rating of Rc 56–59 is ideal for good edge holding with minimum brittleness (assuming that quality steel is used). Most cheap pocketknives run much less than Rc 56, while nearly all high-quality knives fall into the 56–59 range. Some special steels, hardened to Rc 60 and beyond, are used on a limited basis for expensive custom knives. Only diamonds are harder than zircon-oxide (ceramic) blades, whose Rc ratings approach 100. However, ceramic knives are much too brittle for serious outdoor use.

Smooth edge or serrated? A lion's share of today's outdoor knives have serrated edges, which are great for cutting through wrist-thick rope and metal doors. But how do they slice salami and pine? Not very well. And they are difficult for the average person to sharpen! A folding saw, hand ax, and thin-bladed knife, in combination, will outperform any Rambo-style survival blade on the planet. Believe it!

How to Care for Your Edged Tools

I occasionally spray working saws and axes with Balistol or oil. I wipe kitchen knives with digestible canola oil or occasionally cut salami or cheese. **Caution:** Do *not* use petroleum oils on knives that will be used to cut food!

Flitz and Wenol are terrific metal polishes if you like a mirror-bright finish on your knives. RIG Universal—a Vaseline-like product that is available at gun shops—provides superb long-term protection (even against salt water) for carbon-steel tools. And plain old petroleum jelly (Vaseline) also keeps rust away.

Sharpening: Don't ever sharpen a knife on an electric sharpener or one of those mechanical wheeled gadgets sold at supermarkets. You'll ruin the knife beyond repair. Instead, use sharpening hones.

You'll need a coarse hone and a fine hone. The quality of the abrasive is more important than whether the stone is natural or synthetic. Indeed, Amazon natives still use water-worn rocks to sharpen their machetes—and they obtain whisper-sharp edges. My favorite stones are the natural Wachita and Arkansas oil stones and diamond hones sold by Smith Abrasives. The cheap carborundum stones you buy in hardware stores are about the only stones I dislike. But even these will produce a good edge if you know what you're doing.

The jury is out on whether you should lubricate your hone with oil or water or use it dry. I lubricate fine stones, not coarse ones. Final lubrication seems to produce a smoother, more polished edge. I use light oil (WD-40 or kerosene) with natural stones, water with diamond hones. Don't use conventional oils—they gum up the stones. *Tip:* Whetstones eventually gum up with oil and metal flakes. You can restore performance by boiling the stones in water for about 5 minutes.

This procedure produces a wickedly sharp razor edge:

Use the coarse stone first, without lubrication. Keep the back of the blade raised 15 to 20 degrees (the shallower the angle, the better the geometry of the final edge) and cut into the stone. A trick to maintain the proper angle is to adjust an overhead light so that it casts a shadow along the back of the blade when the blade is laid flat on the stone. Raise the blade until the shadow just disappears and you'll have

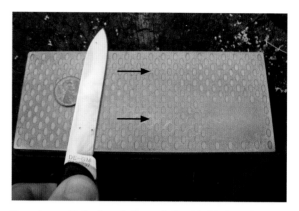

If you have a Swiss Army knife or similar thin-bladed knife, you can approximate the correct sharpening angle if you prop the back edge of the knife on a penny. This method works only with narrow blades like those on Swiss Army knives and jackknives.

the recommended angle. If you can't maintain the proper sharpening angle, try using a circular motion of the blade instead. A circular motion isn't recommended, however, because it makes it harder to keep the same angle (blade bevel).

Tip: If you set the back of the blade of a Swiss Army knife on the edge of a penny, the sharpening angle will be roughly correct. Hold this angle while sharpening the blade and you're good to go. The "penny angle" method works only with narrow blades like those on Swiss Army knives and conventional jackknives.

Hone one edge until a burr appears on the opposite side—you can feel the burr with a fingernail. Then hone the other side until a burr again appears. Now switch to the fine hone and continue honing, using an equal number of strokes on each side of the blade. Maintain a film of very thin oil to float away steel particles that otherwise clog the pores of the stone. Clean the stone (wipe off the surface and apply clean oil) after every twenty strokes or so. This prevents suspended grit from dulling the knife edge.

Exotic-looking tools that clamp to the knife blade are sold for the purpose of maintaining the proper sharpening angle. These tools work great for people who don't know how to sharpen knives by hand.

If you want a polished razor edge, finish by honing on a superfine Arkansas or straight razor stone, then strop the sharpened blade on a piece of leather that's impregnated with jewelers rouge. Strop the edge away from the leather—one stroke per side.

Clean your sharpening stones: With use, grit builds up inside the pores of your sharpening stones and the stones become "finer" (smoother) over time. You'll prolong their life if you occasionally "boil them out." Simply submerge the stones in a pot of boiling water (with a few drops of detergent added) for a few minutes.

To check for blade sharpness: A knife is considered sharp if it will shave hair from the back of your hand. A less barbaric method is to shine a bright light on the sharpened edge. You should see no flat spots, no inconsistencies . . . nothing!

Sharpening (butcher's) steels do not sharpen a knife, they merely realign the microscopic teeth of the blade edge. A steel is handy for touching up a knife (it's simply a coarse version of a leather strop), but it can't take the place of a genuine whetstone.

Tip: If you dip the blade of your knife in boiling water for about 30 seconds, it will be much easier to sharpen.

A good way to carry a hefty folding knife is in a pocket sewn into the back of your field trousers. Sew a line of stitches through the pant leg and pocket as illustrated (Figure K-1) and attach a snap flap or Velcro tab at the top. Equip your

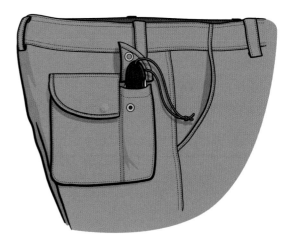

Figure K-1. Carry large folding knives in a pocket sewn into the back pocket of your field trousers.

knife with a nylon lanyard so you can pull it out with one hand.

This system is more secure, less obtrusive, and more comfortable than a leather sheath worn on the belt.

Make a Custom Knife/Tool Sheath

Some friends were lining their canoe around a dicey rapid when the tail of the craft got too far out in the current (a dangerous situation!). The man controlling the bow line tried to compensate by letting out rope, but the rope tangled in some bushes and the canoe spun sideways and began to fill with water. Fortunately, I drew my sheath knife and cut the rope before the craft went under. My knife saved the day because it was sheathed in a "quick-draw," Native American–style case I made myself. I've tried other types of sheaths but none work as well as this traditional design. Here's why:

- The sheath fits the knife like a molded pistol holster—the blade is secure even when you tumble downhill.

The author made each of these sheaths in about an hour. They are form-fitted so keeper straps and snaps aren't needed.

- The knife tells you when it's properly sheathed—it locks in place with an audible click.

- A simple pull releases the blade—there are no straps or snaps to get in the way.

- The blade won't catch on leather—or cut you—when it is quickly pulled or blindly holstered.

- The knife doesn't flop around when you run, or poke you when you sit.

Materials Needed

A rectangular piece of full-grain leather that's $\frac{3}{32}$ to $\frac{1}{8}$ inch thick and is as long as the knife and four times as wide; 6 feet of heavy, waxed shoemaker's thread; two light harness needles; electric drill with $\frac{1}{16}$-inch-diameter bit; contact cement; rivets; small pliers; heavy scissors; file

and sandpaper or grinder; shoe polish. Or you can rivet the sheath and nix the needles and thread. A riveted sheath is bulkier than a sewn one but it's easier to make. If you rivet, you'll need about fourteen $\frac{1}{2}$-inch-long rivets (for the sheath) and four $\frac{3}{8}$-inch-long rivets (for the belt loop). Get two-piece rivets that are designed for leather work. You can order everything you need from Tandy Leather Company.

Procedure

1. Make a cardboard pattern like the one shown in the photo. Enlarge the pattern width by $\frac{1}{4}$ inch to allow for a leather edge

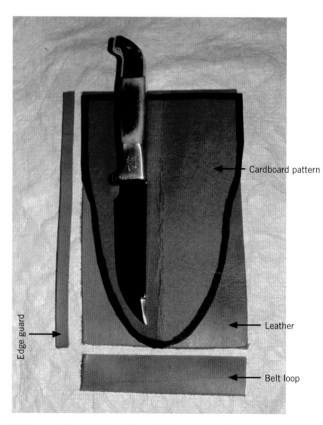

Make a cardboard pattern. Transfer the pattern to the leather and cut out the leather. Allow space for $\frac{1}{4}$-inch-wide edge guard and $\frac{3}{4}$-inch-wide belt loop.

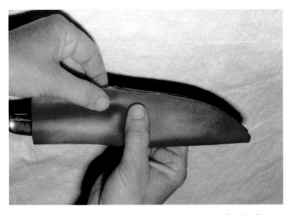

Fold the wet leather to form a sheath and try the knife for fit. Mold the leather to the contour of the knife.

guard. Add ¾ inch at the bottom to make a belt loop.

2. Soak the leather in water until it is supple, then cut out the belt loop and edge guard and set these two pieces aside.

3. Transfer the cardboard pattern to the leather and cut it out.

4. Fold the leather in half to form a "sheath" and try the knife for fit. Mold the wet leather to the contour of the knife. Don't extend the sheath too high—enough

handle should be exposed so that you can easily grab it. Trim excess leather for a perfect fit.

5. Decide how high on your hip you want the knife to ride—a high sheath is more stable when you run and more comfortable when you sit. But it's easier to insert the knife in a low sheath. Then, sew or rivet the belt loop.

6. Glue in the edge guard, then glue the two parts of the sheath together. No need to wait for everything to dry—you can contact-cement damp leather. Sewing or riveting comes next.

7. Sew or rivet. A shoe-repair shop can sew your sheath in less than a minute, or you can do it yourself. If you sew, you'll need to drill ¹⁄₁₆-inch-diameter holes to accept the stitching. Space the holes about ⅛ inch apart. Rivets should be set about ½ inch apart. Remember that rivet heads smash

Glue in the edge guard and rivet on the belt loop.

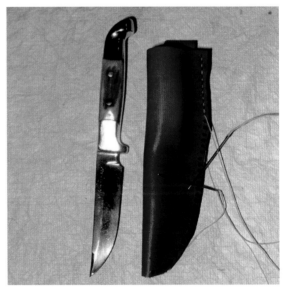

Sew the sheath. Note the use of two needles.

out fairly wide so you'll need to make a wider sheath and edge guard if you rivet.

When the holes are drilled, thread a needle onto each end of your long waxed thread and double-stitch the holes—i.e., each needle goes through the same hole from opposite directions. Figure Y-1 (page 204) shows the procedure. Small pliers are helpful to pull the needles through the tiny holes. Or you can use a Speedy Stitcher, which has been around for decades. It has a self-contained bobbin and a strong replaceable needle. Every leather shop has them.

8. The final fitting: Wet the sheath to restore flexibility, then fit the knife. Again mold the wet leather to the shape of the knife. Press hard on the area around the guard. When you're satisfied, remove the knife from the sheath (the leather will remain formed) and allow the sheath to dry overnight.

9. Use a power grinder or a coarse file and sandpaper to smooth the edge of the sheath.

10. The last step is to apply stain (if you prefer). Otherwise, several coats of shoe polish will do fine. Don't use boot greases or oils on sheaths—they will soften the leather.

That's all there is to it. While you're at it, why not also make a fitted case for your Swiss Army knife and multitool?

Knots, Hitches, and Lashings

While canoeing Manitoba's North Knife River in the summer of 1991, my crew experienced 3 days of wind-driven, icy cold rain. Temperatures in the 30s and wind speeds of 30 miles per hour threatened to shred our paired (12-by-12-foot) nylon rain tarps. I used every trick—and length of cord—to keep the shelter tight and well drained.

When the skies cleared we had one last admiring look at our storm-defying roof before we began its disassembly. I'd used 200 feet of parachute cord, 100 feet of nylon rope, and two Prusik knots to keep things taut, and it

The finished sheath.

Outdoor handbooks define dozens of knots. But for camp use, the half hitch, power cinch (trucker's hitch), and sheet bend are usually enough. Here, the author is using a trucker's hitch to secure his canoe to the pontoon of a floatplane. The pilot (front) looks mighty impressed!

resembled Charlotte's web. "Nice rig," remarked one man, "but how'll we ever get it down? Wet knots are murder to untie!"

"Just watch," I replied with a knowing grin. One pull of each "slippery" loop severed the lines in a matter of seconds. In all, barely 5 minutes were needed to coil ropes and cords and to stuff the flies into their awaiting sacks.

Fabric shelters must be tightly stressed to withstand high winds and prolonged rain. Guy lines and hemlines must be drum tight yet release easily (with a single pull!) when the storm subsides. The alternative to quick-release knots is to pick, swear, and cut them apart. Experienced outdoors people always end their knots with the "slippery" loops illustrated in this chapter. In Figure C-10 on page 69, a quick-release knot is used to secure the mouth of a nylon stuff sack.

Outdoor handbooks define dozens of knots. But for camp use, the half hitch, power cinch, sheet bend, and bowline are enough. Occasionally, you may find use for the Prusik loop and the two common lashings illustrated here.

Use two *half hitches* to anchor a rope or cord to an immovable object like a tree or rock. This is a good hitch to use when mooring a boat. You'll be able to untie the knot more easily if you end

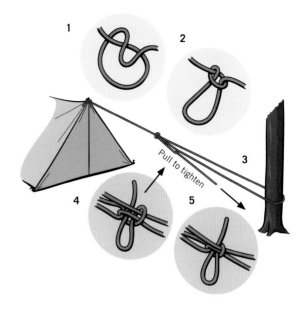

Figure K-3. Power cinch (Trucker's hitch)

the second half hitch with a quick-release loop as illustrated in Figure K-2. Simply pull the line on through if you don't want the quick-release feature.

The *power cinch* (a modification of the trucker's knot; see Figure K-3) provides the block-and-tackle power you need to snug tent and tarp guy lines and keep them tight. The hitch ties and unties in a flash and is much more powerful, secure, and versatile than the tautline hitch touted in old-time camping books. Use the power cinch for rigging a clothesline, tying canoes on cars, securing a package on cartop carriers, and any place you need a tight lashing that won't slip. See my book *Basic Illustrated Knots for the Outdoors* for other practical uses of this ingenious hitch.

Begin the power cinch by forming a simple overhand loop, as shown in Figure K-3, step 1. Pull the loop through as shown in step 2, forming the loop exactly as shown.

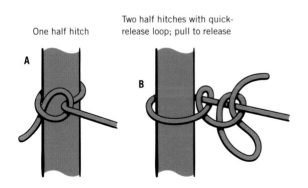

One half hitch

Two half hitches with quick-release loop; pull to release

A

B

Figure K-2. Two half hitches

Single sheet bend

Figure K-4. Sheet bend

Quick release (slippery) half hitch;
pull to release

For absolute security, use
the double sheet bend

If the loop is formed as in step 2, a simple tug on the rope will eliminate it. This is preferable to the common practice of tying a knot in the loop, which after being exposed to a load is almost impossible to get out.

If you are tying a boat on top of a car, tie the long single line (shown attached to the tent) to the boat's bow or stern (use two half hitches or a bowline) and run the double line through a steel S hook on the car's bumper. Now apply power, as illustrated in Figure K-3, step 3. You'll have a tough pulley with a 2:1 mechanical advantage!

If you want a reliable knot, complete the hitch by tying a double half hitch around the body of the rope. If you want the hitch to release with a single pull, end it with a single half hitch and quick-release (slippery) loop as illustrated.

The *sheet bend* (Figure K-4) is the knot of choice for tying two ropes together. Ropes tied with a sheet bend won't slip under a load, and they come apart easily even after being pelted

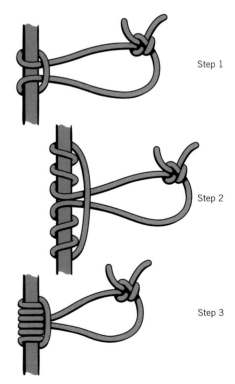

Step 1

Step 2

Step 3

Figure K-6. Prusik loop

Pull

Figure K-5. Bowline

by heavy rain. When rope sizes are dissimilar, use the smaller-diameter rope to make the bend and quick-release feature. If you want absolute security, as in rescue work, use the double sheet bend.

The *bowline* (Figure K-5) is an absolutely secure knot that won't slip. Use it any place you need a nonslip loop at the end of a line. Mountain climbers use the bowline for securing climbing ropes around their waists. If you require absolute security (especially with slippery polypropylene ropes), secure the tail of the finished knot around one arm of the loop with a couple of half hitches.

Scenario: Rain is pooling on a portion of your nylon cooking tarp. An aerial guy line would solve the problem, but there is no place to anchor it. You could run a rope between two poorly situated trees, then secure your guy line

to it, but the pull would be parallel to the rope and the knot would slip down it. What to do?

Why, rig a *Prusik loop* (Figure K-6), of course! Use the Prusik whenever you want an absolutely secure loop that won't slip along a tight line. Mountaineers use this knot for footholds to climb a vertical rope. The Prusik loop slides easily along a tight rope, yet it jams solidly when a horizontal or vertical load is applied. Make the loop from an 18-inch length of parachute cord, completed with a sheet bend.

Lashings

Use a *modified shear lashing* (Figure K-7) to connect short spars together to achieve the pole length (around 6 feet) you need to heighten the roof of a rain tarp. A *diagonal lashing* (Figure K-8) will connect spars in an X configuration and allow you to erect a tight ridgeline when rope is in short supply.

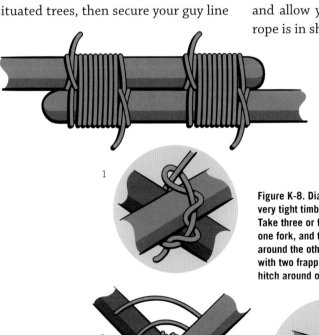

Figure K-7. Modified shear lashing. Place the poles parallel to one another and tie a clove hitch around one pole. Then wind your cord tightly around both poles several times and finish with a clove hitch.

Figure K-8. Diagonal lashing. 1. Begin with a very tight timber hitch around both poles. 2. Take three or four turns side by side around one fork, and three or four more side by side around the other. 3. Then tighten the lashing with two frapping turns and end it with a clove hitch around one of the poles.

L

Lightning

Lightning is a more serious threat than most campers are willing to admit. Next to hypothermia, it is the most dangerous hazard in the outdoors. Realities of backcountry travel necessarily expose travelers to some risk of being struck by lightning, but this risk may be sharply reduced if you religiously follow these guidelines:

1. Lightning ordinarily strikes the highest object in its path, so if you pitch your tent in an open field or plateau, be certain there are trees or rock formations of significantly greater height nearby.

2. A cone of protection (Figure L-1) extends from the tallest trees or landmass (as the case may be) about 45 degrees outward. Pitch your tent or walk, canoe, etc., within this cone of protection, but stay far enough from its source so that lightning can't jump from the object to you. Lightning may jump a dozen feet or more across water, so don't snug against the shoreline if you're canoeing or boating in an electrical storm. Instead, keep within the cone of protection offered by the shoreline trees.

   A note about the cone of protection: A guideline from the National Outdoor Leadership School (NOLS) questions the "cone of protection" theory. NOLS advises hikers to avoid stands of trees and instead seek rolling terrain. The theory is that strikes are most common near tall, lone trees and that the ground surrounding these trees becomes highly electrified. NOLS says lightning doesn't often hit rolling regions that are sparsely treed, so you should be safe there. This makes sense, but only if there's cooperative topography nearby. Consider this example from my own experience canoeing the Gull River in northern Ontario:

My friend Al Todnem was in the lead when lightning suddenly lit up the sky and rain fell so furiously that I could barely see my bow partner. The river was maybe 200 feet wide at this point, and trees choked the shoreline to the water's edge. There was no safe landing in sight.

The distance of a lightning strike can be estimated by dividing the number of seconds between the flash and thunderclap by five. At the 2.5-second strike (meaning lightning was half a mile away), Al turned sharply toward shore and poured on the coal. I stayed near the middle of the river and hollered for him to come back. But he couldn't hear me above the roar of the rain.

When Al was just offshore, lightning struck the top of a tall birch at the river's edge. The top exploded into flame and showered cinders in all directions. The burning top—which probably weighed several hundred pounds—splashed down an arm's length from his canoe! Al back-paddled furiously as burning embers showered his boat. Fortunately, no one was injured.

Yes, boaters should get to shore as quickly as possible when lightning strikes, but only if there's a safe landing spot away from tall trees. Often there isn't. Unforgiving topography—a steep, slick, or vegetation-choked beach—is one reason

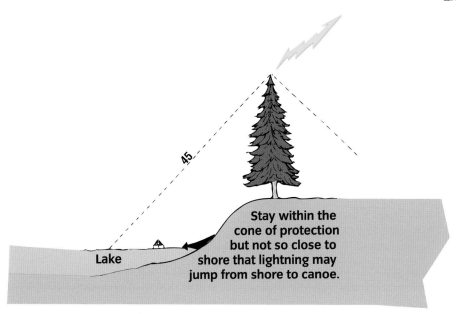

45

Stay within the cone of protection but not so close to shore that lightning may jump from shore to canoe.

Lake

Figure L-1. The cone of protection

why; another is that the sunlit opening of river valleys encourages tree growth near the water's edge. The result is that the tallest trees often grow right next to the river—at the precise place you plan to land. Go there, and as the above case illustrates, you're asking for trouble!

3. Lightning may travel along tree roots, which may extend dozens of feet outward. If roots are close to the surface of the ground, as in rocky areas where there is little soil cover, sufficient energy may be transmitted along subsurface roots to pose real danger to anyone standing on the ground above them. Keep this in mind when pitching your tent.

4. If you're caught outside the cone of protection and suddenly feel electrical energy building (dry hair will stand on end), immediately get as low as possible to reduce the human-lightning-rod effect.

5. The notion that nonmetal boats are safer than metal ones in a lightning storm has no basis. A lightning strike generates millions of volts, enough to fry anything in its path. Steel ships are occasionally struck by lightning, usually with no ill effects. This suggests that aluminum boats and canoes may in fact be safer than nonmetal ones, simply because they more readily dissipate current around the hull into the surrounding water.

6. If lightning flashes all around, get down low in your boat (below the gunnels) to reduce the lightning-rod effect. Again, try to maneuver into the cone of protection offered by the shoreline.

7. Always check your campsite for tall, leaning trees, especially dead ones, which may come crashing down on you in lightning or wind storms.

8. *If you're in a tent and lightning strikes* all around: Sit up immediately and draw your legs to your chest so that only your buttocks and feet contact the ground. A foam sleeping pad (preferably doubled) placed beneath you may provide enough insulation to keep you from being grounded. If you have no foam-rubber sleeping pad, substitute any material that will insulate you from the current.

It is absolutely essential that you maintain the recommended "sitting" position during an electrical storm. In the unlikely event you are struck by lightning while in this position, only your feet and buttocks are apt to burn. But if you're lying flat, electrical energy may pass through your heart and cause death.

Note: Use of a ground cloth inside your tent is highly recommended as it ensures you'll have a bone-dry tent. All your preventive efforts to outwit lightning will be dashed to the winds if your bedding gets wet. See Tents, page 172, for a thorough discussion of the importance of an interior ground sheet.

After the Strike!

Lightning strikes a tree at the opposite end of your campsite. You run to your friends, one of whom is unresponsive and not breathing. One of his shoes is missing and there is a small deep burn on the sole of his foot. You check for a pulse. There is none.

Treatment: Lightning usually kills people by producing cardiac arrest. It may also paralyze the respiratory system. If your friend is alive, the burns are probably minor and you can attend to them later. Right now, you've got to get the heart and respiratory system working.

Begin CPR immediately! If you can restore heart rhythm and breathing, you can probably save your friend.

Keep the patient warm and send for help immediately. Electric shock may cause disorientation, coma, seizures, and spinal-cord injuries. It may also rupture the eardrums. All you can do until help arrives is to keep your friend immobilized and warm and convince him that he'll be OK.

Lyme Disease

According to wildlife experts, there are now more white-tailed deer in Minnesota, Michigan, and Wisconsin than existed in the entire United States at the time of Columbus. Good news to hunters perhaps, but not to hikers who may contract debilitating Lyme disease, which is carried by deer.

Lyme disease is on the rise! In the 1990s around 15,000 cases nationwide were reported to the US Centers for Disease Control and Prevention. At this writing (2020), the number approaches 476,000, although the CDC believes the real figure is much higher due to under-reporting. Just 12 states account for 94 percent of the cases: Connecticut, Delaware, Maine, Maryland, Massachusetts, Minnesota, New Jersey, New Hampshire, New York, Pennsylvania, Virginia, and Wisconsin. And one-fourth of the victims are children, probably because they spend more time outdoors than adults. Several species of *ixodes* (deer/bear) ticks carry the disease. *Ixodes* ticks are very small, about the size of a sesame seed. Their color is dark brown to black; the female often has a rusty brown appearance.

You must be bitten by an infected tick to get Lyme disease. Other insects can carry the

Lyme-producing bacteria, but they can't spread it to humans. Pregnant women can transmit the disease to their unborn infants.

Symptoms: You won't feel the tick bite—it's painless. Symptoms may appear days (or years) after being bitten. In the early stages, there's a red rash or lesion that may migrate to other areas of the body or spread in size. The lesion can be solid red or look like a bull's-eye. The rash is usually about 4 inches across but can be much smaller or larger. You may experience fatigue, headache, fever, and muscle or joint aches. If Lyme disease goes untreated, it can cause arthritis, meningitis, and facial palsy. The disease has caused miscarriages, birth defects, and other health problems.

Prevention

There's no vaccine for Lyme disease, so prevention is everything. Here are the most practical recommended field procedures:

1. Wear long-sleeved shirts and long pants. Tuck your pants into high socks or rubberband or tape the cuffs to keep ticks from crawling up your legs. I prefer to tuck my pants into 12- to 16-inch-high boots.

2. Ticks generally crawl upward, so a shirt collar may prevent ticks from crawling down your neck. Spray the collar with insect repellent.

3. Wear light-colored clothing. It's easier to see ticks on light-colored clothes than on dark ones.

4. Select tight weaves. It's harder for ticks to hold onto tightly woven fabrics than loosely woven ones.

5. *Apply insecticide!* An insecticide plus repellent is your best protection.

An insecticide that contains 0.5 percent permethrin will kill ticks on contact. Spray permethrin on your boots, pant cuffs, and shirt sleeves but do not get any on your skin. Permethrin should be sprayed on clothes and tent openings at least 3 hours before use, then allowed to dry in a well-ventilated area. Dried permethrin will kill ticks for up to 2 weeks and will last through several rains and washings. Permethrin kills slowly; affected ticks may live an hour or more, which is not enough time for them to posture and dig into your skin. When used as directed, permethrin is safe and effective. Most sporting goods stores carry it.

Use skin-safe repellents that have a high concentration of N,N-diethyl-metatoluamide (Deet) on the exposed parts (avoid lips and eyes) of your body. Spread spray-on repellents by hand so you don't miss any spots. Treat arm and leg holes in clothing (tick entry points) with both repellents and permethrin.

See pages 32 and 33 for instructions on how to remove an embedded tick.

M

Maps and Map Tricks

Topographic maps, in the largest scale you can get, are best for finding your way in the backcountry. The smaller the denominator of the map scale fraction, the larger the scale and more useful the map. The numerator of the fraction indicates map units; the denominator equals ground units. Thus, a scale of 1:24,000 would be interpreted as "one unit of distance on the map equals 24,000 units of distance on the ground." Some representative comparisons are shown below:

1:24,000	1 inch on the map equals 2,000 feet on the ground
1:50,000	1¼ inches equal 1 mile
1:62,500	1 inch equals approximately 1 mile
1:250,000	1 inch equals 4 miles

For average field use, American maps in 1:62,500 scale or Canadian maps in 1:50,000 scale are most versatile. Order USGS maps from the US Geological Survey map store (https://store.usgs.gov) or phone (888) ASK-USGS.

The USGS is your complete source for US topographic maps and aerial photos. Request a free index and the UTM (Universal Transverse Mercator) fact sheet. The USGS accepts checks, money orders, and popular credit cards.

To order charts and tide tables of US coasts, the Great Lakes, sections of major rivers, and contoured fishing maps, visit the National Oceanic and Atmospheric Administration (NOAA), https//oceanservice.noah.gov. *Canadian topographic maps and map indexes* must be ordered through a registered map dealer (many are listed on the web). I've had good luck with World of Maps.

Map index: Request a free index to topographic maps if you do not know precisely what to order. The index will tell you what maps are in print, in what scale, and at what cost. If you roughly define the area of your interest (to the nearest state or Canadian province), you'll receive the correct index from the US Geological Survey or the Canadian map distributor.

Colored or monochrome maps? Some 1:50,000 scale Canadian maps may be ordered as monochrome (black-and-white) editions. Monochrome maps are as accurate and easy to understand as colored versions but are less expensive. They also photocopy perfectly—something to consider if you want to provide low-cost maps for a large number of people.

Provisional maps (white prints): Most topographic maps are old; some were last field-checked decades ago. Topographic features won't change, of course, but man-made ones—roads, trails, buildings, power lines—will. If, for example, you're going fishing in Canada, you'll want a map that indicates the location of recently built roads that service the area. Only the most recent topographic maps will indicate the features you want.

However, there may be provisional or white-print maps available that have the information you need. Logging and mining companies and provincial Ministries of Natural Resources (MNR) use provisional maps in their daily work. If these current if unspectacular maps are available, the MNR or the logging or mining company that services the area will know where to find them. The tourism office in the province of your interest will supply the addresses of

MNR area offices. You may also call or write the Canadian Consulate for this information.

Aerial photos are available from the USGS and Canada National Air Photo libraries, but now that we have Google Earth, few people use them anymore.

Internet Maps: Mytopo.com is an internet company that offers custom-printed maps. You choose the scale and coordinate system (latitude/longitude and/or UTM). You add your own title and select the map center location. You preview the finished map, then print from your computer or order a full-sized map printed on waterproof Tyvek paper. There are also "Mobile Maps" that can be downloaded on smartphones with complete coverage of the United States and Canada. Very cool.

The National Geographic digital maps and paper Trail Maps (Guides) of popular wilderness areas are excellent!

Four Ways to Waterproof Your Maps

1. Insert them in ziplock plastic bags. Giant 12½-by-16-inch bags are available from most office-supply stores.

2. Cover them with clear contact paper—makes maps waterproof but you can't write on them.

3. Paint on Stormproof or one of the special waterproofing treatments manufactured by Aquaseal or Nikwax. Every camp shop has them. Products formulated to waterproof convertible boat and car tops will waterproof paper maps (and tent and tarp stitching). Treated maps are water-repellent, not waterproof. You can write over them with pen or pencil.

4. Thompson Water Seal (available at hardware stores) has long been my go-to product for waterproofing paper maps and tent/tarp seams. Regrettably, the Thompson company has changed to a water-based formula which they don't recommend for use on fabrics and paper. There are a wealth of dedicated seam-sealers: Gear Aid, Texsport, and Coleman are most popular. They all work well but (unlike the old TWS) take a long time to dry. And you may need several of the small, pricey tubes to seal the seams on a large tent.

Tip: Use a felt-tip highlighter to mark your course of travel on your map. Highlighter ink won't run or bleed, and you can see topographic features through it.

Learning to Use Map Features

UTM (Universal Transverse Mercator) Coordinates

If you have tried to plot a location on a map to the nearest 100 meters using degrees, minutes, and seconds of latitude/longitude, you know it isn't easy. That's because latitude/longitude is not a rectangular grid.

Enter the UTM grid. It is perfectly rectangular, and coordinate values are in meters. UTM coordinates are referenced or overprinted on all US and Canadian topographic maps. Every GPS unit can be set to read them.

Briefly, here's how UTM works: The Earth is divided into sixty zones. Lettered bands of latitude divide the zones. This creates a rectangular grid. The UTM coordinate designation for the church in Figure M-1 is 357400E /5476200N. You always read "right, up"—that is, you read the easting coordinate first, then the northing one.

If you enter the above coordinates as a way-point into your GPS unit, you must specify the *zone* in which you are located (example: 16T), and the map *datum* (example: NAD27). The datum is the "Earth model" that was used to make the map. If you program your GPS with the wrong datum, the coordinates of your position may be inaccurate. Datum and zone information are printed in the margin of every topographic map.

The details of using UTM are too complicated to detail here. For a complete treatise on the subject, see Michael Ferguson's excellent book *GPS Land Navigation*. Canoeists and kayakers have special needs and thus may want to read the UTM section in my flagship book, *Canoeing Wild Rivers* (Fifth Edition).

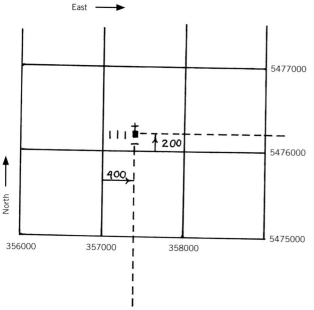

The UTM coordinate designation for the church is 357400E / 5476200N. If the church were located in zone 16T, a GPS would read 16T 357400E / 5476200N. Note that the GPS places a 0 before the first number in the easting coordinate. The zone number (there are sixty zones) is printed in the margin of every topographic map. You MUST include it when you plot a map position using UTM coordinates.

Contour Lines

The light brown lines overprinted on topographic maps are called contour lines. They indicate the elevation (above sea level) of land features and thus permit you to view the topography in three dimensions rather than two. Entire books have been written about contour lines and their interpretation. However, you'll get along quite nicely if you master these basic rules:

- Contour lines connect points of equal elevation. You will gain (or lose) elevation only when you travel from one contour line to another. If you walk along a contour line, you will be "on the level."

- The closer the countour lines, the more severe the drop or rise; the farther they are apart, the more gentle the rise or drop. (Figures M-2 and M-3).

- The contour interval (CI) is the vertical distance between contour lines. Its value in feet or meters is stated in the map margin. If the CI is 50 feet, each

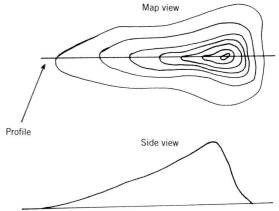

Figure M-2. Basic contour of a long sloping hill indicating the significant drop on the right side of the hill and the gentle slope at left.

successive contour line on the map increases or decreases (as the case may be) in elevation by exactly 50 feet.

- The contour interval is not the same for all maps, so look closely. Convert meters (all the new Canadian maps are metric) to feet (1 meter equals 3.3 feet) if you're confused by the metric system.

- The larger the contour interval, the less clear are the characteristics of the area. In short, a map whose CI is 10 feet gives a clearer picture of the topography than one whose CI is 100 feet.

- Where contour lines cross or run very close together, you'll find an abrupt drop—a falls or canyon (Figures M-3 and M-4).

- The closed or V end of a contour line always points upstream (Figure M-4).

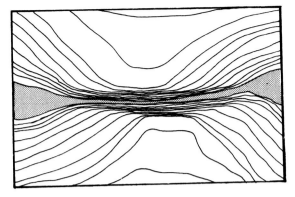

Figure M-3. Contour lines that run very close together and parallel the banks of a waterway indicate canyons.

Using contour lines to determine the drop of a river: For safety's sake, you should know the drop per mile or kilometer of any river you boat. Drop figures suggest the nature of rapids that lie ahead. By comparison, a drop of:

- 3 to 5 feet per mile is easy canoeing— suitable for novices.

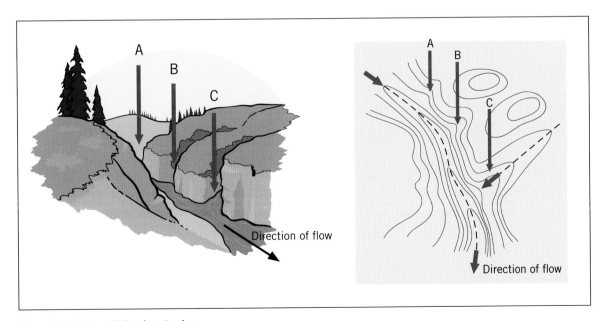

Figure M-4. A, B, and C flow into the river.

- 6 to 10 feet per mile indicates easy rapids—some canoeing experience is desirable.

- 10 to 15 feet per mile is real whitewater—best know what you're doing!

- More than 15 feet per mile—watch out, big rapids! You may have to portage.

Caution: These are rough indicators only. Other factors, like the volume of water, exposed rocks, and how the drop occurs (whether gradually or all at once), determine whether you will paddle or portage a particular rapid.

To compute drop:

1. Draw an arrow wherever a contour line crosses the river. Write the elevation in feet or meters next to the contour line, as illustrated in Figure M-5. Circle the number so you won't confuse it with other map data.

This man is making a map profile—he's determining the drop in feet per mile of a river.

2. Determine the difference in elevation and the distance in miles or kilometers between the contour lines you've marked. Some canoeists prefer to make a table like the one illustrated in Figure M-5.

3. Divide the difference in elevation (vertical distance) by the horizontal distance between points. In the example: From A to B, the river drops 100 feet in 5 miles, or 20 feet per mile—a probable portage. From B to C, the drop is 100 feet in 10 miles, or 10 feet per mile—fun canoeing! My book *Expedition Canoeing* provides more sophisticated examples for those who are canoeing in harm's way.

Monofilament Fishing Line

If you're camping out and lose the screw that holds the rim of your glasses to the bow, here's how to fix it. Tie a knot in a piece of monofilament fishing line and thread it through the screw hole. Knot the other end, then use a cigarette lighter to melt both knots to form a tight rivet. The repair will hold for quite some time.

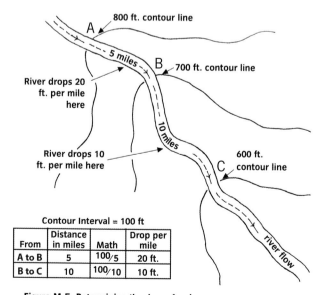

		Contour Interval = 100 ft	
From	Distance in miles	Math	Drop per mile
A to B	5	100/5	20 ft.
B to C	10	100/10	10 ft.

Figure M-5. Determining the drop of a river.

N

Nalgene Bottle Trick

The plastic leash that secures the plastic cap to a Nalgene bottle acts like a spring when the cap is open. You must hold the cap firmly away from the bottle when you take a drink or the tensioned leash will cause the cap to snap shut in your face. The solution is to remove the cap with its attached leash and reverse the leash on the mouth of the bottle. This twists the leash and holds the open cap away from the bottle and your face! (Thanks to Pat Padden of BP Associates in Minneapolis for this clever tip.)

Netted Bags

Strong, netted (mesh) nylon bags with draw cords are popular because you can see what's inside. Here are some uses for these bags on a backwoods camping trip:

- Put dirty clothes inside and "rinse wash" (no soap) the bag in a nearby waterway. Or loosely pack wet, newly washed and rinsed clothes in the mesh bag and tie the bag to your hiking pack. Clothes will dry in a few hours in the hot sun.

- As an anchor for your boat or canoe: Put a rock inside the mesh bag and attach the bag to an anchor rope. This is not as strong as a basketball net anchor.

- To weight the end of a rope that will be tossed over a high tree limb.

P

Packs and Packing Methods

Care of packs: Abrasion (dirt!) is the major enemy of the polyurethane coatings used to waterproof packsacks, so wash your packs with a good detergent at least once each camping season. Tree sap (pitch) may be removed with a small amount of cleaning fluid or gasoline. Don't overdo it though—harsh chemicals may dissolve waterproof coatings!

Allow packs to dry thoroughly before you store them. Wet canvas will mold and damp polyurethane coatings will mildew and peel.

Extending the closing flaps of packsacks: Some packsacks have closing flaps that are too short. The easiest way to extend them without cutting leather or nylon fittings is to sever the flap just behind the closing straps. Sew in a flap extension and reattach the severed piece.

To improve the abrasion resistance of a soft pack, install a double bottom of the same or heavier fabric. An upholstery shop or shoemaker can do this for you quickly and inexpensively.

The bottom corners of packs are subject to considerable abrasion. An early (and still excellent) solution was to crown them with glove leather. You can sew small pieces of lightweight leather to abrasion-prone spots or simply paint these areas with epoxy resin. Epoxy will stiffen the fabric and make it virtually tear-proof. Use epoxy to stabilize frayed threads and small holes that are awkward to patch with a sewing machine.

How to pack a soft pack: Now that nearly all packs have internal or external frames, many campers discount the importance of proper packing. This is unfortunate, for any pack—and

Figure P-1. Tent pole bag secured beneath modern packsack flap

your back—will benefit by doing it right. Here's the proper procedure:

1. Pack in *horizontal*, not vertical, layers. Why? Because your pack should follow the spinal curve of your back. An unyielding upright (tent pole, rolled sleeping pad, etc.) spoils the s-curve. Soft items like sleeping bags and clothing should be placed against your back.

2. Packing will go more easily if you place loose items in colored nylon stuff sacks. For example I keep my extra clothing in a lobster-red nylon stuff sack; my camp shoes go in an orange bag, rain gear in a blue bag, etc. Sacks that reach wall-to-wall across your pack will maximize pack space and eliminate small gaps that are hard to fill. **Note:** The nylon material of stuff sacks may be waterproof, but the stitching and mouth of the bags are not. So don't depend upon waterproof nylon

bags to rainproof your outfit. You can buy pricey waterproof bags or use the *Reliable Waterproofing* "sandwich method" described later in this section.

3. Generally, you should pack in the *reverse order* you'll need things—food on the bottom, tent on top, etc. *Exceptions:* Place heavier items near the top (keeps weight closer to your back) when hiking groomed trails. Set heavy things near the bottom for better control when bushwhacking.

4. Some tents have poles that are too long to fit the confines of a packsack. Consequently, tents and poles should be packed separately, as follows:

    Stuff your tent (don't roll it—rolling takes too much time and identically creases the fabric) into its nylon tent bag. Pack poles and stakes into a special heavy-duty pole bag with drawstring closure. Sew a loop of nylon webbing to each end of the bag and attach lengths of parachute cord to the loops.

    Place your stuffed tent inside your pack and set the pole bag horizontally under the pack flap (Figure P-1). Snake the closing straps of the pack through loops in the cord end. Now your poles can't possibly fall out of your pack!

Reliable Waterproofing: Most books that describe camping techniques recommend that you waterproof your gear by placing it inside a nylon stuff sack (or pack) that has been lined with one or two plastic garbage bags. If you've ever tried this procedure, you know what happens—the thin plastic liner destructs within a few uses. Of course, you can always carry along "a few" extra plastic bags . . .

Here's a better way—one that won't fail 3 days into your camping trip:

1. Stuff your sleeping bag, clothing, or other articles into a nylon sack (an abrasion liner), which need not be waterproof.

2. Place this sack inside an absolutely watertight plastic bag. Twist, fold over, and secure the mouth of the plastic bag with a loop of shock cord.

3. Set this unit inside a second nylon bag, which need not be watertight. Your articles are now completely protected against rain and a canoe capsize. Note that the delicate plastic liner is sandwiched between two layers of tough nylon, out of contact with abrasive materials. Use this sandwich-bag method to pack everything you must keep dry. This is the best way to protect a sleeping bag that rides obtrusively on the outside frame of a backpack.

If you prefer to use a commercial waterproof stuff sack (dry bag with roll down closure) instead of the "sandwich system" described above, do this: First, stuff your sleeping bag into its protective stuff sack (which need not be waterproof). Then, set the stuffed bag into the dry bag. This will prevent the zippers and cord locks on your sleeping bag from abrading the inner waterproof coating of the dry bag. The dry bag will remain watertight for many years if you follow this procedure. *Tip:* Microorganisms will attack the waterproof polyurethane coatings inside stuff sacks. After your trip, turn your stuff sacks inside out and allow them to dry thoroughly.

An Easy Way to Waterproof the Contents of a Pack

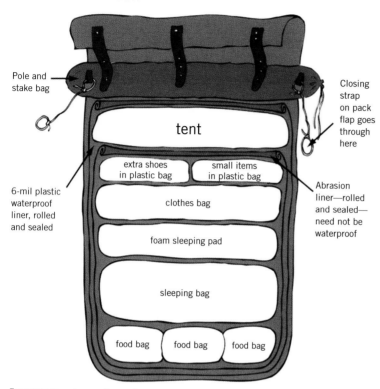

Pole and stake bag

Closing strap on pack flap goes through here

tent

extra shoes in plastic bag

small items in plastic bag

6-mil plastic waterproof liner, rolled and sealed

clothes bag

Abrasion liner—rolled and sealed— need not be waterproof

foam sleeping pad

sleeping bag

food bag

food bag

food bag

Easy way to waterproof a pack

1. Line the pack with *two* heavy-duty plastic trash bags. The inner bag is an "abrasion liner"; the outer bag is the "waterproof liner."

2. Pack things in the rough order shown in the illustration. Note that the tent (which may be damp or wet) is sealed between the abrasion and waterproof bags, out of contact with dry items below. Pack tent poles above the tent if they are short enough to fit. Otherwise, secure them under the closing flap, as illustrated.

Hip belt and tumpline: Most backpackers know the advantages of a hip belt, but few appreciate the worth of a tumpline. A tumpline consists of a wide leather or fabric strap that is secured to the "ears" (sides of the pack at shoulder level) of a packsack. The packer places this strap just above her forehead, grabs the tumpline near her head, leans forward, and trucks confidently down the trail. The early voyageurs carried hundreds of pounds of furs by this method; packers in undeveloped countries still rely on this system.

Tumplines are most useful when ascending steep hills, as they take considerable weight off the pack straps. To make a tump strap for your pack, simply sew a D ring to each side of your pack below the shoulder line, and mount the tumpline across them.

Tip: Place awkward bundles like day packs, fishing rods, and canoe paddles under the tump strap in the hollow of your back, as shown below. When your neck and head begin to ache, cast off the tumpline and shift the load to the shoulder straps. Change back to the head strap when the pain is gone.

Note: A properly adjusted tumpline will *not* strain your neck. The key is "properly adjusted." The strap must be placed *above your brow* (as shown in the photo), not against your forehead, as commonly thought. A tump strap that is too short or too long (half-an-inch can make a difference!) will be ineffective. Get it right and you'll be amazed at how comfortably you can carry heavy loads, especially uphill. Himalayan porters rely exclusively on tumplines. If shoulder straps and hip-belts worked better, they would use them!

Pack pockets: Sew up some small envelope-style pockets and attach them to the outside of your pack with heavy-duty glove snaps or Velcro strips. These pack pockets will add versatility to your hiking outfit. If you attach mating strips of Velcro to the inner walls of your tent, sidewalls, or thwarts of your canoe or boat, etc., your pack pockets can be quickly remounted to provide added convenience.

Pack padding (shown here): You can stiffen the sides of a pack and soften its back by inserting a closed-cell foam sleeping pad inside. Just slip the rolled mat into the pack and let it unroll against the sides. Hard objects, like stoves and saws, won't gouge your back, and foods and beverages will stay cool in the midday sun. The pack will stand upright by itself, which will make it easier to pack.

Pillow

Everything should be multipurpose on a back-country camping trip, even your pillow. A practical pillowcase can be made from a lightweight terry cloth towel. Fold the towel lengthwise and sew up the two long sides. Set a Velcro tab or snap in the open end. Stuff your down or polyester vest into the pillow case. Add more clothes if you want more thickness. Terry cloth breathes and it won't slide on the slick floor of your tent. You can use your pillowcase as an emergency sponge, bathing towel, dirty clothes bag, or stuff sack. One friend made a luxurious polyester-pile pillowcase and sized it to fit his head so he would have an extra hat!

A tumpline makes heavy loads easier to carry, especially uphill. Note that the tump strap is attached to the pack well below the shoulder straps (important!).

You can stiffen the sides of a pack and soften its back by inserting a closed-cell foam sleeping pad inside.

R

Rain Gear

Rain gear has become quite stylish. Some parkas now feature hoods with integral bills that turn with your head, underarm zippers for better ventilation, drip-proof pockets, waist and hem cords, and much more. These niceties are nice, of course, but they won't keep you dry. What will is a sensibly designed garment that is constructed of genuinely waterproof material.

Fabrics: There are those that work and those that don't. Some work sometimes. And the difference between fabrics is not necessarily a function of price. In fact, some of the best (most watertight, that is) rainwear costs less than some of the worst!

Rain gear has become quite stylish. But bells and whistles won't keep you dry. What will is a good functional design and a reliable fabric. Camp-bound on a cold, snowy day along the Poreno River, Norway. Note the smiles: Everyone is warm and dry and having a good time, despite the miserable weather. Location: the Norway-Finland border. Note the reindeer fence.

If you want reliable rain gear at a reasonable price, see what the professionals are wearing. Foresters, wildlife management people, and construction workers all require tough garments that are absolutely waterproof. Rain garments like these are available at every industrial supply store. The new industrial rain suits are constructed of fabrics that are similar or identical to those used on the best foul-weather sailing suits. But because there are no pockets, no underarm zippers, and often no hoods to boost the price, the cost is much lower.

I used to think that a bulky foul-weather sailing suit was the best protection one could buy for camping in prolonged rain. Every lightweight suit I'd tried failed minutes into a major storm. Still, I yearned for something lighter and more compact. So I tried an experiment: I replaced the bulky sailing jacket with two lightweight, unlined Gore-Tex raincoats. Together they were much lighter and more compact than my killer raincoat.

Jacket 1 goes on at the first sign of rain. If the storm picks up, I add jacket 2, which slips easily over the first. Water that gets past the first jacket is stopped by the second. I stay dry in any rain. And I have two quick-drying garments that can be worn alone or layered for warmth. If I'm canoeing, I wear one raincoat under my PFD (personal flotation device) and one over it. This encourages ventilation and discourages condensation—and my PFD stays dry.

Gore-Tex is relatively cool and comfortable. It breathes under most conditions, even on hot muggy days. Modern Gore-Tex rainwear is quite reliable, even in showers that last for days. Leaks are usually due to bad design, not to failure of the Gore-Tex substrate. Pay particular attention to the closures at the wrist, neck, and waist. Zippers should be covered with double-overlapping flaps to seal out blowing rain, and double cuffs to help stop dribbles. Slash pockets must have protective rain flaps or they'll become ponds. And beware of armpit zippers: I haven't found one yet that doesn't leak in hard rains! Jackets that have fully waterproof zippers (pricey!) are the exception.

Naturally, heavy-duty two-ply construction is more rugged, reliable, and expensive than lightweight single-ply construction. You can buy several conventional rain parkas for the price of a good Gore-Tex one—something to consider if cost counts.

Style: Whether you hike, canoe, motorcycle, backpack, or sail, you'll be happiest with a generously sized two-piece rain suit. Ponchos provide inadequate protection and may be dangerous in a boat upset. Below-the-knee rain shirts are ideal for casual fishing and auto camping but are otherwise impractical.

You'll put on and remove rain gear frequently between showers, so select garments that are easy to slip on and off. Pants that have an elastic or corded waistband are much more versatile than those with bibs.

Tip: Remove the elastic waistband of rain pants and substitute a fabric cord and cord lock. Elastic loses its strength over time, and rain pants will fall down. A cord provides quick, positive adjustments. If you want to stick with the factory elastic waist cord, add a second cord lock. The twin cord locks won't slip when the pants become heavy with rain.

Avoid pants with snaps or Velcro tabs at the bottom. These restrict ventilation. Besides, primitive man learned long ago that water doesn't flow uphill! Ankle closures are only useful for mountaineering above the timberline.

Pant legs should be oversize so you can easily slip them on over heavy trousers or boots. Some expensive rain pants feature baffled zippers at the ankles. Straight-cut pant legs go over boots just as easily and are less costly to manufacture. Zippers eventually gum up with debris and fail—they're just another gimmick to drive up costs.

Tip: If you want to learn all there is to know about good rain gear, check out the best foul-weather sailing suits. The only frills you'll see on these garments are ones that work. Now compare your observations to rain garments in camping shops!

Jacket fit: Buy your rain parka a full size larger than you think you need, large enough so you can wear several layers of clothes beneath. Rain gear that looks trim in the store will be hot and restrictive in the field.

Color: Color is a personal choice, though navy blue garments outsell all others by a wide margin. And that's unfortunate, for this color attracts mosquitoes, which invariably come out between showers!

Hoods: A traditionally styled sou'wester hat is much more functional than a restrictive hood. However, if you select a hooded parka, be sure the zipper comes right to your nose. Those that stop at the chin must have a throat strap to seal off the neck area or they'll admit cold air and rain. I have an aversion to garments that have removable hoods or hoods that zip into collars. These styles don't protect your head and face as well as traditional hoods.

Pockets, seams, and zippers: Two covered pockets are more than enough in any rain jacket. Additional pockets add weight, bulk, and cost and threaten the integrity of the waterproof construction. The fewer the seams in any rain garment, the more watertight it will be. Except to close the front of a jacket, the value of zippers is overrated. Underarm zippers (which are added for ventilation) keep out rain only if you don't raise your arms. And zippered flies in rain pants usually leak within seconds.

Waterproofing standards: The US Army requires a garment to withstand a minimum of 25 pounds per square inch (PSI) water pressure in order to earn the title of waterproof. At first thought, this industry-accepted minimum seems adequate, that is until you realize a person may exert that much pressure (or more!) simply by sitting on the edge of a boat seat. Kneel down or plant your elbows firmly in the duff and you may experience similar results. In all likelihood, minimally rated rainwear will not keep you dry!

Good rain clothes will withstand two or three times the amount of water pressure specified by the military, but even this may not be enough for strenuous field use. Then there's the matter of abrasion. Every time you put on or take off your rain parka, or move while wearing it, a microthin layer of waterproof chemical is scraped off the fabric. In time, leaks develop.

One answer to the abrasion problem is to sew a liner into the garment. But liners add weight, cost, and bulk. They also absorb sweat and are slow to dry. A better solution is to insist on a fabric with a minimum 100 PSI waterproof coating. And for really severe applications (like foul-weather sailing), you may want to consider the merits of a fabric that boasts a 150 PSI (or greater) rating.

Unfortunately, manufacturers of rainwear do not usually advertise the PSI ratings of their products. For comparison: A Kenyon Industries light polyurethane coating (Light K-Kote, as specified on the garment label) will average 25 to 50 PSI on the Mullen hydrostatic test, which is used to determine waterproofness of fabrics. But a Super K-Kote (double) treatment will run 100 PSI or more, which makes it suitable for all but the meanest applications.

Tip: You'll increase the effectiveness of your rain gear if you double the thickness of abrasion-prone areas—knees, elbows, and especially the seat. All you need is a sewing machine and some matching fabric. And don't forget to seal the seams you've sewn!

Rain gear for children: See the section Children, page 47.

When not to wear rain gear: Some authorities suggest you eliminate a windbreaker from your clothing list and instead rely on your rain parka for wind protection. Frankly, I think this is bad advice. Every time you lean against a tree or scrape a rock, abrasion takes its toll. In no time leaks develop. If you want your rain gear to last more than a season or two, use it only for its intended purpose and switch to a wind shell when the need arises.

Tip: If you wear your raincoat over your nylon wind shell, you'll reduce abrasion to the waterproof inner coating (the shell acts as a liner). Twin jackets will also keep you warmer and drier than a single waterproof garment.

What to wear under rain gear: Don't wear cotton! It absorbs perspiration and supercools the body. Since perspiration cannot escape through a waterproof covering, a wet, clammy feeling is guaranteed.

If you wear a pure wool shirt over a wool, polyester, or polypropylene undershirt, you'll stay dry—or at least comfortably dry.

Tip: Store rain clothes in a nylon stuff sack between uses. This will keep them clean and eliminate the abrasion that results from stuffing clothing into packs.

Care and repair of rain gear: Hand-wash rain gear in detergent. Air-dry it thoroughly before storing. Store rain gear on hangers so air will circulate. Don't keep these items in confining stuff sacks—polyurethane coatings will mildew!

Patch holes and tears with matching material. One way to get matching fabric is to cut up the stuff sack that came with the garment. Be sure to seal the seams you sew.

Ropes and Rope Tricks

To most campers, a rope is a rope, and they make no distinction between manila, polypropylene, Dacron, and nylon. That's too bad, because different rope materials and weaves excel in different applications. What works best as waterskiing towline is completely inappropriate for rigging a rain fly. Here are three points to consider when choosing ropes:

1. *Flexibility:* Flexible ropes accept knots more willingly than stiffer weaves but are more likely to snag in their own coils. Choose flexible ropes for tying canoes on cars and for any place a proper lashing is essential. Stiff ropes are best for throwing lines (lifesaving), boat mooring and tracking lines, and general use around water.

2. *Slipperiness:* A slippery rope is always a nuisance. Some ropes, notably those made from polypropylene, are so slippery that they will not retain knots.

3. *Diameter versus strength:* Modern synthetic lines are very strong. Even ⅛-inch-diameter parachute cord has more breaking strength than you will probably ever need. However, large-diameter ropes are easier to handle and less likely to snag than small-diameter ones. Quarter-inch-diameter rope is about minimal for heavy-duty camping applications. One-eighth-inch-diameter parachute cords are the recommended camp utility cord.

Note: There are several grades of parachute cord. Avoid the cheap stuff that's commonly sold at hardware stores.

Types of Rope

Nylon: This is the most popular fiber for utility rope, and for good reason. It's strong, light, immune to rot, and inexpensive. On the negative side, it stretches considerably when wet and shrinks when dry. This makes it a bad choice for mooring boats, for canoe-tracking lines, and anywhere you need a rope that won't change dimensions. Nylon also degrades in the sun. A nylon rope may lose half or more of its strength in a single season if it's continually exposed to the weather.

The two most common weaves are the three-strand braided and the sheathed core. Braided rope is very soft and flexible but it cannot be flame whipped after it's cut. The ends of nylon and polypropylene ropes are usually sealed after cutting by melting them in the flame of a cigarette lighter. Three-strand braided rope simply unravels when heat is applied. It must be whipped the traditional navy way by winding the ends with waxed string or by dipping them in plastic whipping compound (available at marinas).

Sheathed nylon ropes (there are many variations) feature a central core surrounded by a woven nylon sheath. This construction is slightly less flexible than the braided type but is pliant enough for camp use. Sheathed ropes flame-whip easily and do not unravel. Quarter-inch-diameter stock is ideal for rigging clotheslines, tying gear on cars and trailers, and other utility applications.

Polypropylene: The choice lies between round, three-strand stiff-braided line and the cheap flat-woven stuff sold in hardware stores. It's no contest; the stiffer line excels in every category. Sailors prefer polypropylene to nylon because it floats and it doesn't stretch when wet. It also comes in bright colors.

Ropes for mountaineering: Some types of mountaineering rope make excellent utility line. The choice lies between the three-strand hard lay construction or the kernmantle type (a core of braided or twisted strands, the kern, is covered by a protective braided sheath, the mantle). Three-strand rope is much cheaper than kernmantle, and it has a stiffer hand, which makes it ideal for lining canoes, mooring boats, and anywhere you need a snag-free rope that won't fail.

Dacron (polyester) line is the material for sailboat sheet and mooring lines. It's wonderfully strong, beautifully soft, and frightfully expensive. If you're a sailor, you know all about Dacron line. Advantages of Dacron over nylon include 1) very little wet stretch/dry shrinkage and 2) immunity to the degrading effects of sunlight—a feature important on boats exposed to the weather. My favorite for tent and tarp lines is ⅛-inch-diameter, 450-pound test "reflective yellow tracer" polyester cord. It glows brightly in the dark when you shine a light on it and it doesn't stretch in the rain or absorb as much water as nylon cord. Available from Cooke Custom Sewing, in Lino Lakes, MN.

Manila and hemp have almost gone the way of the passenger pigeon. These natural-fiber ropes (manila is far superior to hemp!) have a nice hand; they coil beautifully, offer a textured grip, and even smell nice, but they rot easily and for their weight aren't very strong. I can think of no reason to use natural-fiber ropes when better synthetics are available for about the same price.

Tip: Abrasion is the major enemy of rope, so occasionally wash your ropes with detergent to remove ground-in grime. You'll prolong the life of your ropes considerably.

Coiling Tricks

Nylon utility ropes are best coiled and bound by the old navy method, described in the four steps below (see Figure R-1):

1. Coil the rope and put your thumb through the coils to hold them in place. Leave about 3 feet of rope uncoiled.

2. Grasp the rope in one hand and pinch it at the waist to form an "eye." Coil the free end (tail) around the rope and upward toward the eye. Overlap the first coil to lock it in place. Wind evenly and tightly.

3. Form a loop near the end of the tail and pass it through the eye.

4. Grasp the collar (wound coils) in one hand and the rope body in the other. Slide the collar up to the rope to lock the loop in place. (It may be easier to hold the collar firmly in one hand and pull downward on the body of the rope.) The rope is now secured; a pull on the tail will release it.

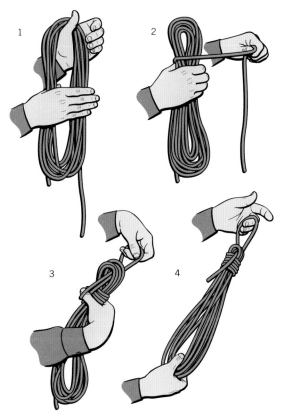

Figure R-1. Coiling a rope—old navy method.
Step 1: Coil the rope and hang it from your thumb.
Step 2: Pinch the waist and coil the free end around it.
Step 3: Make a loop and insert it through the eye of the coils.
Step 4: Snug the collar. Note the handy loop for hanging.

The Throwing Coil: Use this method for large-diameter ropes and throwing lines. The old sailing method is faster to wind and release, but the coils are more likely to snag when the line is tossed.

A. Coil the rope carefully, taking care to rotate your coiling hand downward so as to give each coil a half turn before you lay it in place. The half turn keeps the strands of the rope aligned and prevents the coils from twisting. It is the secret to coiling a rope so it won't snag when you throw it.

B. Wind the tail tightly around the coiled rope. Overlap the first winding to lock it in place.

C. Make a loop near the tail and work it under your last winding. Pull the loop to tighten the winding. A pull on the tail will release the rope.

You can carry the coiled rope over your shoulder, hang it on a nail or cleat, or secure it around a rod or canoe thwart as illustrated in part D of Figure R-2.

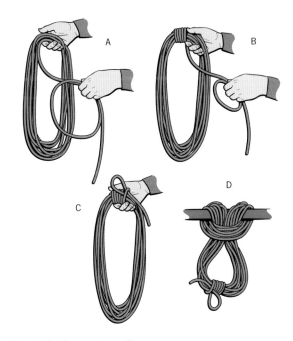

Figure R-2. The throwing coil

S

Saw (Folding)

A folding saw is one of your most useful camp tools. On a rainy day you may be unable to get a fire going without one. Triangular metal saws are flimsy and they won't cut big logs.

The FastBucksaw I've recommended in previous editions has long been my favorite full-frame folding saw, but it is now largely out of production. The Boreal 21 by Agawa Canyon is the new kid on the block—and it is outstanding! This tough-built saw has a strong aluminum frame and an all-toothed (no rakers!) 21-inch-long blade that cuts fast. Assembly takes seconds and, unlike other folders, you don't have to touch the blade when putting it together. Lock-up is vault solid.

Agawa Canyon, Boreal 21 packsaw. The author's favorite. Cr. Agawa Canyon.

If weight and bulk are a concern, consider a compact "jack knife" folding saw like those sold at garden shops. The "Silky" brand folding saws which are made in Japan are phenomenal!

Some saw thoughts:

- Long blades are more efficient than short ones.

- Lightweight saws feel great when you pick them up, but they lack the heft to run easily through wood.

- The more space between the blade and the frame, the larger the diameter of the logs you can saw.

- A folding saw that assembles fast is a blessing.

Saw blades: Some saw blades have rakers, others don't (Figure S-1). Rakers don't cut—they just remove resinous sawdust that becomes trapped in the saw kerf. You need more rakers to cut green softwood than to cut green hardwood, and you need no rakers at all (for example, a carpenter's saw) if the wood is dead and dry and nonresinous. A blade that has one raker for every four teeth (fairly standard on a multipurpose blade) will lose 20 percent of its cutting efficiency. You don't need rakers on a camp saw that is used to cut dead, dry wood. Indeed, cutting green wood in most campsites is a crime! But rakers look cool, so saw makers

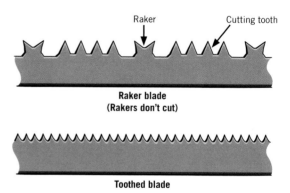

Figure S-1. Saw blades

offer them. The good news is that you can buy rakerless replacement blades at most hardware stores.

Tips: Keep your folded saw in a fabric bag with drawstring closure. This will keep the parts cleaner and speed assembly time. Occasionally wipe tree sap from saw blades with a rag dipped in gasoline, alcohol, or WD-40. This will improve cutting efficiency and keep the blade from rusting.

Shovel

A ¾-inch-diameter, foot-long aluminum tube, flattened at one end, makes an ideal camp shovel. Use it for burying fire remains, fish viscera, and human wastes where proper disposal facilities do not exist. (See Ethics in the Wilderness, page 76, for the proper way to dispose of waste in the backcountry.)

Shower

You can make an effective portable shower by attaching a light plastic hose and showerhead to a folding plastic water jug. Use a long hose and drive the system with foot pressure. If stove fuel or wood (to heat water) is in short supply, consider bringing along a commercial Sun Shower, which is similar to the above system except for its special heat absorbing fabric. Sun Showers can be purchased at most camp shops and marinas. They are quite popular with yachtsmen.

Signal Gear

Only those who are going in harm's way really need signal gear. A minimal kit would include a whistle, signal mirror, fire starters, and maybe a few orange smoke distress signals (available at marinas). Naturally, you should include a cellphone if you have coverage. Flares are valuable on water but are very dangerous on land—they can start a forest fire.

A more advanced kit might include the following:

Satellite phone: Iridium and Globalstar are the major companies that serve civilians. Iridium has complete world coverage; Globalstar has some blackout zones. If you're going where help is an airplane ride away, a satellite phone is the best protection you can buy. Satellite phones operate just like regular phones, except that calls must be dialed in international mode. In the United States and Canada, dial 001, followed by the area code and number.

Rent or buy? When customers return their rented satellite phones, the rental companies usually just charge the batteries and mail the phone to a new customer. Often, the batteries are many years old and/or have experienced too many charging cycles. I've observed two occasions—both, deep in the heart of Canada—where rental phones failed due to bad batteries. Better to buy a used phone and a NEW battery (about $100) then to take a chance on a rental unit. There's an active market for used sat phones—check the internet. My ancient 9505 Iridium model still works like new.

VHF aircraft transceiver: Even on remote trips it's not uncommon to see an airplane every day. Any plane you can see is probably within 10 miles of you—close enough to be reached on a handheld VHF aircraft transceiver. The typical VHF transceiver has a 15-mile range—enough for about 8 minutes of talk time at propeller plane speeds, or less than a minute for jets. In a life-threatening situation, you may broadcast on the restricted emergency frequency (121.5 megahertz). But for other concerns you must stick with the frequencies that are assigned to local companies. Be aware that transmitting without an FCC license isn't strictly legal! In the bush, however—and given the short range of handheld transceivers—everyone looks the other way. **Note:** Many bush pilots prefer satellite phones to VHF radios for personal communications. They will usually provide their phone number if you ask.

VHF marine radio: Looks and works just like an aircraft model but operates at a lower frequency. Boats on the coasts and Great Lakes all have them. Channel 16 is the emergency channel; use channel 13 to contact a ship when there is danger of collision.

CB radio: People in Alaska and the Canadian north converse mostly on CB radios. Most power boats have them.

Channel 9 is reserved for emergencies but it is poorly monitored. A cellphone (if there's service), satellite phone, or VHF radio may be more reliable.

PLB (personal locator beacon): A PLB emits a distress signal that allows rescue personnel to hone in on you. The units provide precise positioning. A PLB is strictly a signaling device—you can't talk or receive messages on it.

Satellite Messengers

Satellite messengers, like the Garmin inReach and SPOT models, run off satellites, not phone towers, so they work almost everywhere (there are blackout zones) in the world. Garmin models run on the Iridium satellite system; SPOT uses Globalstar. Both allow you to communicate your geographic position (generally to within 20 meters) via email or text. Garmin inReach and top SPOT models feature two-way text/email messaging. All satellite messengers

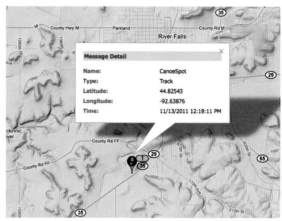

A SPOT GPS location as it appears on Google Maps.

provide continuous tracking data which can be viewed on a cellphone or computer. An SOS emergency button will send help your way. Additional features (depending on model) may

SPOT GEN4 provides GPS positioning and tracking, HELP/OK, custom messages, and emergency SOS. It runs off four AAA batteries.

The palm-sized Garmin inReach features location sharing, two-way messaging, weather forecasts, and more. An internal, rechargeable lithium battery provides up to 90 hours of use.

include pre-loaded topo maps, satellite imagery or coastal chart downloads, and weather forecasts. Satellite messengers are lightweight, compact, waterproof, and rugged. They are great peace of mind if you're going in harm's way.

Warning: Electronic communication and navigation devices should never be your first line of defense! Batteries can fail, units can break, and satellite signals can be blocked by terrain and weather. Always carry a paper map and needle compass if you're going in harm's way! Bring extra batteries for all devices, and always tell your friends where you're going!

Skis (Cross-Country)

Under certain conditions; the surface of cross-country skis will load up with crusty snow and impede performance. To prevent this ice buildup, occasionally apply a paste wax to the top of your skis.

Sleeping Bags

This is your most important item. With care, a good sleeping bag will last half a lifetime, even with almost regular use.

Principles of Sleeping-Bag Design

1. The smaller the bag, the less area it will have to insulate. **Translation:** Confining mummy bags are much warmer for their weight than roomy rectangular ones.

2. Most heat loss from a sleeping bag occurs through the open head end. It's nearly impossible to seal the open end of a

Most people choose sleeping bags that are too warm! Summer temperatures in the continental United States seldom fall much below freezing, and for this, a summer-weight (minimum 40°F) sleeping bag is usually enough. The temperature inside a tent is about 10 degrees warmer than the outside air. If you wear wool long johns and a stocking cap when you sleep, you'll effectively add another 10 degrees.

rectangular-style sleeping bag so that warm air won't escape. (One solution is to install a collar—see Figure C-7 for details.) For this reason integral hoods are mandatory on sleeping bags that will be used for cold-weather camping.

Tip: An effective makeshift collar can be tailored from a sweater or scarf. Drape the garment across your chest and bunch the fabric around your neck and shoulders. This will eliminate drafts and increase warmth.

3. Inexpensive mummy-style sleeping bags and all rectangular models are built with a flat foot, which means the material is simply folded in half at the foot end and a zipper is installed around the edge (as in a typical station-wagon sleeping bag). A boxed-foot design, though more costly to manufacture, is much more comfortable. Here, a foot-high circular panel is sewn in at the bottom (like the end of a tin can), which allows you to maintain a comfortable toes-up position without bearing against tight material.

4. A full-length zipper running from foot to chin is a must. Bags with half-length zippers become impossibly hot in warm weather. *Tip*: Getting out of your bag quickly can be important if there's an emergency like a tent fire or bear attack. So don't buy any sleeping bag until you've climbed inside it and worked the zipper. It should run flawlessly. In an effort to cut weight and bulk, some manufacturers have downsized their zippers. The new smaller ones don't seem to run as well (they catch on fabric) as bigger zippers from decades ago.

Categories

Down and synthetic sleeping bags are generally categorized as:

- *Summer weight*—comfortable in temperatures to near freezing.

- *Three season*—warm to about 10°F to 15°F.

- *Winter*—good to 20 degrees below zero or more. There are some special arctic bags that go much lower than that.

Note: "Comfort ratings" are speculative. Few sleeping bags are as warm as their manufacturers suggest. And numerous tests have shown that women need warmer sleeping bags than men.

Which Sleeping Bag Is for You?

Most people select three-season models, thinking they represent the greatest value for the money. Wrong! The typical three-season sleeping bag becomes too warm when temperatures rise much above 50°F.

Only if you do considerable primitive camping in the spring and fall should you buy a three-season bag. Otherwise, a lighter, less-costly summer bag will be a better buy. Tent temperatures commonly run about 10 degrees warmer than the outside environment, so a good summer bag will keep you toasty to near freezing. In really cold weather, you can mate your summer bag with an outer or inner liner or with a blanket. Or, just use two sleeping bags, one inside the other.

Down or synthetic? Down bags are lighter, warmer, more compact, and have a more "gentle hand" than any of the synthetics. If you've ever slept under a down comforter, you know what I mean. Good down is also much more resilient and long-lived than synthetics. For an equivalent weight of fill, down has a lower and wider temperature comfort range. This means down will keep you warmer when it's cold, and cooler when it's warm, than will a synthetic. Eight years are about the useful life of most synthetic bags that are used regularly. Down, on the other hand, will never wear out—at least not in your lifetime!

For example: Consider two three-season sleeping bags, one down, one synthetic. Both bags are rated to 10°F. The finished weight of the down bag will be at least a pound less than the synthetic and it will compact into a much smaller space. The synthetic bag will become too warm when the temperature reaches 50°F, while the down bag will remain quite comfortable.

However, good down sleeping bags are more expensive than equivalently rated synthetic ones, and you can't beat them around as much. Wet down is almost impossible to dry under typical field conditions. Because down is a natural fiber, it absorbs body moisture, which in damp winter conditions can be a serious problem. For this reason, experienced winter hikers usually select synthetic-fill sleeping bags.

Question: If down dries so slowly, shouldn't we eliminate it from consideration for summer use too? Absolutely not! If you sandwich pack your sleeping bag as I recommend in the Packs and Packing Methods section (page 124) and stormproof your tent accordingly (see page 182), you will never get your bedding wet. I guarantee it!

Waterproof Down Bags?

Yes, there are "waterproof down bags"—well . . . sort of. The down is treated with a chemical to make it resist water. A soaked "waterproof down" bag will be warmer and dry more rapidly than a similar drenched conventional bag. But drying time in the field for either will be measured in days, not hours! Comparative tests show that synthetic fill outperforms waterproof-treated down when soaked. So if you commonly camp in the wet, or are allergic to down, a synthetic sleeping bag is the way to go.

Sleeping Bag Shells

Most nylon sleeping bag shells are factory treated with a durable water-resistant (DWR) chemical. DWR treatment makes the shell water-resistant, not waterproof. A waterproof shell would trap body-produced moisture inside the bag, which would result in a cold, damp, night's sleep. You would be in big trouble if the temperature was below freezing and moisture froze inside the bag!

Bottom line: A sleeping bag MUST allow moisture to exit the bag. And the quicker it leaves, the more comfortable you will be. Waterproof/breathable fabrics such as Gore-Tex and its competitors are waterproof and breathable. Again, sort of! Water molecules rush through the large pores of uncoated nylon; they trot through the pores of DWR-coated nylon, and they crawl through the microscopic pores of waterproof/breathable membranes. The point is that restricting the flow of air through a sleeping bag or active garment is not a good idea.

Buy what you can afford; but whatever you buy, make sure it has a hood to keep your head warm, a full-length two-way zipper to keep your feet cool, and a temperature range that matches the environment in which you'll camp. If you choose a mummy bag—and most experienced campers do—try it in the store before you buy it. Mummy bags come in different lengths and girths; some are quite restrictive while others are surprisingly roomy. If a bag feels tight in the store, you won't like it in the field.

Winter sleeping bags are roomier than summer bags to allow dressing space inside. Winter campers usually take their clothing and canteens to bed so they need space for all these "rummage sale" items. The typical synthetic-fill winter bag weighs 5 pounds or more. Summer-weight bags may weigh half that.

Packing the Sleeping Bag

Sleeping bags (discounting station-wagon types) should be stuffed, not rolled. Zippers should be closed to prevent galling of the material. Just grab the foot end of the bag and stuff it, handful by handful, into its nylon sack. This is easier on the fabric and fill than traditional rolling.

Do not store sleeping bags in stuff sacks; you'll wear out the filler in no time. Instead, keep sleeping bags in a breathable cotton sack (a pillowcase works fine) or store them flat or on hangers.

When to Clean Your Sleeping Bag

Once every year or two is often enough, even if you use your bag a lot. A down bag will lose some loft and resiliency with the first washing. Additional washings seem to have no adverse effect.

Some campers never wash their sleeping bags; they believe that washing will ruin them. But body oils and dirt will accumulate and the insulative value of the bag will decrease accordingly. It's a catch-22. My advice? Keep your bag as clean as possible and wash it carefully when the occasion demands.

How to Clean Your Down Sleeping Bag

Hand washing is the best way to clean any down-filled item. Nonetheless, manufacturers often recommend dry cleaning on down product labels simply because so many down items have been ruined by improper machine washing. Make no mistake: Dry cleaning with powerful perchlorethylene solvents will reduce the loft and warmth of a down bag. But it will not destroy it. Improper washing will!

Recommended Procedure for Handwashing

1. You'll need a huge basin to wash your sleeping bag. A bathtub is ideal.

2. Use lukewarm water and any mild soap. I've had good luck with Woolite, Ivory Snow, Ivory Liquid, Basic-H, and other liquid dishwashing detergents. There are also some special down soaps that may or may not be worth their high price.

3. Place the sleeping bag into the soap solution and sponge the shell thoroughly. Rub gently at stubborn spots. Do not use Spray 'n Wash or stain removers! The shells of sleeping bags are tightly woven to contain the down, so it may require many hours for wash water to work through them.

    Allow the bag to soak in the wash water for an hour or so, then squish the bag gently with wide-spread hands. Carefully work wash water well into the down. A couple hours of additional soaking and frequent "squishing" should remove most of the dirt.

4. To rinse the bag, drain the tub and gently press soapy water out of the article with

both hands, fingers spread wide. Don't lift or wring out the article. A water-filled sleeping bag is very heavy, and the delicate baffles may tear if you roughhouse the project.

A minimum of two rinse cycles is recommended. You absolutely must get all the soap out or the down will mat when it dries.

5. Gently place the thoroughly rinsed sleeping bag into a large plastic clothes basket for ease of handling. Now, it's off to your Laundromat with several dollars of change in hand.

6. Place the incompletely rinsed bag into an extractor (a high-speed centrifuge) and spin out the remaining water. If your Laundromat does not have one of these machines, a large washing machine set on spin dry will work. One pass through the extractor machine or two passes through the washing machine will safely exhaust nearly all the water.

7. Next, place the bag in a large commercial clothes dryer set on very low heat. Be sure the dryer puts out low heat! If it does not, run it with the door ajar (jam a magazine through the door hinge over the safety button so the machine will continue to run) to bleed heat. Check the progress of the bag every 10 minutes.

Some people place a terry-cloth towel into the dryer to absorb the static electricity. This seems to speed drying.

It will take you a full day to wash your sleeping bag!

Warning: Do not attempt to dry a sleeping bag in family-sized clothes dryers. The heat is concentrated over too small an area. You may, however, safely spin dry your sleeping bag in your home washing machine if a commercial extractor is not available.

Method 2: Machine Washing

Machine washing, even in a big Laundromat-size machine, is much harder on a sleeping bag than washing it by hand. Still, if you're careful, the bag should come out fine. Simply place the bag, along with down-safe detergent, in a large, commercial front loading washing machine. DO NOT use a "home sized" machine, even if it is a front-loader. Set the temperature to the coolest "warm" setting. When the machine has stopped, follow steps #6 and #7 above.

How to Wash Synthetic-Fill Sleeping Bags

Synthetic-fill sleeping bags and garments cannot be dry-cleaned. The cleaning fluid will destroy the fill. These garments are best handwashed in the same manner as down bags. Yes, you can machine wash them successfully. However, most sleeping bags are too large to be safely washed in family-size washing machines—some abrasion, stretching of stitches, etc., is sure to result. If you must machine wash your bag, use one of the large front-loading commercial machines. Even then, my vote goes to handwashing.

Synthetic-fill jackets, vests, and other small items may be safely washed in most home machines (gentle cycle only). But, they must be dried with low (under 120°F) heat—or better yet, no heat!

Dos and Don'ts for Sleeping Bags

- *Don't* roll sleeping bags; stuff them.

- *Don't* yank sleeping bags out of stuff sacks; pull gently.

- *Don't* leave sleeping bags stuffed for long periods of time.

- *Don't* machine wash down sleeping bags in small (home-sized) washing machines.

- *Don't* dry-clean synthetic-fill sleeping bags.

- *Don't* wash down bags with harsh detergents.

- *Don't* pick up a wet down product without adequately supporting it.

- *Do* air and fluff sleeping bags after each use.

- *Do* store sleeping bags flat, on hangers, or in large porous sacks.

- *Do* sponge clean the shell of your sleeping bag occasionally.

- *Do* wash your sleeping bag when it gets dirty.

If you're on the move, air-dry your bag in direct sunlight for about 10 minutes each day.

Tip: You can get along surprisingly well in summer without a sleeping bag if you fold a blanket or two in the manner illustrated in Figure C-6. You can also increase the warmth of any station-wagon-size sleeping bag by applying the procedures outlined in Figure C-7.

Sleeping Pads, Air Mattresses, and Sleeping Systems

Toddlers and teenagers can get along quite nicely without a foam pad or air mattress, but these items are a must for most adults. In general, air mattresses are more comfortable than foam pads, but they are cold to sleep on and they frequently fail. For this reason, most expert campers choose open- or closed-cell foam pads over more traditional air mattresses.

Some things to consider when choosing a trail mattress:

- *Weight matters:* Most of the best sleeping pads weigh under 2 pounds; some are well under a pound.

- *Bulk:* The best sleeping mats roll to football size or smaller.

- *Warmth:* Some people are cold sleepers; others are warm sleepers. Hence, there is no industry-reliable method of determining the warmth of a sleeping pad. Suffice it to say that except in the heat of summer, a noninsulated pad is not a good choice. The difference in weight between a lightly insulated three-season pad and one suitable only for summer is maybe 4 ounces.

- *Speed of inflation and deflation:* The best trail mattresses inflate in less than a minute. Deflation should be nearly instantaneous. Struggling to inflate or deflate your bed will adversely affect your attitude!

- *Comfort:* The shoulder area should be wide enough to keep your elbows from falling off the pad onto the cold ground.

The best foam mats inflate in less than a minute. Deflation takes seconds. Struggling to inflate or deflate your bed will adversely affect your attitude! It's obvious that this camper is not having a good time!

Sleeping with your body on the pad and your elbows "hanging down" can be quite uncomfortable, more so if the pad is very thick and your arms drop several inches.

Air mattresses: Except for car camping, the traditional single-valved air mattress is extinct. Such mattresses require too much time to inflate and deflate to be practical on backwoods trips. Except in the heat of summer, air mattresses cannot be used with down sleeping bags. Body weight compresses down to near zero thickness, and air mattresses do not have sufficient insulation to make up for this loss. In fact, the circulating air in an air mattress simply moves the cold from place to place. Even thick polyester-fill sleeping bags (polyester doesn't compress as much as down) may get cold when the temperature drops below freezing.

Tip: Place a thin closed-cell foam pad on top of an air mattress for the ultimate in warmth and comfort.

Hybrid air mattresses: A few companies produce air mattresses that are insulated with goose down, foam, or synthetic fibers. These mats are light, extremely comfortable, and very warm. The bad news is that oral inflation introduces moisture that can freeze or at best reduce the warmth of the mat. A special pump (provided) eliminates these concerns. These built-in inflation pumps are very fast, compact, and reliable.

Closed-cell foam pads: You can choose PVC (polyvinyl chloride), polyethylene, EVA (ethyl-vinyl acetate), or a number of mix 'n' match types. EVA is so superior to other closed-cell foams that it defies comparison. EVA is unaffected by sunlight, heat, and most solvents. It is almost immune to abrasion. It's expensive and worth it!

A ¼-inch-thick closed-cell foam pad will provide plenty of insulation for summer (but not much comfort). For winter, you'll need at least a ⅜-inch thickness, more for subzero temperatures. Closed-cell foam pads are immune to water and mild abrasion so it is not necessary to cover them with materials.

Open-cell foam pads: These have largely gone the way of the passenger pigeon, and for good

NEMO Cosmo Insulated sleeping pad. Note the luxurious polyester microsuede cover. Regrettably, these covers are no longer available—you'll have to make your own.

reason. They weren't very comfortable and the polyurethane foam absorbed water.

Air-filled foam pads: The Therm-a-Rest began the revolution—now there's lots of competition, and variation. Basically, these consist of a low-density (soft and cushy) open-cell foam, chopped foam, or foam sheet that's sealed in an envelope of vinyl and nylon. One or two oversize plastic valves control the air flow. Open the valve and the pad inflates itself. Close the valve to lock in the air. Some pads have a built-in air pump. The result is a comfortable, incredibly warm (suitable for subzero use), and very reliable mattress. I've used Therm-a-Rest mats for decades and never had a problem. I've also had great luck with Exped and NEMO pads (my favorites).

Tip: Make a fabric cover (one side cotton, one side soft wool) for your air-filled foam pad. The cover will protect the pad from punctures and keep it from sliding on the slippery tent floor. Most important, the cover will absorb the imperceptible perspiration that becomes sweat against your back. On hot nights keep the cotton side up; turn the wool side up when it's cold. When it's too hot for any cover, sleep with your bare skin against the cool cotton cover and use your sleeping bag as a blanket. *Tip:* A thin polyester cover is nearly as comfortable as a cotton/wool one and it weighs much less.

A crinkly "space blanket" (every discount store has them), placed silver side up under your sleeping pad, will increase the efficiency of your sleeping system.

If you find yourself sleeping on an uncomfortable incline, level out your sleeping system by placing folded clothes beneath your air mat or foam pad. You can make an intolerable sleeping situation quite bearable by this method.

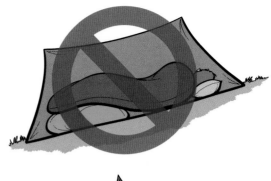

You sleep "on the level."

Figure S-2. Sleeping comfortably on an incline

Tip: If you are stuck with an inclined site, pitch your tent perpendicular to the drop (one side lower than the other), rather than parallel to it with the entrance high, as suggested in most camping books. It's easier to level a sunken side than a lowered end. Figure S-2 shows why.

Snow Glasses

Dark sunglasses are necessary to prevent snow blindness in dazzling white conditions. You can make an emergency pair by applying parallel strips of electrical or duct tape to the lenses of standard glasses. Leave a narrow horizontal slit to see through.

Snow Shelters

It's a well-kept secret that winter camping is a whopping good time. After all, when it's 20 below, only fools and "them's that knows what they're about" are apt to be out there. Along with predictable solitude comes exquisite beauty and awesome silence. Camped on a pristine blanket of white, there are no footprints or garbage to muck up the view. Touch the crispness of dawn, hear the harsh stillness of night. Like those who lived here millennia ago, you are part of the land, not meaningless passersby. What was in summer is no more. Everything is covered by sterile white.

Getting around in 4-foot snowdrifts requires new technique. You shuffle along on snowshoes or glide on skis. Equipment is carried in special backpacks or on classic toboggans, polyethylene sleds, or fiberglass pulks. Fire building becomes an art as well as a lesson in tedium. First you establish a base of logs so flames won't sink into oblivion, then you split dry kindling from the heart of a snow-drenched log. A folding saw and ax and a good sharp knife are essential tools in the winter woods.

And if you go above the tree line, there are new challenges and equipment. Instead of fires, there are gasoline and butane stoves, low-slung mountain tents with cook holes and tunnel doors; baffled parkas, balaclavas, and face masks; vapor-barrier liners, tinted goggles, and frost cream. And when tents fail—or for those who just disdain them—there are snow caves and trenches, quinzees and igloos. To the uninitiated, "sleeping out" in the dead of winter flirts with death. To those of us who know and live by nature's rules, it's hyacinths for the soul.

If you have a warm sleeping bag and a thick foam pad, a winter shelter can be as simple as a nylon tarp or lean-to. In fact, for winter camping, a nylon tarp beats an unheated tent on these scores: It's lighter and more compact; you can build a reflector fire out front; and you don't need to worry about frost condensation

A winter snow shelter can be as simple as a tarp, a sleeping bag, and a thick foam pad.
Alan Wenker

falling on your face while you sleep. Of course, the classy way to winter-camp is with a canvas tent and sheet-metal stove (see Winter Tents on page 180). But this outfit is heavy and slow to pitch. If you're on the move and want to travel light, a snow shelter is the way to go. Ask an experienced winter camper if he or she prefers unheated tents to snow houses and you'll get ten to one in favor of the huts. That's because unlike tents, snow structures are warm inside. Sometimes too warm. Everyone knows that snow is a great insulator, but you won't believe how good until you've crammed three people into a snow cave built for two. Add a candle or two for light and warmth and watch the thermometer rise. Keep a close eye on the temperature, for when water starts dripping from the inner walls, you've got problems. Snow is porous but ice doesn't breathe. And if your home freezes solid inside, air won't get in. Overheating a snow house is a very real concern—one that newcomers to winter sport don't take seriously enough.

Warnings aside, snow huts are comfortable and eminently safe, and as every kid will attest, they are fun and easy to build. And they are much stronger than any tent. If you have to wait out a blizzard, a snow hut is the place to be. Here are some ideas to get you started.

Quinzee Hut

A quinzee is the white man's version of the traditional Eskimo igloo. It's made by piling up snow, then digging out the center, rather than by carefully laying snow blocks. Quinzees are as warm, as strong, and as spacious as igloos, but they take much longer to build. Compared to igloos, they are terribly ugly. An Eskimo snow house is a work of art; a quinzee retains the appearance of a schlocked-together snow pile (which is exactly what it is). Nonetheless, quinzees are practical for base camp travel in winter and as emergency-survival dwellings. Kids build them just for fun and occasionally someone makes news by carving a garage-size quinzee from a giant snowbank. Quinzees are similar to snow caves, which are also built from packed snow. Snow caves, however, are hollowed out from an existing packed drift, which is faster and simpler than piling snow. Both

This quinzee is nearly complete. All that's needed is to porcupine it and "dig it out." *Important:* Always keep a shovel with you inside a snow hut in the event the entrance is closed by blowing snow while you sleep.
David Wescott

structures serve the same function—that of keeping you warm and dry regardless of the weather outside.

You don't need a thick layer of snow to build a quinzee. You can simply haul in what you need or scrape a thin surface layer of snow to provide sufficient building material.

Building the Quinzee

1. First decide on the size. A 10- to 12-foot diameter is about right for two people. Most snow campers make their huts too small, so err on the large side. You can easily adjust the interior dimensions to a custom fit when you dig out the structure.

2. Pile up snow to a height of about 7 feet. This will provide comfortable sitting room inside for both occupants. You'll speed manufacture of the hut if you occasionally pack the snow pile with your shovel.

3. When the snow pile is complete, insert foot-long sticks into the structure at approximate 18-inch intervals.

Piling up snow to build a quinzee hut.
David Wescott

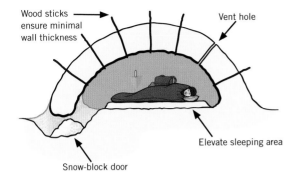

Wood sticks ensure minimal wall thickness

Vent hole

Elevate sleeping area

Snow-block door

Figure S-3. A quinzee

"Porcupine" the hut with these sticks all around and on top. Don't stop until the quinzee resembles a medieval mace. These sticks provide a gauge by which you can judge the thickness of the walls when you dig out the center. It is essential to maintain a minimum 8-inch wall thickness. Without the "gauge," you'll shovel right through the sidewalls, and once you've gone too far, repair is difficult.

4. If you want a tunnel entrance, now's the time to build it. Don't forget to porcupine the tunnel.

5. Now comes the hard part—finding something else to do for the next few hours. The structure needs time to settle; the snow must contract and harden. How long this takes depends on temperature, humidity, and age of the snow. If the snow is fresh and dry and it's very cold, the pile will take much longer to set. On warm days the molecular change will occur much faster. Eight hours is usually enough time, regardless of the weather. Do not throw water on the hut to speed its cure; you'll wind up with an ice ball—one you can't dig out or breathe inside of!

6. When the structure has hardened, prepare to dig. You'll need a small shovel and a friend. You'll get very wet from falling snow, so wear rain gear or highly water-repellent clothing. Dig out the tunnel entrance through to the center, passing carved snow to your partner outside. Now it's simply a matter of sculpting the interior to suit your fancy. Just remember to stop digging when you see the porcupine "hairs." You need to maintain an 8-inch minimum wall thickness. Do not remove the porcupine sticks from the structure—doing so will weaken the hut.

7. *Finishing the interior:* As everyone knows, warm air rises while cold air does the opposite. For this reason, you need to elevate the sleeping area a foot or so for additional warmth. While you're doing this, you can also carve some "pockets" into the sidewalls, in which to place small items. Make a small shelf for your candle—a single candle will light the entire structure and raise its temperature considerably.

8. *Vent hole:* It's not absolutely essential to cut a vent hole in the roof, but it will make for a better exchange of air if you do. Simply punch a ski pole through the roof or pull out one of the porcupine sticks. Don't panic if the hole eventually fills with snow and closes. You'll get plenty of fresh air through the doorway, and the quinzee walls are porous.

9. *Doorway:* If you have a tunnel entrance to break the wind, you don't need a door. However, a snow block, angled across the entryway, will reduce heat loss without

significantly affecting ventilation. Just be sure you don't close the snow-block door completely.

Tip: A length of nylon parachute cord makes an acceptable snow knife for cutting blocks. Just saw the cord back and forth through the snow until the block is free. This procedure will only work with "old snow," whose molecular structure has compacted.

Warning: The heat generated by two or three bodies in a small quinzee will easily maintain an interior hut temperature of 20°F or more. In fact, the temperature may rise above freezing if you're not careful. The danger is not in being too cold; it is in allowing the structure to overheat. If the temperature goes above freezing, the interior walls will melt and ice up, ventilation will cease, the structure will drip water, and you'll have an intolerable mess. So watch your thermometer—and your hut temperature—carefully.

Sleeping Inside the Quinzee

As stated, interior temperatures are apt to maintain a balmy 20°F even in subzero weather, so you don't need an arctic sleeping bag for comfort. Any three-season bag will do, provided you have plenty of insulation beneath you. You're sleeping on ice, remember?

Your first sleeping layer is a waterproof plastic ground sheet. Atop this place foam pads, carpeting, cardboard—anything that will insulate your body from the cold ground. If you have an open-cell-foam trail pad, a 2-inch thickness (or greater) will be required for comfort. A ⅜-inch-thick closed-cell foam pad may provide enough warmth. You need much more insulation below than on top!

Common fears: There are two: 1) "I'll die from carbon-monoxide poisoning," and 2) "The hut will collapse and smother me." Both concerns are unfounded. You'll get plenty of air through the entryway and vent hole, even in the unlikely event the quinzee freezes over. As to strength, there is no contest. Snow huts gain strength as they age. I doubt a polar bear could crush a week-old quinzee!

Tip: If you plan to use the shelter for several nights, chip away the ice buildup on the inner walls each day. This will maintain breathability of the structure.

Important: The entryway of a quinzee or snow cave should always be placed on the windward side of the structure. If wind-driven snow begins while you sleep, sufficient snow could pile up on the leeward side of the hut to seal a leeward entrance. This could be quite serious (deadly!) in a snow cave, especially in a blizzard. It's always wise to keep a small shovel in a snow hut, just in case you need to dig out in the morning.

One-Person Trench Shelter

You can use a nylon tarp in a variety of creative ways to construct a trench shelter. One plan is illustrated in Figure S-4.

1. Make a snow pile 6 feet by 12 feet by 3 feet deep. Like the quinzee, let it set awhile before you begin the process of digging out. If you can find a snowdrift of these dimensions, you may begin digging immediately.

2. Dig a trench 9 feet long, 3 feet wide, and 2 feet deep. Make the entrance a foot lower than the sleeping platform so cold air will be drawn out of the structure.

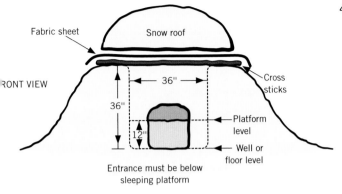

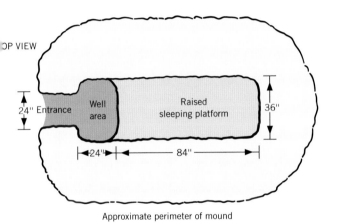

Figure S-4. A trench shelter

4. Retrieving your tarp: If you leave snow on your tarp overnight, the snow will compact and make the tarp difficult to remove in the morning. One solution is to allow the snow to set for a few hours, then pull out the sticks and remove the tarp from inside the trench (better have smooth sticks or you'll tear the tarp). Expect some falling snow, but the roof should hold. Like a quinzee, the trench shelter will grow stronger with time.

Vaulted-Roof Snow Trench

If you have a snow knife (machete) and old snow, you can build a vaulted roof like that shown in Figure S-5. Be sure to cut the blocks long enough so they'll butt at the peak. Fill cracks with loose snow.

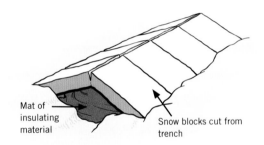

Figure S-5. Trench shelter with vaulted roof

3. Span the structure (side to side) with a couple dozen closely spaced sticks. Then set your tarp over the crossbars and cover it with an insulating layer of snow.

   You won't need cross-sticks if you substitute two 7-foot-long aluminized space blankets for your nylon tarp. Merely overlap the cold-stiffened space blankets so they'll cover the 9-foot trench, then anchor the sides with snow. A real advantage of the space blankets over a conventional tarp is that they reflect much more warm rising air back to the sleeper below.

Sleeping on Snow

Sleeping on snow requires extra preparation. As mentioned, you need substantial insulation under your sleeping bag. Here are some other tricks that will add to your comfort:

- Place dry outer clothing in your sleeping bag before you retire. The clothes will absorb some of the bag's cold and reduce the size of the area your body must heat.

Remove the clothing as the bag warms up.

- Wear long johns, a balaclava, and down or synthetic booties to bed for extra warmth. Don't bring down parkas into your bag with you; they will absorb imperceptible perspiration and become damp. Use the parka as a pillow or as extra insulation to cover your feet.

- If you eat some high-energy food before you retire, your body will produce more heat as you sleep.

- Make a draft collar for your sleeping bag by placing a wool sweater or scarf across your chest and neck. Tuck the sweater sleeves around your shoulders to prevent air loss at the head of the bag.

- Don't cover your face with your sleeping bag if your nose gets cold. Your bag will not be able to eliminate the moisture from your breath. The moisture may even ice up on the outside—a dangerous situation! Instead, use a sweater or shirt as a face mask. You can easily breathe through this porous material.

- A midnight urination call at 20 below is no fun. Carry a special poly bottle for elimination. Women may want to try the Go Girl feminine urination device.

- In winter your sleeping bag cannot easily dissipate all the moisture your body produces, so air out your bag in the sunlight for several minutes each day.

- A candle will raise the temperature of your tent or snow shelter by 10 or 20 degrees. **Reminder:** Batteries don't work well when they're cold, so insulate them until they are needed. Lithium batteries are almost essential in severe cold.

Snowshoes

For deep, open snow, select long, slender snowshoes with high-turned toes (the Alaskan or Pickerel style is best). Low-toed models plow deep under fluffy snow and double your work output.

For crusty snow or wooded areas, a small maneuverable shoe is best. My favorite "woods shoe" is the narrow cross-country model, which is basically a miniature version of the old Alaskan, though with a lower toe. The Sherpa bearpaws with their ingenious binding and integral traction are excellent for deep woods/mountain trails. The common Michigan/Maine pattern is a good compromise style, though its low toe makes it a poor choice for fluffy snow. The Ojibway model (see photo) works well in

These traditional Ojibway-design snowshoes work well for deep snow. A number of manufacturers offer nylon-laced snowshoe kits based on this simple but functional pattern.
David Wescott

woods and deep snow—most snowshoe kits use this design. No one snowshoe will do everything well.

Plastic and aluminum snowshoes: Most of today's recreational snowshoes are made from aluminum and plastic. How do these perform when compared to traditional (and beautiful) wooden models? The answer is "better and worse." Synthetic shoes are better on groomed trails and in tight brush where speed and maneuverability are important—and their built-in claws are awesome on ice. They are also much lighter than wooden shoes, which makes them the clear choice for running or competition. Finally, they are maintenance free, something that can hardly be said for wood and rawhide.

There are downsides: The neoprene foot beds can load up with snow; you may get a painful "freezer burn" if you touch an aluminum frame with your bare hands in subzero weather; a broken neoprene lace may completely unravel; a cut rawhide lace won't retreat beyond the cut. Break an aluminum frame and you've got trouble. Broken wood can be pinned, spliced, and lashed—an easy field repair.

Modern recreational snowshoes with traction bindings.
Chris Coleman

Negatives aside, synthetic recreational shoes do what traditional snowshoes don't—that is, they get large numbers of people out in the woods in winter. And that alone is enough to recommend them.

Snowshoe Bindings

Snowshoe bindings keep evolving. Here are some popular types:

- *TruTrak:* Designed to end pigeon-toeing and provide security in deep snow.

- *Speed:* Goes on in less than 30 seconds!

- *Floating/spring-loaded:* The shoes pivot and move with your feet.

- *Pivotal-Hinge:* Tail falls to the ground as you walk so you slide easily along. Negative: You can't walk backwards.

- *Boa (like the snake) closure:* Extremely secure, wraparound fit; very fast and easy to adjust. Negatives: Somewhat heavy; snow/ice buildup can be problematic.

All the top bindings have some sort of "traction device," which helps on icy snow and when ascending steep grades.

Binding Straps

- *Leather:* still manufactured but are now largely seen on traditional wooden snowshoes that are "lookers not users." Leather bindings stretch when wet and they're less secure than modern types.

- *Nylon webbing:* Highly adjustable but less supportive than other modern types. Nylon, like leather, will stretch when wet.

- *Rubber and polyurethane:* Less wet stretch than nylon.

- *Ratchet straps:* Similar to snowboard bindings—highly adjustable, fast, and easy to use.

Soaps

Backcountry soaps should be biodegradable and lather in cold water. They should also be highly concentrated for maximum efficiency. Bar soaps should not melt in the sun or crack in extreme cold. These are the traditional backwoods soaps:

- *Kirk's Coco Hardwater Castile:* Comes in bar form and lathers wonderfully in cold water. Very stable in heat and cold.

- *Dr. Bronner's Peppermint Soap:* The label provides hours of tireless entertainment. Surprisingly, a lot of the label's trivia is true. Dr. Bronner's formula works well for everything from washing dishes to hair. I've even used it for shaving and to brush my teeth. The nice peppermint smell is compelling. Every earth-friendly co-op and specialty store has it.

- A number of *specialty liquid camp soaps* are similar to Dr. Bronner's. A few contain citronella which keeps mosquitoes away. Barely.

- *N/R Laboratories No-Rinse shampoo and body bath* are among the most interesting products to come along in recent years. Just rub them in to create a rich lather, then strip off the floating dirt and oil with paper or cloth towels. No water—or only a very small amount of water—is necessary. For example, 1 ounce of the body bath in a quart of water is enough for a full sponge bath! No water is needed when you shampoo. There is no residue, so no need to rinse. No-Rinse cleaning products were first used on hospitalized patients who could not bathe normally. Now NASA's astronauts have discovered their merits. No-Rinse products are ideal for backpacking trips where clean water is hard to find.

Solar Charger

If you're camping off the grid and need to charge electronic gear, you'll want a solar charger. But before you run out and buy one, be aware that "power-wise" you get exactly what you pay for. A petite, business-envelope-size unit may be suitable only for low-energy devices like iPods and cellphones. Satellite phones, cameras, and other units with big batteries require a fair amount of power to recharge in a reasonable time. For example, my solar charger puts out 26 watts at full peak. Still, it can take several hours in the field to charge my satellite phone—a feat accomplished in about 30 minutes at home. The point is that even in bright sunlight, charging usually takes longer than you think. Buy more solar charger than you think you need and you won't be disappointed!

Sponge

A small sponge is one of the most useful and forgotten items on a camping trip. It will clean your tent floor, remove accumulated water from your canoe or boat, dissolve mud from your boots, mop up a tent leak, and more. A natural sponge is much more absorbent than the best synthetic.

Stool (Camp)

A camp stool is worth its weight and bulk on all but the lightest "go light" backpacking trips. Camp chores—cooking, washing dishes, sharpening edged tools, etc.—go easier when you don't sit on the ground. I most appreciate my stool when I must wait out a storm under my rain tarp or endure a long tour of kitchen duty.

Friends scoffed when I first began to bring a camp stool on my wilderness canoe trips. Now they all follow suit. I've tried all manner of stool designs and have ultimately settled upon a simple collapsible model like those used at competitive shooting events. Be sure you get a stool that sits on two parallel aluminum rails. Avoid individual pointed legs that can sink into soft ground. My favorite camp stool weighs 30 ounces and has a canvas storage pouch beneath the seat. When not in use it folds flat and clips (with bungee cords) to my backpack (see photo). It is available from Piragis Northwoods Company. *Tip:* Keep a seat-sized square of closed-cell foam inside the zippered pouch. It will provide flotation for the stool in the event

A folding stool is worth its weight on a camping trip. This one has a handy storage pouch and tube legs that won't sink into the ground. It folds flat and can be secured to a pack with a bungee cord.

of a boat capsize. If the seat is wet, set the dry foam piece on top and sit on it.

Stoves

There are gasoline, kerosene, alcohol, butane, propane, multifuel, and wood-burning trail stoves. Here's how they differ:

Butane stoves don't have to be primed, pumped, or filled with gas. Just turn the adjuster knob and light. Refueling with a new canister takes seconds. Because butane burns clean, there are no clogged fuel jets to clean. However, the efficiency of butane is directly proportional to the outside temperature, and the altitude. Stoves run better when it's warm; they lose pressure when it's cold (there are butane-propane blends for better performance). When temperatures slip to well below freezing, they quit working altogether. Butane stoves are affected by altitude: the higher you go, the more pressure they generate and the more efficient they run. Butane fuel is bulky and fairly expensive (compared to other fuels) so it's not a good choice for extended camping trips. Most butane stoves have poor windscreens or none at all.

Propane stoves burn hot and clean, even in subzero temperatures. Like butane, you just turn the adjuster knob and light. Propane gas containers are refillable, but also heavy and bulky.

Gasoline stoves are hot, reliable, and inexpensive to operate. Gasoline has the highest heat output of all stove fuels.

Most gasoline stoves accept only white gas or Coleman or Blazo fuel (highly refined forms of naptha). An important distinction must be made between additive-free white gas (difficult to obtain these days) and additive-packed automotive unleaded gasoline. Unleaded gas is more volatile than white gas and may produce excessive pressure in stoves designed for white gas only. Best stick with Coleman or Blazo fuel. Most white gas stoves have very effective windscreens.

Kerosene has about the same BTU rating as gasoline but it's less volatile. Where a gasoline stove will explode, a kerosene one will burn. Kerosene stoves must be primed with alcohol (recommended) or gasoline.

Alcohol stoves: Just light the burner, wait a minute for the fuel to vaporize, then start cooking. They run dead quiet but are slow to heat. By comparison, my Primus Omnifuel gasoline stove will boil a quart of water in a covered pot in about 4 minutes. My Swedish Trangia needs 10! HEET in the yellow can (available at gas stations), an efficient and inexpensive alcohol fuel. Alcohol stoves work fine in any temperature and at any altitude. They are the lightest and most reliable of all trail stoves. Many long-haul hikers swear by alcohol stoves, which they make from empty aluminum beverage cans. Plans are on the web.

Dual-Fuel and Multifuel: Dual-fuel stoves burn white gas (naptha) and unleaded auto gas. Multifuel stoves burn kerosene, diesel, jet fuel, white gas, and unleaded auto gas. These stoves run best (cleanest) on white gas, so it makes sense to pay extra for the multifuel feature only if you need it. Changing fuels generally means changing jets—a hassle in the field.

Wood: Compact, wood-burning stoves have become quite popular. My favorite is the ultralight stainless steel Littlbug. It assembles in seconds and burns twigs and logs up to 3 inches thick. Cranked up, it doubles as a campfire. The Littlbug assembles in seconds and takes up almost no pack space. Set it on a high-sided aluminum baking pan and it meets federal fire-pan regulations in places where

Littlbug stove (left) and Emberlit stove (right) are two of the author's favorites. The Littlbug burns twigs and wrist-thick wood and doubles as a campfire. The Emberlit only burns twigs. These stoves are ultralight and super compact.

WHAT'S WRONG WITH TWO-PIECE GASOLINE TRAIL STOVES?

Modern gasoline trail stoves have a separate fuel tank and armored fuel line. You must connect the line to the tank every time you use the stove—then disconnect it afterwards. This frequent connect/disconnect cycle wears the connector and/or O-ring and in time, may cause a fuel leak. Foreign matter can also become lodged in the valve or connector when the stove is assembled or disassembled. If this happens, it's game over—you'd best know how to build a fire!

This said, two-piece stoves are remarkably safe. Those who report problems tend to cook for large groups, which means bigger pots, longer running times and hotter (higher-pressure) tanks. Still, given equal materials, a one-piece stove will be more trouble-free than a two-piece stove.

Why Two Parts to Put Together?

The idea of splitting a stove into two parts—burner/fuel line and fuel bottle/pump assembly—began as an advertising stunt that enabled manufacturers to list the weight of the stove sans fuel tank and pump. Twisted thinking? Yes. But lightweight sells and most buyers don't know they are being duped.

A two-piece stove can have a long fuel delivery tube that keeps the tank away from the hot burner. That's a good safety feature, especially if you use large pots that reflect heat onto the tank. But fuel lines on some stoves are too short—they don't allow enough space between the burner and tank—so for safety, you should ALWAYS use the aluminum windscreen that separates the two.

Disassembly: When you're done cooking, just turn off a one-piece stove, release the pressure, then pack it away. No need to unhook a fuel line (and get gas on your hands) or fold carbon-black burner supports.

fire-pans are required. I also like the Emberlit stove which packs much smaller but won't burn big wood. The Emberlit is remarkably strong for its weight—it easily supports my 20-pound Dutch oven!

Troubleshooting a White Gas (Naptha) Stove

Problem: Flame sputters; stove won't reach normal operating temperatures.

Solutions:

1. Problem is likely due to *dirt in the mechanism*. Turn off the stove and pour about half the fuel out. Recap the tank and shake the stove vigorously for a few seconds to dislodge the clogged dirt particle. Then pour out the gas and refill the stove with fresh fuel. If this doesn't work, drain the stove and force high-pressure air (from an air compressor) through the filler cap opening. If this fails, the stove must be disassembled and cleaned.

2. The *safety valve*, usually located in the filler cap, is damaged. Squirt a small amount of liquid detergent on and around the cap and look for air bubbles. If the valve is blown, replace the filler cap.

3. *Stove needs more pressure.* If additional pumping doesn't do the trick, check the leather washer on the pump stem. Lubricate the washer with oil or grease. Most new stoves have synthetic (plastic) pump washers that don't work as well as the old leather ones. Consider replacing a plastic washer with a leather one. Check the plumbing section of your hardware store. Some leather stool washers fit some stoves perfectly. ***Note:*** In subfreezing temperatures stoves must be insulated from the cold ground to maintain operating pressure.

4. *Check for improper fuel.* You cannot use lead-free automotive gasoline in white-gas stoves. Naphtha (Coleman or Blazo fuel) is the cleanest burning of the stove fuels, and it is prefiltered.

5. *For Optimus/Svea stoves that don't have pumps:* The nipple may have become enlarged by improper cleaning (a bent cleaning needle will do it). The nipple (a low-cost item) must be replaced. Overpriming can burn the cotton wick and reduce its absorbent qualities. The remedy is to replace the wick—something that is best done by one who is familiar with the process.

6. *For MSR stoves with manual "shaker jets" or Brunton/Optimus stoves* that have weighted cleaning needles that are activated by a magnet: If the stove is run for a long time with a yellow flame, the jet orifice can become caked with carbon, which can prevent the cleaning needle from passing through the jet to clean it. Eventually, the hole becomes so caked with carbon that the stove will not produce a hot, blue flame. Or if the stove is run at full blast for an extended period, with a large pot on top, the weighted cleaning needle may become so hot that it welds itself to the stove. I've had this happen twice with two different stoves! If either of these events occur, your stove is out of business. **Solution:** At the first sign of a sticking needle, stop the stove immediately and *remove* the cleaning needle. The stove will run fine without it. Use a thin wire—like that designed to clean Svea stoves—to manually clean the jet. After you've suffered one of these events, you may prefer to clean the jet manually and never again trust the stove's built-in cleaning device! ***Note:*** Some of the old, high-end stoves—like the no-longer-manufactured Optimus 8R and 111B—featured a geared cleaning needle that was completely reliable. Regrettably, most of the new stoves have dropped the geared

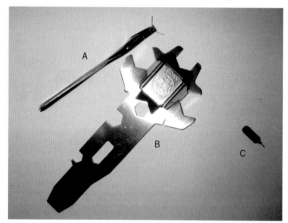

A) "Svea-style" wire tool is used for manually cleaning stove jets. B) Brunton/Optimus stove disassembly wrench with built-in magnet. The magnet pushes the stove's weighted, magnetic needle upward into the jet to clean it. C) A weighted, magnetic cleaning needle that has been removed from a stove—note the carbon black deposit on the weight.

system, probably to save money. New ideas are not always best!

Problem: Stove stays lit for about 20 seconds, then slowly goes out. Pumping it revives the flame.

Solution: Invariably this is the result of a slow leak in the tank-filler cap. Either the safety valve is blown or the silver solder around the filler neck has melted. Replace the pressure cap or resolder the neck. Determine the exact location of the pressure leak by squirting liquid detergent around the pressure cap. If the safety valve checks out OK, the gasket in the filler cap is probably at fault. Replace the age-hardened gasket with a new one. If the tank is a removable aluminum fuel bottle, replace the synthetic gasket on the bottle neck. If the stove is used often and hard, it's wise to replace this gasket every year.

Problem: Butane (or butane-propane mix) trail stove loses pressure after it has run a while.

Solution: The burners of early butane stoves were mounted on top of their fuel canisters— the cooking pot reflected heat onto the canister below and kept it warm (and pressurized). The plus to this design was improved cold-weather performance; the minus was that an oversize pot could radiate enough heat to the canister below to cause it to overheat and explode!

To eliminate this danger (and potential lawsuits), most butane stoves now use a long armored fuel line to separate the canister and burner. This eliminates overheating but encourages supercooling of the tank and accompanying loss of pressure. The longer the stove runs, the colder the tank gets (frost may even form on the surface). When this happens, you must either live with the low flame or warm the canister to

increase the pressure. One solution is to set the canister in a pot of hot (but well below boiling) water. Another is to make a "canister cozy"— simply fit a cylinder of closed-cell foam around the tank, add a foam bottom, and glue or tape the pieces together. If the flame drops while you're cooking, pour some hot water into the cozy. Keep the cozied canister in your sleeping bag at night so it will be warm in the morning.

Priming

Most white-gas and kerosene stoves must be preheated or primed with gasoline or alcohol to bring them to sufficient temperature to vaporize raw fuel. You don't need much heat to prime a gasoline stove. On a hot day the sun or heat from your hands may generate enough pressure to cause fuel to stream from the nipple.

Pumps do not vaporize fuel, they simply allow you to maintain greater pressure in the fuel tank, which makes the stove easier to start and maintain, especially in cold weather.

Procedure for priming pump-equipped stoves:

1. Clean the nipple. Most stoves have a built-in cleaning needle.

2. Be sure the pressure cap is tight and the adjuster knob is closed. Then pump the stove a half-dozen times.

3. Crack the adjuster knob a quarter turn for about 4 seconds and watch fuel stream into the spirit cup below the burner head. Do not fill the spirit cup more than one-third full of gas!

4. Close the adjuster knob and ignite the fuel in the spirit cup. While the fuel is burning, give the stove another dozen pumps. When the flame has nearly died, crack the

adjuster knob to permit the entrance of gas. An instant blue flame should result. **Note:** Overpriming (too much gas in the spirit cup) wastes gas, carbons up parts, and may overheat and damage stove parts. Underpriming makes stoves difficult to light. Learn to strike a compromise.

To prime stoves that don't have pumps:

1. Clean the nipple.

2. Remove the tank filler cap and withdraw an eyedropper full of gas from the tank. Replace the filler cap. Squirt the dropper full of gas into the spirit cup.

3. Ignite the gas in the spirit cup. When the flame has nearly gone out, crack the adjuster knob with a one-fourth turn. You should see a bright blue flame.

Note: The Optimus minipump, which is sold for use in cold weather, is unnecessary if you follow the eyedropper method of priming. Cupping stoves in hands, as is recommended by some stove makers, is slow, unreliable, and painfully cold in chilly weather.

Stoves: Dos and Don'ts

- *Do* carry fuel only in recommended containers. Sigg, MSR, Primus or Brunton/Optimus aluminum liter bottles, or the original container, are recommended.

- *Do* frequently check the temperature of your stove's fuel tank by feeling it with your hand. If the tank is too hot to hold, reduce pressure and/or pour water on the tank to cool it.

- *Do* carry extra stove parts and tools. An extra pressure cap and leather pump washer is usually enough. Bring a small screwdriver and pliers.

- *Do* empty the fuel in your stove after each trip. And burn the stove dry at the end of the camping season. Impurities in fuel left in stoves can cause malfunctions.

- *Do* keep your stove protected in a rigid container when it's not in use.

- *Don't* loosen or remove the filler cap of a gasoline stove when the stove is burning. This could result in an explosion!

- *Don't* refuel a hot stove. There may be sufficient heat still available to ignite the fumes. Be especially careful in cold weather, as gasoline vaporizes much more slowly then.

- *Don't* set oversize pots on stoves. Large pots reflect excessive heat back to the fuel tank, which may cause overheating of the stove. Run stove at three-fourths throttle if you use oversize pots.

- *Don't* start or run a stove inside a tent or confined area or any place where there is insufficient ventilation.

- *Don't* enclose a stove with aluminum foil to increase its heat output. The stove may overheat and explode!

- *Don't* fill gasoline or kerosene stoves more than three-fourths full. Fuel won't vaporize if there's insufficient room for it to expand. Some stoves erupt into a ball of fire when they're overfilled.

End-of-Season Stove Maintenance

Once a year fill the tank one-fourth full with fresh gas and add a capful (no more) of engine fuel-injector cleaner. Burn the tank dry. The injector cleaner will remove harmful deposits that could cause clogging. Lubricate the pump washer with nongumming high-grade gun oil or synthetic motor oil. Spray exterior stove parts with oil to prevent rust. Wipe the stove dry with paper toweling and store the stove in a dust-free environment.

Storing Fuel over the Winter

- For stoves with integral tanks: Empty the tank, fire up the stove, and burn it dry.

- For stoves with removable aluminum fuel bottle tanks: Either empty the fuel bottle or fill it to the brim with fuel so as to remove as much air from the mix as possible.

Stuff Sacks

Nylon bags with drawstring closures are useful organizers for food, clothing, and small items. Camping shops sell these bags in a variety of shapes and sizes. You can easily sew your own from nylon taffeta in a few minutes (see Yard Goods and Repair Materials, page 204).

Note: Ordinary fabric shops usually don't stock waterproof nylon, but the best camping shops do.

Survival

Anyone who has spent much time in the woods has, at one time or another, become lost. In his memoirs, Daniel Boone tells how he once became "mightily confused" for 3 days. As a young forester, I once shared a similar experience while working in western Oregon for the Bureau of Land Management. I did an incredibly stupid thing—one which I am naturally embarrassed to share with readers. But I was barely 21 at the time, so I'll blame my incoherence on youth.

I'd just finished marking a timber sale near Coos Bay when I was told the sale was canceled. My instructions were to remove from the trees the yellow plastic ribbons that denoted the cutting line. Now, most people of normal intelligence would simply follow the flagging to the end, then remove it. Not me. I began picking ribbons off the trees the moment I entered the woods. I realized the folly of this almost immediately, but I continued on. After all, I'd established the cutting line, which for the most part followed a ridge. Yeah, there were some crossovers, but these were "obvious." I was certain I wouldn't get lost.

By noon that day I was "mightily confused." By dark I was hopelessly lost. Sure, I knew the rules: "Stay put, build a fire, and someone will find you." But it was Friday and the government doesn't work on weekends. Monday was a holiday and I had Tuesday off for elk hunting. No one would even think of looking for me till Wednesday—5 days from now! Besides, this was the Pacific Coast Range, where Douglas fir trees grow tall as skyscrapers. Crown cover here was close to 100 percent. Even a combat chopper pilot couldn't spot me beneath all that foliage. And making a signal fire in the persistent December rain was out of the question. Suddenly, "survival" became a meaningful word.

Space does not permit sharing the details of my ordeal. Suffice it to say that I set my compass for due west—the direction of the ocean and Highway 101—and struck off into the rain-drenched forest. Clothed in woolens and waterproof rain gear, I also had a knife, compass, cigarette lighter, Thermos of coffee, and my lunch. Water abounded everywhere.

Three days later I walked into the sunlight of an unimproved logging road, which I followed to the whistle-stop town of Remote, Oregon. From there, I hitched a ride back to my jeep. I never told BLM about my adventure. Why? Because *foresters don't get lost!*

In this section we'll examine some personal survival shelters and techniques for coping with a wilderness emergency. You'll find no energy-draining thatched-roof lean-tos that take hours to build, for when you are lost, food is at a premium. Better to keep things simple by modifying natural shelters (caves, downed trees, brush piles, etc.) to meet your needs.

Frankly, a positive mental attitude is your most important survival tool. I vividly remember praising my Silva compass at the end of my 3-day ordeal. Without it—and the knowledge to go west—I probably would have died in the Oregon woods, shelter or no. The tools of survival are less important than believing you'll get out alive!

Shelters

Possibilities are endless if you have a tarp. If not, the rule is to modify an existing shelter. Can you remove the lower branches of a downed tree to create a small nest? Or burrow into the hollow at a tree's base (Figure S-6)? Perhaps you can stack some brush or logs along one side to block out the wind. A tiny reflector fire will help you weather the storm.

Before you move in, check for potential dangers—dead trees that may blow down on you, loose rocks, dry wash, etc. Make your crawlspace large enough to stretch out but small enough to conserve heat.

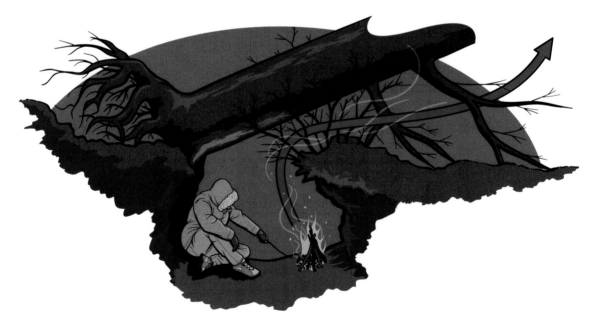

Figure S-6. It's best if you can modify an existing shelter.

Next comes bark or boughs to insulate the floor and walls. If it's raining, divert the water with makeshift guttering. Otherwise, shingle fresh-cut browse. This is no time to think environmentally: Cutting vegetation and trenching your home are tenets of survival.

Now crawl inside and try the fit. If you're cold, use evergreen boughs or leaves for a blanket. Perhaps if you rearrange the layering of your clothes you will add some warmth. For example, suppose you're wearing (from the skin out) a cotton T-shirt, cotton-polyester long-sleeved shirt, and wool sweater. Cotton wicks away body heat at a rapid pace, while wool does not. So wear your sweater next to the skin and the cotton garments over it. Don't overlook the value of nontraditional insulation like newspaper, leaves, a life jacket, or your packsack. Even rope, coiled about your body, will provide warmth.

If you have a vehicle, you have lots of options. All you have to do is dissect the expensive upholstery and sew the pieces into clothing. Any sharp object will function as an awl. Fabric ravelings and electrical wire provide thread (have you tried dental floss?), sticks become buttons. No formulas, just ingenuity.

Survival Kit

Most commercial survival kits have cutesy items—like wire, fish hooks, Band-Aids, and safety pins—that you will never use. The result is a heavy, bulky unit that's more likely to be left at home than carried to the wilds. At the other extreme are impractical belt-size kits whose miniaturized components defy productive use. For example, one enterprising company offers a wallet-size "survival card" that comes with a magnetized disk (compass?) that points north when you float it in water. How absurd!

The kit illustrated in Figure S-7 is recommended by the Minnesota Department of Natural Resources. There is at least one documented case where quick thinking and some of its components saved a life. Here's the story:

A Minneapolis teenager was snowmobiling when a blizzard created whiteout conditions. Fortunately, the boy had recently completed an outdoor education class in high school, and he had a simple survival kit in his possession. When the young man could no longer see to drive, he used the coffee can to scoop snow from under the machine. Then he put on the plastic-bag "rain suit," wrapped himself in the space blanket, and spent the night inside the hollow. His snowmobile suit kept him warm, the "rain suit" kept him dry, and the reflective space blanket helped retain body heat. Here are the contents of his survival kit, along with some proven extras.

Suggested survival-kit contents:

- Two large leaf-and-lawn-size *plastic bags.* Cut out the bottoms and duct-tape them together to form a continuous tube that can double as a tent and rain suit.

- *Space blanket.* Get one of the compact versions at any outdoor store. Don't open it: You'll never fit it back into the container! These space blankets are actually too small to cover an adult. Best use them to supplement your trash bags or to help warm a victim of hypothermia.

- Fifteen to twenty *wooden strike-anywhere stick matches,* a large plumber's candle (which will burn for hours), and a solid fuel chemical fire starter enable anyone to make a blaze in any weather.

- If space permits, add *bouillon cubes, tea, and sugar.* Be aware, however, that food is a low-priority item when you're lost. Your main concern is shelter, warmth, and getting found.

- A 2-pound *coffee can* with a fitted plastic lid makes a handy pot, snow shovel, and container for everything.

- Carry a *whistle* (the pealess designs take up little space) and a small mirror for signaling.

- Two *ziplock bags.* Use them as a cold-weather vapor barrier (wear them against the skin) on your feet or hands and as a container for berries, minnows, tinder, etc.

- Twenty-five feet of strong *nylon line* suspends your tube tent from trees or becomes a belt to secure your "rain gear." **Warning:** Never seal the ends of a nonporous plastic tube tent. Doing so could cause suffocation!

- Large cotton *bandanna.* Doubles as a neck warmer, sun and bug hat, cravat, bandage, and spare sock. Use it to strain minnows and crawfish.

- Small, single-bladed *knife.* A razor blade is no substitute for a sharp knife. If you include a compass in your kit, make it a real one.

Pack everything in the coffee can and seal the lid with several feet of duct tape, which you can use to rig shelters and mend holes in plastic bags.

A Smart Survival Kit for Remote Trips

Say you're hiking a remote area where help is days away. These items will fit into a small fanny pack:

- Knife

- Compass

- Paper map

- Two disposable butane lighters or at least twenty waterproof matches

- Forty feet of ⅛-inch-diameter nylon cord, cut into approximate 10-foot lengths. (Learn the quick-release "sheetbend" and you can daisy-chain cords for added length.)

- 3 Band-Aids, small tube of triple-antibiotic ointment

- 4 feet of Gorilla tape wound around a pencil stub

- Small waterproof notebook (tack a note on a tree; pages can be used to start a fire)

- If near water, two fish hooks and one jig. Fifty feet of high-test fishing line. To cook: cut fish into chunks and boil in metal cup, or hang gutted fish from a tripod over a fire.

- An insect head-net can double as a net to catch crawdads and minnows.

- Space blanket: shelter or sleeping bag (fold in half and tape sides; sandwich "bag" between thick layers of brush)

- Roll of brightly colored plastic surveying tape (mark a trail)

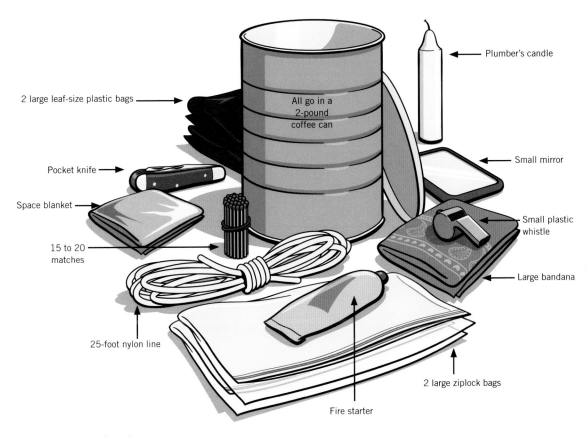

Figure S-7. A survival kit

- Metal drinking cup (heat water)

- Water bottle, water purification tablets or SteriPen

- Cotton "cowboy" handkerchief

- A few energy bars

- Ultralight rain jacket

- Lightweight wool sweater or longjohn top

- Headlamp

- Optional/highly recommended: Satellite messenger

- Optional: Some bouillon cubes in a waterproof bag

T

Tablecloth

You are preparing lunch along the edge of a rain-soaked trail. Every depression is a pond, every leaf a pool. You break out the crackers and slice the swiss and salami. Where can you put them out of the muck?

On a tablecloth, of course! A small (2-foot-square) plastic tablecloth adds dignity to what might otherwise be a dirty free-for-all. My red-checkered tablecloth has painted black ants on top. It always draws a smile, even in rain.

Tarps (Rain Flies)

Tarps are essential in a rainy-day camp. Under them you'll comfortably prepare meals, make repairs, and otherwise enjoy a day that might be soured by rain. The value of a fly is obvious, whether you're camped on a remote mountain

vista or in the gentle confines of a state park. It requires skill and a bit of weather knowledge to pitch a drum-tight fly in a howling storm, yet anyone can learn how in less than an hour. Once you know how, you can pitch a tarp in less than 10 minutes. A well-rigged rain fly exemplifies the expert's edge.

Materials: A 10-by-12-foot (or larger!) nylon tarp for every four people. I ordinarily rig a single fly in modified lean-to configuration, but for severe storms I mate the pair into a

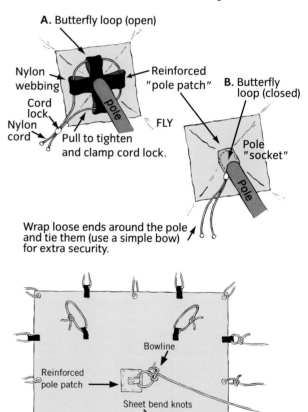

On a rainy, windy day, a tarp creates a protected place to prepare meals, make repairs, and otherwise enjoy your day. Note that the leading edge of this tarp is tied to a tight rope. This distributes wind stress across a wide area. Appropriately spaced trees were unavailable so poles were used for support. Note the colorful tablecloth on the ground at right. A campsite along the Little Missouri River, Teddy Roosevelt National Park, North Dakota. The barren site of Teddy Roosevelt's ranch is just over the hill.
Larry Rice

Figure T-1. A customized tarp

giant open tent that everyone can crowd under. No need to purchase expensive tarps (I suggest you get two). Any waterproof nylon—ripstop or taffeta—is fine.

Customize your tarps according to Figure T-1. Two hours' time and a light-duty sewing machine are all you need.

Tips: Well-sewn nylon loops (get inch-wide nylon webbing at any camping shop) are much more reliable than grommets. If you're a belt-and-suspenders person, you'll replace critically located corner grommets with well-reinforced nylon loops. Allow no more than 18 inches of space between loops or grommets. Be sure to back whatever you sew with heavy material.

Sew an 8-inch-square pole patch of heavy material to the inside center (opposite the center guy line) of your fly, then sew on the two "butterfly pole" loops that are illustrated in Figure T-1. Thread a 2-foot-long piece of parachute cord through the loops and secure the cords with a heavy-duty cord lock. This will allow you to use—and stabilize—an interior center pole when there are no trees to which you can attach an outside guy line. Nylon stretches and abrades easily, so a reinforcing patch is essential if you plan to use a pole.

To use the butterfly pole loops: Center the pole in the socket and tighten the cord lock. The loops will wrap around the pole and hold it in place when the tarp is buffeted by wind. For extra security, wrap the cords around the pole a few times and tie them with a simple bow. In very high winds you may need to stake the pole to the ground—simply run a guy line from the butterfly loops to a stake at the base of the pole.

Attach loops of parachute cord to each grommet or loop. Loops should be large enough to allow insertion of a wire stake. Leave at least

Figure T-2. Quick-release loop

6 inches of "tie" hanging, as illustrated. *Tip:* Braided nylon cord holds knots better than the inexpensive sheathed parachute cord sold at hardware stores.

Attach generously sized chute-cord loops to each of the five webbed loops on the face of the fly (Figure T-1). Loops should be tied with a sheet bend. One 20-foot-long cord should be permanently secured to the center face loop.

Tip: If you sew matching loops inside the tarp opposite those on the outside of the tarp, you'll have a handy place to hang flashlights, candle lanterns, stuff sacks, etc.

Don't Leave Home without These Items!

When suddenly the sky turns black and the wind grows deadly still, you generally have only a few moments to pitch tents and get everything and everybody under a stormproof tarp. There's no time to cut hanks of line; fumble for tent stakes, poles, or ground sheets;

or wonder where you put your pocketknife. Suddenly, your worst foul-weather concerns have materialized.

You'll avoid much embarrassment when the weather turns sour if you gather these materials before you take to the woods:

- One hundred feet of ⅛-inch-diameter parachute cord for each tarp you plan to rig. Cut rope into 15- to 20-foot lengths and burn the ends so they won't unravel. Then tightly coil each hank and secure it with the quick-release loop illustrated in Figure T-2.

  Tip: Choose brightly colored cord that you won't trip over in failing light. As mentioned earlier, my favorite is "reflective yellow tracer" polyester cord. It glistens when you shine a light on it.

- Fifty feet of ¼- or ³⁄₁₆-inch-diameter braided nylon rope (twisted rope unravels too easily) for each tarp. Singe the ends and coil the ropes by the method illustrated in Figures R-1 and R-2 (page 133).

- A sharp knife. A hand ax and folding saw are useful when you need to cut extension poles from dead, downed timber.

- Inexpensive plastic sheeting can be substituted for nylon tarps (please don't leave plastic in the woods) if you have small rubber balls or pebbles. Figure T-3 shows the attachment procedure.

- Waterproof tape for making repairs to nylon and plastic.

Pitching the Fly

When thunderheads loom threateningly overhead and the wind builds to impressive speeds, you generally have only a few minutes to rig a stormproof camp. So keep everything you need to rig your tarp—50 feet of rope, five 20-foot coils of parachute cord, and a dozen stakes—in a nylon stuff sack with cord-lock closure.

Note: Military-specification kernmantle-style parachute cord that has a lightly textured outer sheath is better than rough-braided civilian cord that has no protective outer sheath. Rough cord holds knots well, but plant matter sticks to it. You'll find the best cordage at mountaineering shops.

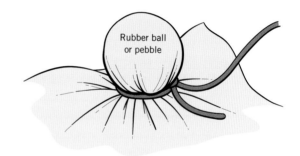

Figure T-3. A simple tarp anchor—all you need is a rubber ball or pebble and cord.

Tip: Stuff your fly, don't roll it. Stuffing is faster and easier on the waterproof coating. Be certain everything is bone dry before you pack it away. Dampness provides a medium for microorganisms to attack the fly. Microbes will not attack nylon, but they will devour the polyurethane coating on it. Ever see a tent floor whose waterproof coating has peeled? More than likely the tent was put away wet!

Rigs

Single Lean-to

This meat-and-potatoes configuration (Figure T-4) can be erected alone in about 3 minutes and will withstand winds of 30 miles per hour. The sloping design spills water effectively and conserves the warmth of a reflector fire.

Procedure:

1. Locate two trees about 15 feet apart and string a drum-tight line between them, about 5 feet off the ground. Use two quick-release half hitches at one end, and a quick-release power cinch at the other.

2. Take the pair of ties at one corner of the fly and tightly wind one tie of the set clockwise around the rope. Wind the other tie counterclockwise. Take at least four turns around the rope, then secure the ties with an overhand bow.

3. Pull the other corner of the open end of the fly tight along the rope and secure it with the ties, winding them around the rope, as above. The tie wrappings will

Back side of a "meat-and-potatoes" tarp rig. Note the cords on the windward side and the heavy rocks on the corner stakes. Boundary Waters Canoe Area, late autumn.

provide tension to keep the corners of the tarp from slipping inward along the rope when the fly is buffeted by wind. They perform the same function as a Prusik loop, but unlike a Prusik, they remain attached to the fly when the fly is packed.

4. Secure all remaining ties to the rope with a simple overhand bow. Note that by securing the fly at several points along the length of its open end, rather than just at the corners, you distribute the strain

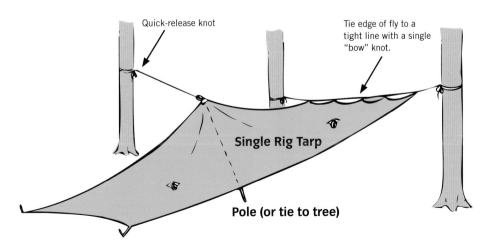

Quick-release knot

Tie edge of fly to a tight line with a single "bow" knot.

Single Rig Tarp

Pole (or tie to tree)

Figure T-4. Single lean-to

across a wide area, thus increasing the strength of the fly. High wind will tear out the corner grommets or loops unless you distribute the load along a main hemline, as illustrated.

5. Pull the back of the fly out so it's tight and stake it.

6. Run the center cord over a tree limb or a horizontal rope strung above and behind the fly. Snug the cord and secure it with a quick-release power cinch. Use an interior center pole if trees are not available. Connect additional lines (use a quick-release sheet bend) to other face loops as needed to produce drum-tight geometry.

In ultrahigh winds, guy or stake the side hems of the fly to the ground or adjacent trees.

Using Campfire and Single Fly Together

A fire built just under the open edge of the fly will provide substantial heat inside the lean-to. However, since the fly acts as a wind eddy, you must backlog (or backrock) your fire (Figure T-5) or it will smoke you out. The bottom of an aluminum canoe works well, as does a large sheet of aluminum foil. You can even use several packs if you keep them well away from the flames. The real purpose of the backing is to draw smoke away from the enclosure, not reflect heat into it. Note that the fire must be completely outside the tarp. The backlogs have insufficient area to make up for the size of the wind eddy created by the huge tarp.

When rigging twin tarps you can foil the smoke with the ingenious procedure illustrated in Figure T-6 and shown in the photos.

For more information, my 90-minute DVD, *The Forgotten Skills* (available on my website www.cliffcanoe.com), shows how to stormproof tents, rig tarps, tie knots, make fires, and more. If you can do everything in the video, you'll be a hero to your friends!

Twin Flies with Fire Slit

Here's a secure, airy shelter that will provide luxurious comfort for up to twelve people. Two people can rig it in about 10 minutes, even in high winds. You'll need two 10-by-10-foot or larger customized flies and all your rope and cord.

The beauty of this arrangement is that you can build a rain-protected warming fire right

Twin flies with fire slit. Later, a back-logged fire will be built just under the ridge of the orange tarp. Along the Fond du Lac River, Saskatchewan, Canada.

Twin flies with fire slit. Notice the clothes drying on the line and the smoke exiting through the slit in back. Along the Kopka River, Ontario, Canada.

Figure T-5. Backlogging a fire

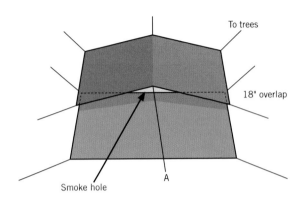

Figure T-6. Rigging twin flies with a smoke hole

underneath the fly. The combination backlog and overhead vent spills smoke through the opening on top. You can "float" the slanted roof, as illustrated, to provide more interior room, or stake it to the ground for protection from blowing wind.

Procedure:

1. Rig the single lean-to configuration shown in Figure T-4. Remember to connect all lines to one another with a quick-release sheet bend.

2. Overlap to the second grommet the hem of the top fly over the hem of the bottom fly. This should provide an approximate 2-foot overlap. Then secure the corner ties of the top fly to the ties on the side hem of the bottom fly.

3. Attach a 20-foot length of chute cord to the center loop of the top fly (point A in Figure T-6) and secure this cord to a tree—or line strung between two trees—directly behind the bottom fly. If you won't build a fire under the top fly, you may guy this line to a stake at the base of the bottom fly.

4. Next you'll need a 6-foot-long aluminum or wooden pole. If you don't have a metal pole, cut one from dead, downed wood, or use a shear lashing to extend several short spars to this length. Tie the top of the pole to the center ties on the top fly. Run twin guy lines from the pole tip to the stakes below. Secure guy lines with a power cinch. Stake or guy out the corners of the top fly.

5. Go to the back of the bottom fly and tighten the overhead "vent" cord (A) until the structure is tight. There should be an approximate 6-inch gap between the overlapped portions of the two flies. The last step is to add additional storm lines on the face and hem of both flies to produce a taut shape that won't pool water. You now have a huge, sturdy shelter that won't pool water or flap in the wind.

Campfire Considerations

Build the fire just inside the hem of the top fly. Backlog it as explained. Smoke will follow the backlogged eddy line to the roof of the top fly and be drawn out through the slit between the two flies. This works slick when there's no wind. You'll have to experiment here, as a good breeze may confuse the eddies and allow the shelter to fill with smoke. You will also discover that if you raise the back of the bottom fly off the ground to provide more headroom, the bottom draft that results will pull smoke away from the vent and into the shelter. Ingenuity and strong backlogging will usually solve most smoke problems.

Special-Purpose Rigs

Cliff and Dan Tundra Tarp

For many years I outfitted and guided canoe trips in northern Canada. I typically traveled with a crew of ten, often in very rainy conditions. Rigging twin flies every night was time consuming, so I left the small tarps at home and instead brought a giant 15-foot-square model that I designed with the help of Cooke Custom Sewing. This tundra tarp, as Dan Cooke calls it, has full bug netting sewn to all four sides. The netting rolls and ties out of the way when it's not

If bugs drive you batty, you'll want a fully netted tundra tarp (cookecustomsewing.com). Along the North Knife River, Manitoba, about 40 miles from Hudson Bay.

needed, yet it releases instantly. Surprisingly, there's no need to kill or shoo away blackflies that are trapped inside the enclosure. The bugs happily entertain themselves by crawling on the inside netting, away from you!

The tundra tarp is ingenious and expensive—and worth every penny when you need a bug-proof structure that stays up in high winds. I've used mine on the shores of Hudson Bay in sustained winds of 50 mph! No problems. The outfit weighs about 14 pounds with four aluminum poles, stakes, lines, and netting. Twelve people can crowd inside. Cooke Custom Sewing will build a tundra tarp to your specifications.

Canoe Prop Method

Prop a canoe on paddles and cover it with your rain tarp, as shown in Figure T-7. If you have two canoes, prop them side by side about 6 feet apart, parallel to one another, and cover them with a tarp. Stake and guy the tarp and push out the center with a paddle so it won't pool water. *Don't trust this setup in a strong wind!*

If it's perfectly calm, you can prop up the back ends of the canoes, as well as the front, to produce a nonsloping shelter with more interior space.

I don't like the canoe prop method. It's hard on paddles and not very secure. But it is useful

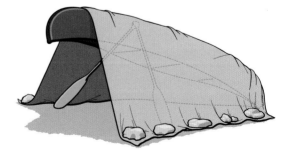

Figure T-7. Canoe prop method

in light rain and handy when you need protection for a small fire.

Tip: A single canoe prop without fly makes a quick shelter for two in a light, vertical rain. I've used it many times to prepare lunch along a canoe portage on a rainy day.

Quick-Rig Tundra Tarp

You're canoeing in the barren lands where no trees and high winds are the rule. Rig a canoe prop, like that illustrated in Figure T-7, and it will go sailing off into the tundra before you can move in. What to do? Why, use your canoes to weight the tarp, of course. And, oh yes, you'll need one 5- to 7-foot aluminum pole.

Procedure:

1. Lay the tarp flat on the ground and weight two adjacent sides with overturned canoes.

2. Hoist the apex of the shelter on a long pole, then guy the pole and remaining

loose fabric in place. Total rigging time? Less than 3 minutes!

Tips:

*   You can construct a more spacious shelter by placing the canoes inside the fly, bellies facing the occupants. Drape the tarp partially over the canoes and tie it to them (you'll need several short lengths of cord).

*   An overturned canoe blocked up on the sides makes a great table (Figure T-8). Remove the side blocks and it becomes a windbreak for your stove.

Single-Walled Sun Tepee

This is similar to the quick-rig tundra tarp illustrated in Figure T-8, except stakes, not canoes, are used to secure the back of the tarp. The sun tepee requires one pole and one or two guy lines. For a taut configuration, you'll need to guy out the midpoint of the fly—impossible

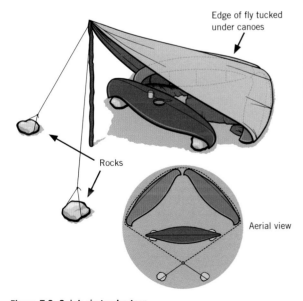

Edge of fly tucked under canoes

Rocks

Aerial view

Figure T-8. Quick-rig tundra tarp

A simple rig pitched for shade in the desert. Since there are no trees, the ridgeline of this tarp could not be tied to a tight line, as recommended. This method is adequate only if the corners of your tarp are well reinforced. The guy line on the front hem adds security and diverts wind (it acts like an airplane wing) over the tarp. Along the Green River, Utah.

if there are no trees. However, stacking gear against the inside back wall will stiffen the shelter considerably.

As you can see, there are dozens of ways to rig tarps. And that's the problem. Most people are so baffled by all the possible configurations that they never master a single design. My advice? Forget about the cute options suggested in survival texts and become expert at rigging the single lean-to (Figure T-4) and twin flies with fire slit (Figure T-6 and photo on page 168). For desert or barren-land camping, the quick-rig tundra tarp or its derivative, the single-walled sun tepee, is most practical. Or just carry three aluminum poles and stick with the basic desert rig shown in the photo.

Tents

And the night shall be filled with music
And the cares that infest the day,
Shall fold their tents like Arabs
And as silently steal away.
—*Henry Wadsworth Longfellow,*
A Psalm of Life

It's been 4 hours now and still it continues. The water comes in sheets, cold and unrelenting. Everywhere the ground is drenched with it; every rut holds a pool, every leaf a tiny pond. Contentedly, you peer through the mosquito net of your nylon tent at the vastness of the forest beyond. The sky, deep gray and foreboding, communicates that "more of the same" is on the way.

Overhead, a small aluminum candle lantern provides some warmth and enough light to permit reading a novel. You laze against the loosely rolled sleeping bag and momentarily stare into the dampness of the day. A smug smile flashes

briefly: Granted, the 5-by-7-foot A-frame tent is a bit cramped for two. But no matter; it is warm and dry. Be it ever so humble, there is no place like home, even when it is a confining backpack tent pitched on a secluded ridge deep in the Adirondacks.

Five states to the west, a similar scenario is in progress. A man, woman, 12-year-old girl, and towheaded boy of 9 peer wistfully through the netted window of their spacious 9-foot-square umbrella tent. The walls of the 10-ounce canvas Eureka tent rustle contentedly to the rhythm of the wind-whipped rain. Outside, tiny icicles drip from the well-bronzed canvas, but inside, warmed by the glow of a Coleman lantern, it is snug and dry. The 6-foot peak provides plenty of room to stand and dress, and the spacious floor plan encourages games and socializing. This family has been confined for 6 hours, but they are having a very good time. Yet all around, as far as the eye can see, the campground is deserted. Where earlier dozens of tents had dotted the treeless field, now there is only grass and rain. Everyone else has gone— casualties of the persistent precipitation.

At the top of the continent, just above the Arctic Circle, two canoe campers ride out a polar gale in their low-slung geodesic dome. The state-of-the-art nylon igloo expands and contracts with every gust of the 50-mph wind, but it holds firm. Thirty-six hours later, two smiling voyagers emerge onto the still, sunlit tundra, grateful that their tent had weathered the storm.

As you can see, there is no such thing as a perfect tent or even an all-around one. What's best for car camping is out of place in the tundra or on the hiking trail. Backpacking in the mountains is not like desert hiking or wilderness

A comfortable camp, pitched on a gravel beach along the Noatak River, Alaska. This is grizzly country so meals were prepared inside the tundra tarp, which is located downwind from the tents. (These Eureka! Tundraline [A-frame] tents are no longer manufactured.)

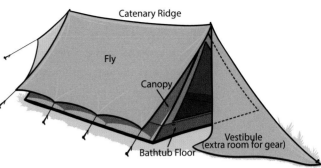

Figure T-9. Basic tent terminology

canoeing. And winter camping imposes new demands. Tents designed to withstand high winds may perform poorly in rain, and vice versa. Those built to withstand snow loads may be too heavy or difficult to pitch. Ones light enough to carry long distances may test your sanity on a rainy day, while larger models may strain the confines of your backpack. And so it goes. When you do find your dream tent, it may simply cost too much.

But don't despair: There is order in the universe. The following principles of tent design and construction will help you separate the wheat from the chaff. Figure T-9 will help you with terminology.

Design and Construction Features

The construction features of most tents are vastly overrated. Thread count, number of stitches per inch, reinforcement of zipper ends, and such are proudly touted by tent makers, but in reality these take a backseat to *good design*—a feature not always associated with quality construction or high price. In all my years of canoeing and camping, I've never seen a well-designed tent come apart at the seams or a zipper rip from its stitching. But I've experienced enough bent poles, torn flies, and broken zippers to know that fabrics and sloppy sewing are rarely the villains.

If you keep uppermost in your mind that good design, impeccable construction, and high price don't always go hand in hand, you'll be on your way to finding the ideal tent for your purposes and pocketbook.

Design Principles

If you ask a boating expert how to tell a seaworthy canoe from one that's not, he or she might use the following analogy:

Pretend your hands are water and place them on the keel line of the canoe. Now slide your hands up toward the rails. Is there substantial flare here? Good. Water will follow that flare away from the hull rather than into it. But if your hands "tumble home" (follow the inward curve of the canoe above the waterline), water will do the same. It's no mystery why flare-sided dories are more seaworthy than hard-chinned rowboats.

Now try this same test on your tent. Follow the fly to the ground, as if your hands were water. Do your hands fall on unprotected seams? If so, rain will pool here and seep into your tent. And seam sealant (glue) won't keep you dry for very long. The most reliable way to keep seams from leaking is to cover them with waterproof material. A fly that stakes right to the ground will do the trick, but few tents come so equipped. To save weight, many tents have short "cap" flies that don't protect the canopy in wind-driven rain. Some tents feature machine-sealed (heat tape) seams like those applied to the best rainwear. These seams won't leak in any weather.

Exceptions aside, you are best advised to avoid any tent that has perimeter seams that are not fully covered by the fly. The floors of some tents, like the Eureka Timberline, are sewn to the canopy several inches above ground. This bathtub construction puts vulnerable seams under the protection of the fly, where they belong. All the best rain tents have bathtub floors!

Now check the tent corners where the floor seams and door zippers come together. Does the fly drip water onto any stitching? If so, find a way to fix it or keep shopping! Even the well-designed Eureka Timberline scores low in this category.

The entrance and windows are other critical components. Are there generously sized awnings over doors and vents to keep rain out? Are exterior zippers protected by weather flaps? Can you easily turn aside a weather flap with your hand? If so, wind will do the same. Many of the best tents use elastic or Velcro to keep weather flaps in place. Perhaps you can make modifications.

Vestibules are worth their weight in gold on a rainy day. They function as an extra room to store packs and wet gear. More importantly, they protect the entrance (all those exposed seams and zippers we are concerned about) against blowing wind and rain, and they provide a place to cook out of the weather when you're too lazy to rig a rain tarp. Vestibules are generally add-on affairs that attach to the tent canopy with clips or shock cord. If you're serious about camping in rain, you'll demand a vestibule!

Geometry

There are A-frames, tepees, tunnels, domes, lean-tos, wall tents, and sophisticated geometric shapes that defy description (Figure T-10).

Domes: In terms of space, domes are the most efficient of tent designs. The high, gradually sloping sidewalls of a dome provide a pleasant spacious atmosphere, and the hexagonal or octagonal floor permits occupants to sleep in any direction—a real advantage if the tent is pitched wrong or on a sloping site.

But domes have plenty of faults. Though they shed rain efficiently, they're poorly ventilated (the fly covers the windows and door) and not very stable in wind. Geodesic domes, which use a lattice of arrow-shaft aluminum poles, are the exception. However, serious geodesic designs are time consuming to pitch and very expensive. All domes (geodesics included) crush in high winds unless they are well guyed and staked. This means running storm lines through slits in the fly to guy points on the poles. Rigging a dome for gale-force winds is quite a task, though once accomplished, the tent usually holds.

By design, domes cannot utilize bathtub floor construction. The many-faceted floor must be sewn to the canopy at ground level,

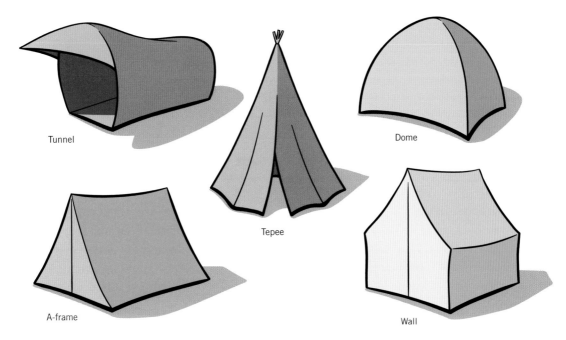

Figure T-10. Tent shapes

which leaves plenty of seams for you to glue. Ironically, some of the best domes have short flies that leave perimeter floor seams exposed to the weather. Such construction guarantees a sponge party in prolonged rain.

Geodesic domes were designed as mountaineering tents. Since they're basically freestanding, can be shoved into small crevices, and don't need to be rotated to face into a changing wind, they are ideal for situations where creature comfort, light weight, small packed size, and wind stability are important factors. Good geodesics are at best mediocre rain tents. And conventional domes are worse. Inexpensive (cheap!) domes that have fiberglass poles and no awnings over the doors and windows are among the worst tents you can buy. Better off with a play tent than one of these!

Tepees: The tepee is perhaps the most efficient and ingenious of tent designs. No other tent of comparable size sheds wind and rain as well and is as cool in summer, as warm in winter, and as versatile. The American Indian knew what he was doing when he designed the tepee.

Indian tepees are actually egg shaped, not round at the bottom as is commonly believed. The long axis of the cone was placed windward to brace the structure against the harsh prairie winds. Ventilation was provided by the doorway and a clever system of flaps at the apex. In winter, fine brush was stacked between the inner tent liner and outer wall to serve as insulation. The original tepee design was ingenious and difficult to improve upon.

The modern nylon tepee is a far cry from its skin-covered ancestor. Aluminum poles provide support and a removable cap fly keeps out the weather. Entry is a zippered door or traditional hole.

Tepees light enough for backpacking share the same wet-weather inadequacies as domes, but they're more rigid, so they remain rock solid in winds that would flatten conventional tents of equal height. However, their flies are slow and awkward to install, they have stakes and guy lines everywhere, and there is no awning over the doorway to keep rain out. Tepees are great for semipermanent camps. Otherwise, forget 'em.

Tunnels are low-to-the-ground affairs that are supported by a network of semirigid aluminum hoops. Designed for severe service, tunnels are among the most wind-stable tents. Their small size makes them light and compact. Inside they are cramped and doghousy, but they're generally more rainproof and better ventilated than domes. For high-altitude work and where weight is critical, tunnels have few peers.

Tunnel tents are among the most wind-stable of all tents. But they lack headroom and their many poles and lines make them slow to pitch. Sophisticated models like the tents shown here usually have side doors that make them easier to access in high winds. However, tents with side entries can be hot and stifling—they are not good warm-weather tents. The red tent is a Swedish Hilleberg Kaitum 3. The white tent is a Cooke Custom Sewing "Lean 3." It has side walls and awning and bug-netting. Headwaters of the Poreno River, Norway, above the Arctic Circles

A-frames are by far your best buy. These tents shed rain and wind effectively, allow construction of water-resistant bathtub floors and protective awnings, are well ventilated and pestproof, and are less costly to manufacture than other styles. In its most elementary form (a single I pole at each end), the A-frame is the lightest, most compact, and strongest of all tents. The design is thousands of years old, but it is still a good one.

Umbrella tents are traditional for family camping. And for good reason. They go up easily on any terrain and are almost entirely self-supporting. There's standing room inside and a generous front awning under which to cook and relax. With full-length flies, these tents are rain- and wind-proof.

The umbrella design is not just for family tents. Some sophisticated backpacking tents are built on this pattern.

Self-supporting tents: Any tent design can be made self-supporting if it's rigged with a tubular exoskeleton and shock-cord suspension system. Note that self-supporting tents remain

Self-supporting tents remain freestanding only if there is no wind. This unstaked dome blew out to sea, and these canoeists hope to catch it before it sinks!

freestanding only if there is no wind—a fierce storm will send any unanchored tent reeling across the countryside. The real advantage of self-supporting tents is that they require fewer stakes to erect than traditional U-stake-'em models. But these tents do require staking . . . nearly always!

Fabrics

Nylon is the most suitable fabric for lightweight backpacking tents. Cotton tents are too heavy and bulky for most forms of self-propelled travel. Nylon tents need a porous canopy to let body-produced moisture out and a protective waterproof fly to prevent rain from getting in. Check the fit between fly and canopy: The two must not touch at any point (even when stressed by high wind) or condensation and dripping will result.

Nearly all American backpacking tents are constructed from polyurethane-coated nylon that meets US fireproofing standards. European tents, however, are mostly built from silicone-treated nylon fabrics that don't meet fireproof specs but are much lighter, stronger, more compact, and better at shedding water than those coated with polyurethane. Tents that don't meet US fire specs cannot be sold in American retail stores, though you can often buy them on the internet. In the unlikely event of a tent fire, silicone fabrics are probably as safe as fire-spec ones. Why? Because all-nylon fabrics will melt and drip before there is a sustained flame. And these drips will cause severe burns. All the world's best tents are now built from silicone nylon. Regrettably, the law does not allow US tent makers to follow suit. It's interesting to note that you can buy silicone tarps here in the United States. You can also buy tents that have silicone flies, provided that the interior canopy

is not silicone. On the horizon are new silicone coatings that will meet fire-retardant rules. Crazy world, isn't it?

Color

Being confined inside a dark-colored tent on a rainy day can be depressing. A bright-colored tent is more cheery. It's also easier to spot from an airplane in a search-and-rescue situation. On the other hand, a drab black or green tent is best when camping in the far north where the summer sun barely sets. Try sleeping in a bright-red tent in blazing sunlight without wearing an eye mask and you'll see why!

Poles and Stakes

Poles should be *aluminum*, no ifs, ands, or buts! There is no such thing as a good fiberglass or plastic composite pole. *Wands* (nonsupporting members) that are used to hold out awnings and vents are an exception, though even here aluminum is better. It follows that large-diameter aluminum poles of equivalent alloy are less apt to break than smaller poles. I prefer ¾-inch-diameter tempered poles if I can get them. Thin arrow-shaft poles are fine if there are enough of them. All poles should be shock-corded for easy assembly.

Tips:

- Tent poles are less apt to jam together if you polish the joints (a one-time effort) with 400-grit *wet* sandpaper, then wipe them with a cloth sprayed with liquid silicone.

- Remedy for stuck pole sections: Heat the joint lightly in the flame of your trail stove. The joint will expand and the poles will part easily.

- Aluminum poles will slide more easily through tight pole sleeves in nylon tents if, before your trip, you squirt talcum powder down the sleeves and lubricate the poles with liquid silicone. One application of silicone and talc lasts several weeks, even in rain. Gun shops sell special dry powdered lubricants that are used for resizing hand-loaded brass cartridge cases. These cartridge-case lubricants work better than talcum powder, but they're much more expensive.

Tent stakes: Twelve-inch-long arrow-shaft aluminum stakes or staples (U-shaped stakes) hold best in sand, mud, and tundra; aluminum skewers are good for mildly compacted soil; narrow steel-wire stakes are ideal for rocky ground; quad-corner "U-pound-'em" stakes are for hard, compacted soil, and so it goes. Carry a variety of tent stakes so you'll always have what works best. And, with rare exceptions, the longer the stake, the better!

Tips:

- Eight-inch-long aluminum concrete nails make acceptable low-cost tent stakes. The heavy steel and plastic U-pound-'em stakes sold at discount stores are useful only on big, semipermanent canvas tents.

- Special stakes are unnecessary for camping on snow or sand. Conventional aluminum stakes can be buried or guy lines wound about wooden sticks and then buried. Tin-can lids (with the edges peened in for safety) make good snow stakes. Run the guy lines through holes in the center and bury the lids.

A   B   C   D   E

Types of tent stakes: A) 12-inch arrow-shaft (for sand, mud, and spongy tundra); B) 10-inch staple (for soft ground); C) 9-inch skewer (general purpose); D) 6-inch pin (general purpose / rocky ground); E) 6-inch quad-corner (U-pound 'em stake for very hard ground). With rare exceptions, the longer the stake, the better.

Features

Bug netting may be standard mosquito type or no-see-um-proof. I prefer the former as it is stronger, easier to see through, and allows free flow of air. Tightly woven no-see-um-proof netting can be stifling on hot nights. When the tiny gnats begin their act, simply spray your mosquito net with bug dope or permethrin, or close the fabric door panel.

Door panel: A well-designed tent has the door panel inside the bug net so you can open the door to peek out without unzipping the screen.

Extras: Some tents have niceties like lantern loops and inside pockets for the storage of small items. These features—which require only a few minutes on a sewing machine to make—add considerable cost to a tent without significantly increasing its utility.

How to Select a Family Tent

My family's first camping tent was a 9-by-9-foot umbrella model with a wet-wax finish, a steel telescoping center pole, and two netted windows with flaps that tied shut. It weighed 52 pounds and, when rolled, barely fit into the trunk of the car. In hot weather it smelled like kerosene and paraffin, and in rain it leaked profusely. But it was inexpensive and it enabled us to see a lot of country on not a lot of money.

Family tents, like the times, have changed. They've gotten more expensive, of course, but they're also lighter, stronger, roomier, and more weatherproof than those of the 1960s. And they're easier to pitch too. Guy lines are passé, as are obtrusive center poles and odors. Ties have been replaced by nylon zippers and Velcro, and shock-corded aluminum poles have succeeded steel ones. Even the largest family tents can be erected in less than 15 minutes.

Your needs: For comfort, you need at least 21 square feet of floor space per person, more if you use cots. Tents with rectangular floors use space more efficiently than those with square or circular floors, which means more room between sleepers.

Weight: Three to 4 pounds per person is the rule for lightweight backpacking tents; 5 to 6 pounds for canoeing and high-altitude expedition tents; and up to 10 pounds for drag-'em-out-of-the-car family shelters. Many of the best tents weigh much less than this.

Height: Waiting out a rain in a tent you can't stand in is no fun. However, low-profile tents with sloping sides spill wind better than high-sided umbrella and wall tents, so you may have to make some sacrifices if you camp where there are big winds.

Fabrics: Though nylon is the most popular and best fabric for the construction of small tents, lightweight cotton is still a good choice for family tents where weight is less of a concern. It's impractical to use double-walled (waterproof fly/porous canopy) construction in large tents, so one layer of waterproof nylon is usually used throughout—a design that encourages condensation inside. Big windows and a porous cotton or nylon roof help dispel some moisture, but not enough to prevent these tents from occasionally turning into saunas.

Nonetheless, if you confine your trips to areas where high humidity and rain are infrequent, then you may like an all-nylon tent. In any case, be sure the tent has at least two rain-protected windows. The best nylon family tents have four-way ventilation—three windows and a door.

Speed of pitching: A tent that requires 10 minutes to pitch in dry, windless weather may require twice that long to erect in a rainstorm. It's faster to assemble poles than to drive stakes and tie guy lines, so choose a tent that is supported mainly by poles.

Modesty curtains: Family tents are commonly used in areas where there are other campers, so they should be designed to provide privacy without sacrificing ventilation. Some tents have a modesty curtain—a short fabric panel that attaches behind the door—in addition to the regular entry flap. On hot days you can leave the door open for ventilation and close the modesty curtain for privacy.

Clothing loops: Convenience dictates plenty of D rings, loops, or brass hooks at the ridge to hang wet towels, clothing, and your battery-powered lantern. ***Warning:*** Mantle lanterns

A canvas wall tent, warmly rigged for winter. The stove pipe runs through a flameproof collar in the side wall and is supported by a makeshift wooden tripod. Note the snow shovel and Ojibwa-style snowshoes in the foreground.
Paul Kirtley

put out enough heat to burn through the roof of flame-retardant tents. And they consume lots of precious oxygen as they produce poisonous carbon monoxide. For this reason, you should hang only flameless lanterns inside your tent. Heaters, except catalytic ones, are also unsafe in tents.

Winter Tents

Most travelers use their three-season nylon tents for snow camping, which works well enough if they rig a frost liner inside. A piece of cotton sheeting, hung from the roof by ties or Velcro, absorbs exhaled moisture that might condense and freeze on the sleeping bags below.

A more gracious style of winter camping, popular a century ago, is again finding favor among those who spend long periods of time in the wilds. A 7-by-9-foot or larger canvas tent is rigged to accept a small sheet-metal stove and pipe. A generously sized canvas fly defies blowing rain, increases interior temperatures, and protects the roof from sparks. The tent must be canvas. Hot sparks will melt nylon instantly and cause serious burns! Most winter campers use wall or pyramid-style tents. Authentic period canvas tents—some of which are wonderful for winter camping—are available from Empire Canvas Works, Duluth Pack, Frost River, and Tentsmiths.

In summary, the best tents are largely self-supporting and have full-length flies and bathtub floors that wrap well up the sidewall. Protective awnings over doors and windows are a must, as are heat-treated aluminum poles and one or more vestibules.

Care and Cleaning of Tents

Canvas tents: Sweep them out, hose them down with water, and let them sun-dry until they are bone dry. Don't use soaps or detergents to clean cotton tents, as these products will remove the waterproof compounds.

Tip: You can restore the water repellency to small sections of cotton tents by rubbing a bar of paraffin across the fibers. Heat from the sun will melt the paraffin and the cotton fibers will absorb it.

Nylon tents should be thoroughly washed at the end of each camping season. Soak the tent for 30 minutes or so in a tub of lukewarm water and mild detergent. Tent manufacturers wisely suggest that you avoid use of detergents and chemical solvents, as these products may dissolve waterproof coatings. However, sparing use of these products will remove abrasive dirt, which is your tent's greatest enemy. Sponge troublesome spots with detergent. Tree sap may be removed with a very small amount of gasoline or alcohol. Don't overdo it though; gasoline is very hard on waterproof coatings.

Never roll and store a wet tent. Even rot-resistant nylon tents are sewn with cotton/Dacron thread, which can mildew. Damp polyurethane coatings provide food for microorganisms. Generally, it's better to stuff a nylon tent than to fold and roll it. Folding produces harsh creases that can damage waterproof coatings.

Caution: Tents like the Eureka Timberline, with exposed metal hooks and pins that can puncture fabric when the tent is packed, should always be rolled, never stuffed!

Sustained exposure to ultraviolet light saps strength from nylon fabrics. A nylon tent may lose half or more of its strength in a single season if it's continually exposed to sunlight. Do sun-dry and air your tent regularly, but don't overdo it!

Nylon tent lines harden and lose strength. They should be replaced occasionally. Tent cords should be brightly colored for high visibility in failing light.

Store tents in a porous cotton or nylon sack. Be sure the bag is large enough. A dry, properly rolled tent that fills its sack when dry won't fit when it's soaked with rain! Never store a tent on a concrete floor or in a damp basement.

Waterproof the seams of a new tent. That said, sealing seams is mostly window dressing. If your tent fly covers every seam and zipper, you can eliminate this step. That's because rain that gets through stitching on the fly will, due to surface tension, slithers harmlessly to the ground. There is no particular advantage in sealing floor seams if you use a ground cloth inside your tent.

A whisk broom and small sponge will keep your tent clean and neat.

Tips:

- Attach a tiny brass hook to the lanyard of your flashlight so you can clip it to a ridge loop or line inside your tent.

- Sew a D ring or nylon loop inside your tent at each end of the ridge. A length of parachute cord strung between the D rings makes a handy clothesline for light items like damp socks. Some campers sew up a miniature hammock of mosquito netting and suspend the hammock from the tent ridge. This "gear loft" will hold all manner of small items.

- It's worthwhile to repeat that a small candle lantern will raise interior tent temperatures by 10 degrees or more and eliminate much dampness.

Stormproofing Your Tent

A sewing machine and 60 minutes are all you need to turn your tent into a bombproof shelter!

You pitch your tent—a four-person Eureka Timberline—on a gentle knoll near a clump of youthful birch trees. There's a better spot 20 feet away—a well-worn area where hundreds of tents have stood before. But there's a slight depression here; a good rain could flood you out. And nearby is a long-dead spruce, its limbs

poised menacingly overhead, waiting patiently for a high wind to send it crashing down.

Slowly it begins with the tap, tap of intermittent rain. Then it intensifies into unrelenting drizzle. For a while, you stand complacently in the gentle shower and curiously watch the blackening clouds approach. Then you suddenly realize that you have only a few minutes to get things under control before the storm unleashes its fury.

First, you string two parachute-cord guy lines from each peak to stakes below (Figure T-11). Next, you weight the corner stakes with rocks then turn your attention to the right sidewall, which is being crushed by the building wind. It would be nice if you could turn the tent into the storm, but the site won't cooperate. Besides, it's too late now; you'll have to make do by shoring up the windward sidewall and poles. You're glad now that you sewed storm-line pullouts to the fly before you left home. As the wall

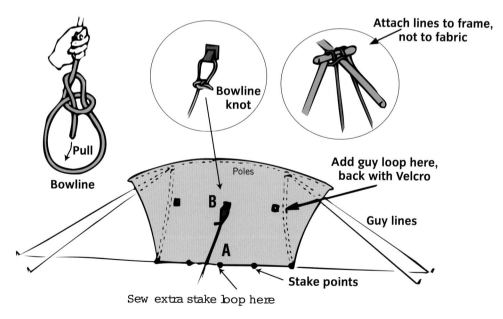

Figure T-11. Customizing the Eureka Timberline tent

firms under these tight guy lines, you wonder why they aren't standard equipment on every tent.

Satisfied now that everything's secure, you retire to the tent, confident you'll stay dry no matter how hard it rains.

Stormproofing Philosophy

Admittedly, staying dry in a deluge requires luck as well as skill. What would you have done if there had been no well-drained spot? Or if rocks or uncooperative ground kept you from placing your tent where you wanted? And don't forget that clump of birch you used for a windscreen.

Nonetheless, even a bad campsite can be made habitable if you correct the shortcomings of your tent and follow these rules.

1. *The right spot:* The section Tent Site: How to Cope with a Bad One, beginning on page 191, reviews some things you can do to make a bad site habitable.

2. *Use a ground cloth inside your tent!* Even well-sealed seams will admit water in prolonged rain. And no tent floor will remain watertight forever. The solution is to always use a 4-mil-thick plastic ground cloth inside your tent. Make the ground cloth large enough so it flows a few inches up the tent walls. If your tent springs a leak, water will be trapped under the groundsheet and you'll stay dry. Do not place the ground cloth under the tent floor (exception—in winter put it under the tent to prevent the floor from freezing to the ground). Surface water may become trapped between the groundsheet and floor and be pressure wicked (from body weight) through worn waterproof coatings and floor seams. You'll really have a sponge party if this happens!

Contrary to the claims of tent makers, you don't need a ground cloth under your tent floor to protect it from abrasion. Holes in tent floors usually develop from the inside. If you don't believe this, begin a trip with a new plastic groundsheet inside your tent, then count the holes it accumulates with each day of use. Old beliefs die hard!

3. *Reinforce seams:* If a seam looks weak, it probably is. Reinforce stress points with heavy carpet thread and nylon webbing.

This tent was flooded by rain. Note the pooled water on the ground. Photo at right shows how an interior ground cloth saved the day!

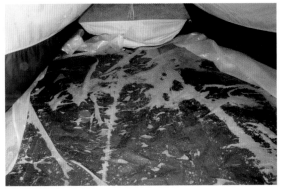

The water inside this tent is trapped beneath the plastic sheet. Anything placed on top of the sheet will stay dry.

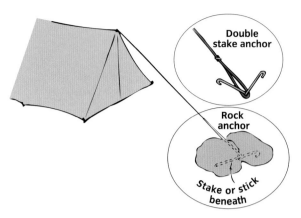

Figure T-12. Soft-ground tent anchors

4. *Add extra stakes:* If the hem of your tent looks like it needs additional stake lines, add them!

5. *Double-stake or anchor guy lines in soft ground:* Inserting two stakes per loop—each through a separate hole and at a different angle—doubles the surface area and holding power in soft ground. In sand, use a rock anchor like the one illustrated in Figure T-12. *Tip:* Tie 3-foot lengths of parachute cord to each stake loop before your camping trip and you won't have to mess with cutting and tying these anchor lines in a rainstorm.

6. *Attach loops of shock cord* or bands cut from inner tubes to all stake points and guy lines (Figure T-13). Shock cords take up the wind stress normally reserved for seams and fittings. Even a badly sewn, poorly reinforced tent can be used in severe weather if it's rigged with shock cords.

7. *Shock-cord your tent poles.* Shock-cording kits are available at most camp shops. Color code non-shock-corded pole

sections and wands for easy assembly. It's frustrating to look for a center ridge section or spreader bar in failing light. Colored plastic tape sticks to poles better than paint.

Old Tents Reveal New Secrets!

The best turn-of-the-century A-frame tents were better foul-weather shelters than modern campers like to admit. Studying one reveals some interesting things about where to place seams, guy lines, and stake points. Let's analyze one of these canvas antiques:

• There's a single vertical pole at each end. The poles are located at the apex of the triangular door and back wall. In essence, they form the "altitude" of each triangle.

• The tent has no floor, so there are no perimeter seams at ground level. A removable rubberized groundsheet, placed inside, protects occupants from flowing ground water and dampness.

• Including the corners, there are five stake points per side hem. A center stake halves the length of the sidewall material; the others split the distance between adjacent stakes. There's that apex-of-the-triangle relationship again.

• Guy lines at each end originate on the poles or at heavily reinforced fabric very near the poles. The exoskeleton—not the fabric—absorbs most of the wind stress.

Rigging storm lines is largely a game of triangles. Locate an apex, put in a stake or guy line. This keeps fabric tight by equalizing strain. As any elk hunter will attest, a modern

Extra storm
lines added
here.

Shock-cord loop
takes strain off tent
fabric when storm
lines are not used.

Storm line

Figure T-13. Stormproofing the tent

canvas-wall tent will withstand quite a blow. That these tents perform much better than their simple geometry suggests is no mystery to those who use them.

Customizing the Eureka Timberline and Similar Freestanding Tents

Let's use what we've learned to beef up the popular Eureka Timberline tent so it will stand up to a major storm.

First, the hem test. Does the fly cover all exposed perimeter seams? You bet! At least along the sidewalls. The Timberline has a full bathtub floor so fly coverage below the elevated bathtub seams isn't necessary, right?

Wrong! Fabrics wear, and the floor sidewalls are no exception. An extra waterproof layer here is always a plus. Seam coverage on the Timberline is adequate for vertical rain but not for wind-driven weather.

Rule: If your tent has exposed stitching or a fly that can be blown aside by high winds, you may want to extend the fly by sewing on

matching material. Make cuts above stake and guy line loops so you won't have to reattach them to the new fabric. Matching (or contrasting) material can be obtained from the tent manufacturer and many outdoor stores (see the section Yard Goods and Repair Materials, page 204).

Move to the corners where the toggle pins plug into the pole ends and note that some corner stitching is exposed to the weather. You'll have to rely on glue (seam sealant) here—a bad idea. Or you can solve the problem instantly by attaching a vestibule to one or both ends of the tent.

Check out the hems along the sidewall. There are just two equidistant stake points, neither of which splits the distance between tent corners. The result is that a strong side wind can compress the center sidewall hem into the porous canopy. Correcting the problem is easy: Just sew a third stake loop to the hem center at point A (see Figure T-11). Note how this one center stake firms the sidewall.

The Timberline is a comfortable, relatively high tent, with lots of sidewall exposed to the wind. Stiffen each wall by sewing a nylon storm loop to the center of the fly at point B of Figure T-11. Be sure to back with heavy fabric whatever you sew.

The aluminum A-frame is your final concern. Standard-issue Timberline poles simply aren't designed for winds above 30 mph. (The expedition poles are much sturdier.) Is there a way to stiffen the framework without adding weight or bulk?

You bet! Sew a nylon guy loop to the fly face at the midpoint of each pole that makes up the A-frame. Back the loop on the inside fly with a length of mating Velcro. When the weather gets nasty, secure the Velcro tabs to the poles and guy the outside loops. Since the Velcro tabs secure directly to the poles, there is no stress on the fly fabric—and no danger of tearing it.

Rule: Whenever possible, guy off the framework rather than the tent fabric!

Now, apply this philosophy to each end of the tent. The Timberline is effectively freestanding; there are no forward and aft guy lines to provide stability in oncoming winds. To account for this, the manufacturer has provided a D ring on the ridge at each end. You can attach guy lines directly to these, right?

Wrong! Reread the rule above and you'll see why. The first good blast of air will tear the D rings right off the tent. There's a better way.

1. Sew a Velcro tab to the underside of the fly, opposite the D ring. Secure the tab to the plastic pole junction tube, *then* guy off the D ring.

2. Or disregard the D ring and secure your guy lines directly to the horizontal junction tubes. If possible, attach guy and stake lines to an immovable object like a tree or rock.

For dome tents: Sew Velcro tabs to the inside fly, adjacent to the poles, as illustrated in Figure T-14. When high winds develop, Velcro around the poles and run guy lines to stakes or trees. Wind stress will be absorbed by the poles instead of the nylon tent fly.

Stormproofing in Summary

Let's review the rules for stormproofing tents:

- Perimeter floor seams (there should be none!) must be fully covered by the tent fly. Check the tent corners. If there's a problem here, adding a vestibule may solve it. If not, sew on an extension of some sort.

- There should be enough stake points (you can never have too many) along the fly hem to prevent wind-whipped rain from getting under the fly and onto seams. If your tent needs more stake points, add them.

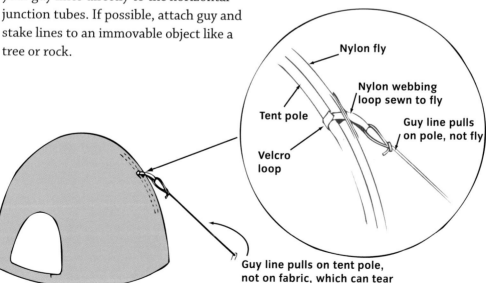

Figure T-14. A good way to attach storm lines to dome tents

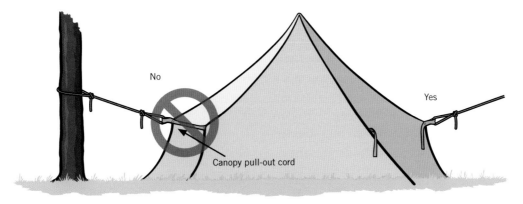

Figure T-15. Disconnect (or cut) canopy cords—they provide a path for rain to enter your tent!

- High-walled tents can be stabilized by attaching a guy line to the center face of the fly. Back your sewing with extra material. Don't run a canopy pull-out cord from the inner fly face to the canopy to increase space inside the tent (Figure T-15). Rain will wick through the stitching on the fly face and slither down the side-pull cord into the sleeping compartment. If your tent already has a canopy side-pull cord, disconnect it the moment rain begins. If this is impractical, tie a cotton shoelace or handkerchief to the cord somewhere between the fly and canopy. Now any water that wicks through will follow the hanky to the ground (at least for a while!) rather than into your tent.

- Whenever possible, guy directly off the framework of a tent. If you must attach lines to fabric, back what you sew with heavy material.

Now stand back and take a long, proud look at your accomplishments. You have a tent that will keep you dry in any rain. Cost of materials? Under $20. Time involved? About 3 hours.

Tents: Classics You Can Make

In the 1950s, when I was a Boy Scout, I owned a Spartan 5-by-7-foot canvas "wedge" tent (Figure T-16). There were no zippers, bug nets, or windows and no floor. A rubberized poncho doubled as a ground cloth, and in buggy weather I wore a head net. With two wooden poles and ten stakes, the little pup tent weighed exactly 7 pounds—a respectable weight for a two-person hiking tent, even by today's standards.

Classic canvas tents like these shown here are available from Duluth Pack, Frost River, Tentsmiths, and others (see appendix B). Left: Whelan lean-to; Right: wedge tent. This section provides plans for making the most popular vintage designs.
David Wescott

187

I used the wedgie in all types of weather—backpacked all over upper Michigan with it—and can recall only one time when I was wet and cold. It was my "go light" philosophy and a cold, 2-day rain that did me in. I got just what I deserved when I placed my dry sleeping bag on top of my wet poncho. From then on, I carried a special ground cloth for use inside my tent.

In the 1960s I bought my first nylon backpacking tent—a three-person Gerry Fireside. More commodious and half the weight of the wedge, it featured true double-walled (waterproof fly over porous canopy) construction. The Gerry had a window in back and an integral floor and bug net. Man, was I living! For more than a decade, the little tent was a constant companion on canoe camping trips in Minnesota and Canada. It never failed me in any weather.

Though I now own more sophisticated tents, I occasionally use the Gerry for solo canoeing. With its built-in (sewn to the ridge) rain fly and shock-corded I poles, the Fireside goes up in less than a minute. Few modern tents can do as well.

Admittedly, for high-altitude and severe-weather use, state-of-the-art tents outshine the old-timers by a wide margin. But for general camping in forested areas, many turn-of-the-century tents are better. At any rate, the best of the nostalgic designs were lighter, better ventilated, and roomier than most people think.

Many of the old tent designs—like the wall, wedge, baker, and forester—are still in production. Attempts to modernize these designs by substituting nylon for canvas have generally been unsuccessful. That's because breathable canvas still is the best material (and certainly the most durable) for large, airy tents. Though I spent considerable time under canvas when I

was a kid, I now prefer nylon tents by a wide margin. Nonetheless, the traditional tents of the past have much to recommend them. Reproduced in Figures T-17, T-19, and T-20 are three of the most popular models from the 1912 Abercrombie Company camp catalog for your interest and amusement. Study the specifications and you'll discover how light and versatile these shelters were. You may even want to build one yourself. Plans for the simplest models are included for your convenience.

Wedge Tent

Simplest of all designs, the wedge is versatile and cozy (Figure T-16). When constructed with a doorway at each end, the structure can be opened to face a fire. Snap or Velcro a mosquito bar to the roof and you have a tent that is similar to the convertible A-tent recommended by the legendary outdoorsman Calvin Rutstrum in his book *The New Way of the Wilderness*. The design is so simple you can easily draw your own plans from the specifications.

Note: A twin-door version of this classic tent is manufactured in mildew-resistant army duck by Tentsmiths.

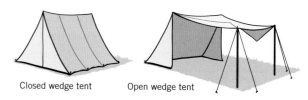

Closed wedge tent   Open wedge tent

Figure T-16. The wedge tent

Forester Tent

This ultralight tent (Figure T-17) was designed around 1910 by *Field & Stream* editor Warren Miller. Nothing more than a tapered tarp, the forester tent goes up fast on any terrain and is very wind resistant. The 1912 Abercrombie catalog lists a weight of just 2¾ pounds for the 8-by-8-foot version—this, in cotton canvas. Try finding a two-person nylon tent that light today!

Build a campfire out front and you'll discover how well the cone-shaped entrance funnels heat to the occupants inside. The forester was a standard offering in Boy Scout catalogs for nearly 50 years. David Abercrombie wrote about the material used in this and other Abercrombie-manufactured tents in the company's 1912 *Camp Outfits* catalog:

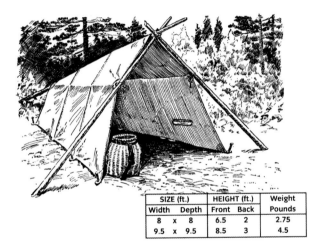

SIZE (ft.)		HEIGHT (ft.)		Weight
Width	Depth	Front	Back	Pounds
8 x	8	6.5	2	2.75
9.5 x	9.5	8.5	3	4.5

Figure T-17. Forester tent, from 1912 Abercrombie catalog

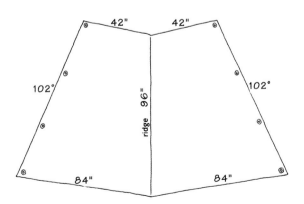

Figure T-18. Forester tent pattern

The cloth is treated by a copper process that makes it waterproof, rot proof and vermin proof, and leaves it perfectly pliable and soft. Even the white ant will not attack it; neither does it burn as readily as unprocessed material and it is not affected by either tropic heat or Arctic cold, changes in temperature making little differences in its feeling.

It is a non-conductor of heat, which makes it a cool summer and a warm winter tent. The color is a great advantage, the green being a shade that is easy for the eyes, and flies and gnats are not so troublesome in a green tent.

Baker Tent

Everyone who has camped out for long eventually comes to know and love the baker tent (Figure T-19). Guy out the fly and build a cheery fire beneath; gather the crew and deal the cards. There's room enough for all, even when heavy rain blows up. Add a sod cloth, bug net, side wings, and a privacy screen out front, and you have a snug four-season shelter that's as much at home in Patagonia as at a friendly KOA campground. Baker tents once were the backbone of

SIZE (ft.)		HEIGHT (ft.)		Weight
Width	Depth	Front	Back	Pounds
6.5 x	3.25	4	1	3.5
6.5 x	6.5	5	1.5	7
8 x	6.5	6	2	9
9.5 x	8	7	2.5	13.5

Figure T-19. Baker tent, from 1912 Abercrombie catalog

every 19th-century hunting camp, and in parts of the American West, they remain so today. Note that the 1912 *Camp Outfits* catalog listed the 8-by-6½-foot model at just 9 pounds—lighter even than today's popular nylon Eureka Timberline.

You can buy a modern baker tent from *Tentsmiths* and many western outfitters.

Miners' Tent

When it comes to efficient utilization of space, the miners' tent is hard to beat. Four pegs and a tie at the top (or interior pole) stabilize this tent in winds that would flatten most conventional designs. Spread the door flaps and feel the heat of your campfire. Button up tight and listen to the patter of rain while you stay dry inside. The miner is great for winter camping too: Just run the pipe of your sheet-metal stove through a thimble in the roof and watch things heat up fast inside.

Pyramid tents like these were popular in the cowboy days and well into the 20th century. Journals of the early arctic explorers praised the miner tent for its light weight, wind stability, and ease of pitching. Look around and you'll discover that this ancient design is still going strong. If you can draw a triangle, you can build this tent.

Whelen Lean-To

The Whelen lean-to (Figure T-21) was designed by the famous outdoorsman Colonel Townsend Whelen. A retired army officer, Colonel Whelen wrote prolifically about guns, hunting, and camping. Even when it was no longer fashionable, he preferred to base his hunts out of tents rather than RVs or motels. Whelen disliked the popular campfire tents of the day because their sloping back walls reflected campfire heat onto the floor rather than the occupants. And everyone had to sleep with their head or feet toward the fire, which cooked one end and froze the other. "Much smarter to sleep sideways, so all parts get done at once," snipped the colonel.

Whelen added a short vertical wall to the back of a conventional lean-to, then he sewed on a generous awning and side flaps. And voilà! The Whelen lean-to was born. It's interesting to note that Eureka and Cooke Custom Sewing offer a facsimile of this still-popular 1926 design—in waterproof nylon, of course!

SIZE (ft.)		HEIGHT (ft.)	Weight Pounds
Width	Depth		
6.5 x	6.5	6.5	5
8 x	8	7.5	6.75
9.5 x	9.5	8.5	9.75

Figure T-20. Miners' tent, from 1912 Abercrombie catalog

Figure T-21. Whelen lean-to

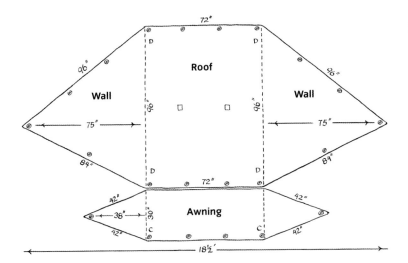

Figure T-22. Whelen lean-to plan

Tent Site: How to Cope with a Bad One

The camping literature is rich with advice on how to choose a good campsite. Requirements generally include high, flat ground with good drainage; a south-facing slope (so you can enjoy the morning sun); and an open vista so a welcome breeze will blow away bothersome insects. In reality, a rank novice can tell a good tent spot when she sees one. Everyone knows enough not to pitch a tent on bumpy ground, on a rock face, or in a depression. However, most camping today is carefully regulated, and some programmed sites are downright awful. In most cases you'll have to accept the inadequacies of the place and make the best of it. Here are some suggestions to do just that:

1. Always use a ground cloth inside your tent. The exception is in winter when you are camping on snow (with no chance of rain). Then the ground cloth should be placed under the tent to prevent the floor from freezing to the ground. Stormproof your tent as suggested in the Tents section on page 172.

2. Know the shortcomings of your tent and correct them. For example, the most weather-vulnerable portion of any tent is the door end, where zippers and seams come together. A vestibule will solve this problem instantly; however, not all tents come so equipped. If the ground slopes,

Good campsites aren't always available. Sometimes you have to take what you can get and make the best of it. This tent is pitched in a swamp—when you kneeled inside your tent, the pressure of your knees would force water up through the floor! Fortunately, our interior plastic ground cloths saved the day. This was the worst tent site I've ever had! A floatplane dropped us off here and a storm prevented us from moving to a better site. Near the headwaters of the North Knife River, Manitoba, Canada.

pitch the tent with the weather-vulnerable end downhill, so groundwater will run away from the seams rather than onto them.

3. If the site drainage is bad and there are a number of tents in your party, pitch each tent far enough away from its neighbor so that tent roofs won't funnel water onto nearby tents. Closely spaced tents act as gutters in a heavy rain!

4. Please do not "improve" the lay of the ground by attacking it with a hatchet and Rambo knife. Instead, use foam pads or air mattresses. Level your sleeping system by placing additional clothing beneath your trail bed.

5. There will not always be trees available from which to rig cooking flies. A set of collapsible tent poles will provide anchor points for tarps.

6. If, despite all your precautions, a heavy rain threatens to wipe you out, create water-diversion bars by placing logs alongside your tent's perimeter. The logs will function much like the erosion-control bars used for trail maintenance. After the rain, return logs to the forest so you'll leave no trace of your presence.

7. An anti-rain dance or thoughtful plea to the Great Spirit will sometimes cause the brunt of a storm to bypass a bad tent spot.

Tools

For predictable outings close to home, a Swiss Army knife or Leatherman multitool and duct tape are all you need. For backcountry trips, add to your kit an assortment of bolts, nuts, and washers; a small coil of light copper wire;

5-minute epoxy; sewing needles and waxed thread (or dental floss), a trail mattress repair kit, a file, and some diaper pins, and you're set for most emergencies.

Towels

Cloth dish towels have no place on a wilderness trip. They trap and spread bacteria and absorb soot and dirt. Once soaked, they usually stay that way for days. Try these as towels on your next campout:

- A synthetic (cloth) chamois will absorb about ten times its weight in water. You'll find this product at kitchen supply and auto shops and at state and county fairs. Outdoor stores sell the highly absorbent PackTowl, which comes in three sizes. A cloth chamois is my first line of defense against heavy spills. It works nearly as well as a sponge but it dries much faster.

- Absorbent paper toweling: Two sheets of paper toweling per meal will dry dishes for four, if you first "chamois dry" your cookware.

- The Boy Scouts consider toilet tissue so useful they call it "AP" (all-purpose) paper. Use it to blow your nose, nurse a cut, clean a stove, etc. Uses are endless. *Tip:* To save weight and bulk, remove the cardboard tube and place the roll inside a ziplock bag. Pull the paper from the center of the roll (tube removed) and you'll have a steady stream of tissue that you won't have to unroll.

- A cotton bandanna, lightweight cotton dish towel, or cloth baby diaper is the only wash towel you'll need on a wilderness camping trip.

U

Ultraviolet Protection

If you want to make your plastic canoe, poly-ethylene dry box, car dashboard and rubber moldings, carpeted cartop carriers, and other sun-sensitive materials last almost forever, treat them regularly with 303 Protectant. Many vinyl makers and canoe manufacturers recommend 303 by name. A 303 customer treated one panel of a nylon life vest with 303 Protectant and placed it on an aluminum roof in Portland, Oregon. He checked the vest 4 years later and discovered that the 303-treated panel looked fine, while the rest of the vest had completely disintegrated!

You won't find any petrochemicals, silicone oils, or petroleum distillates in 303 Protectant. It's not greasy or oily and it repels dust, dirt, and stains. I store my canoe trailer outside year-round and regularly use 303 to preserve the tires. It works!

V

Vapor-Barrier Liners (VBLs)

A vapor barrier is a waterproof fabric (urethane-coated nylon or plastic) that you wear next to your skin. Warm clothes are layered over that. Perspiration can't get through the waterproof fabric to dampen your clothes and reduce their insulating properties, so you stay warm even when you're inactive. It's like wearing a wet suit—you're warm but not very comfortable. Some people don't mind the damp feeling; others can't tolerate it.

VBLs were popular in the 1970s, especially for use as sleeping-bag liners. But the choir has quieted. In 2003 I attended an arctic survival school in Spitsbergen, Norway. It never warmed above 24 degrees below zero. Our instructor was a top winter-survival expert in the Norwegian army. He did not recommend vapor barriers.

W

Wanigans

Wanigans are rigid boxes commonly used in the fur trade to carry hard goods like knives, guns, and axes that would be uncomfortable in a standard soft pack. Modern campers can use wanigans for the same purpose. For auto camping, nothing beats a well-organized wanigan camp kitchen, which has compartments for tin cans, utensils, and soft goods. Most commercial models have a plywood lid that doubles as work area and cutting board. You can get detailed plans for making a camp kitchen from many scout and YMCA camps.

Smaller hard packs are handy for canoe camping, picnicking, berry picking, and any activity requiring a strong, rigid container. The traditional hard pack for canoeing is the Maine pack basket, which is available from L.L. Bean and Duluth Pack. If you place a woven ash basket into a waterproof sack (the army-surplus

Wanigans, from left to right: pickle barrel with Ostrom Outdoors harness; 18-inch-high Maine pack basket inside Duluth Pack #2 canvas Cruiser Pack (note the two waterproof pack liners); and Cooke Custom Sewing foam-lined food pack (the foam provides rigidity and insulation).

waterproof clothes bag is just the right size), then set this unit into a tailored backpack, you'll have a strong, watertight container that's comfortable to carry.

Tip: Make a number of narrow fabric pockets and attach these to the inside rim of your pack basket. Store sunglasses, a fillet knife, and other small items in these handy organizers.

A less-expensive solution is to nest a cheap rectangular plastic trash container inside a soft pack. This outfit will protect all your breakables.

A medium-size plastic ice chest (cooler) can also be pressed into service as a wanigan. It will be easier to carry if you strap it to a tubular aluminum pack frame.

Aluminum and plastic wanigans (usually called "dry boxes") are available from western raft companies.

Round wanigans: Many years ago a resourceful Canadian canoeist, who was on the prowl for a low-cost wanigan, tried an experiment: He packed some hard items that would gouge his back in a giant plastic pickle barrel. His canoe capsized and everything in the barrel came through dry. The word that there was a new round wanigan in town spread like an Ontario bush fire, and soon everyone copied the plan. Then capitalism reared its ugly head, and the smelly plastic jars that were once free for the asking began to sell for big bucks. (Any relationship to the true story of how this all began is purely coincidental!)

Pickle barrels are more watertight than any wanigan, but they are a pain to pack and portage. The pack-makers Granite Gear offers comfortable foam-padded harnesses, which help. Barrels were unpopular in the States until recently; now most every canoe shop has them.

Pickle and olive barrels, like this one being carried by Canadian canoe expert Toni Harting, are strong and watertight. But they *are not* bear-proof!

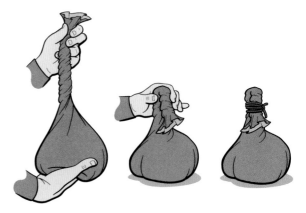

Figure W-1. How to gooseneck and secure a plastic bag

Waterproof Bags and Boxes

To make a plastic bag waterproof, tightly twist the neck of the bag and fold it over. Secure the gooseneck with a rubber band (Figure W-1). This procedure is recommended by the Boy Scouts.

aLOKSAK waterproof and waterproof/odor-proof plastic bags: These inexpensive plastic bags look like ordinary ziplock bags, but they are much stronger and are waterproof to depths exceeding 190 feet, even when placed under mild compression. They have a patented triple seal and come in sizes to fit everything from passports and cellphones to topographic maps and bulky clothes. Odor-proof (they block all odors!) versions, originally developed for the safe disposal of hazardous biological wastes, are also available.

Waterproof boxes: A waterproof box is only as good as its seal. Quality control is never 100 percent, so carefully eyeball the seal, inch by inch, before you buy. A magnifying glass will show imperfections. The slightest dent or cut will let water in.

After each use in the field: It takes just one tiny plant seed, blade of grass, or dirt particle to corrupt the seal of a waterproof box. You'll get a perfect seal every time if, just before you close the box, you wipe the full length of the seal with a cotton bandanna, preferably one moistened with water. I've religiously followed this procedure for years and I've never had a problem, even when my canoe capsized and the box was submerged in a pounding current for many minutes.

A few times each season: Use a Q-tip to clean the seal with water. Rubbing alcohol will remove tree sap and insect fragments. Apply silicone spray and you're done.

Tip: Plastic deteriorates and becomes brittle after long exposure to sunlight. Occasionally (once a year is enough) spray the outside of your waterproof plastic boxes with a nonoily ultraviolet protectant (I prefer 303 Protectant).

Water Treatment

There are few places in North America where you can safely drink water from a lake or stream. And conditions don't seem to be improving. Water quality—and just plain availability of water—remains a major environmental concern. Unless you always camp where the quality of drinking water is guaranteed, you should carry your water or treat it by one of these methods.

Using a purifier/filter to purify drinking water in the Boundary Waters Canoe Area. Important: To avoid contamination from hands or the ground, keep the outlet end of the filter hose secured in a plastic bag when you're not using it. And don't touch the inside of the bag with your hands!
Mike Rapatz

Field Methods of Water Treatment

1. *Boiling* is the most reliable way to kill almost everything. Even cryptosporidium, which can survive exposure to iodine, chlorine, and bleach, is killed by boiling. If you are uncertain about the quality of your drinking water, boiling is the best way to make it safe. Simply bring your water to a rolling boil then shut off your stove. There's no need to adjust boiling times for altitude.

2. *Filtration:* Mechanical filters have improved steadily since the first edition of *Camping's Top Secrets.* There are a lot more options than a decade ago. If you opt for mechanical filtration, choose a large-capacity unit whose pores will remove the smallest infectious agents you are likely to encounter. By comparison, a filter with a 4-micron absolute pore size will stop giardia; a 1-micron filter will halt cryptosporidium. "Absolute" pore size means that no hole in the filter is smaller than the diameter indicated. Generally, large pores mean fast delivery, while small pores slow the flow. The industry standard for removing bacteria is 0.45 microns (absolute). Be sure you can easily replace or clean the filter. Naturally, it's wise to carry a spare.

   Note: Some filters use iodine to "purify" the water after it has been filtered. The drawback is that the iodine imparts a bitter aftertaste that some people find objectionable. An optional carbon cartridge removes some of the bad taste.

3. *Chemical treatment:* Halazone tablets are an old standby that have been available from corner drugstores for years. If you use Halazone, take an unopened bottle on each trip. The product loses considerable strength when exposed to air and heat.

Aqua Mira (called Pristine in Canada) is the latest high-tech water-purification pill. It comes in two bottles. You mix drops of each together, and the chlorine dioxide that is formed kills microorganisms in about 30 minutes. It's easy to use and it has very little chlorine aftertaste.

MSR Aquatabs contain the chemical sodium dichloroisocyanurate which has been used by the World Health Organization for many years. Aquatabs meet EPA purifier standards for viruses, bacteria, and giardia cysts. They have a stable 5-year shelf life. Unlike typical chlorine and iodine-based tablets, Aquatabs leave little to no aftertaste. One tablet purifies two quarts of clear water. When using a microfilter, you can use Aquatabs after filtering when viruses are a concern.

MSR has an impressive Magic Marker–size purifier called the MIOX, which uses electricity and salt to produce a powerful disinfectant that kills everything. Simple and fast, it's ideal for purifying large volumes of water. The water has minimal aftertaste.

Important: Any chlorine-based system will leave an aftertaste if you don't allow the chlorine gas to evaporate. No problem if you purify your water in an open container (pot or bucket). If you don't, you should aerate the mix before you drink it—simply pour the water back and forth from one poly bottle to another several times.

Chlorine: Liquid chlorine bleach with 4 to 6 percent available chlorine may be used to purify water. Use two drops of bleach per quart of clear water and four drops per quart of cold or cloudy water. Let treated water stand for 30 minutes before using. You should be able to smell the chlorine gas. If not, repeat the dosage and let it stand another 15 minutes before using. If the water is very cold or cloudy, let it stand overnight before using.

Note: None of the chemicals work very well in cold, cloudy water. Under these conditions your best bet is to boil your water.

Tip: You can sterilize your camp dishes by simply adding a splash of chlorine bleach to the final rinse water. Or add a convenient EfferSan tablet. EfferSan tablets have 30 percent available chlorine in a handy dry form.

Iodine: Place six grams of iodine (your pharmacist will weigh it out for you) in a one-ounce amber bottle. Fill the bottle with water. The iodine crystals will dissolve until a saturated solution results, then no more crystals will dissolve.

Sterilize a 1-quart canteen of water by pouring about half (the amount isn't critical) the iodine solution into the canteen. Let the canteen stand at least 30 minutes before drinking. Allow additional time for cold or cloudy water.

Recharge the iodine bottle with fresh water after each use. Only a small amount of iodine will dissolve from the crystals each time, so you may continue to use the "iodine decant bottle" dozens of times until no more crystals are visible.

Caution: Do not allow any iodine crystals to enter your canteen. Large doses of iodine can be fatal! (Iodine is a rather heavy metal and is visible in solution, so you'll have no trouble seeing the crystals or containing them in your bottle.)

You may also treat your water with a commercial tablet that releases iodine. Potable Aqua (sold nearly everywhere) is highly recommended.

A 2 percent tincture of iodine solution may also be used to purify water. Use six to eight drops of iodine per quart of drinking water. Let the chemical work for at least 30 minutes before you drink the water. Double the dosage and working time if the water is cold or cloudy.

Note: Products that release chlorine will not destroy giardia cysts under all conditions, and they won't destroy cryptosporidium cysts under any conditions! If you suspect contamination by these parasites, boil your water or use a water filter with an absolute pore size of 1 to 2 microns or smaller. Authorities generally agree that compounds that release iodine are more reliable than those that emit chlorine.

4. *Ultraviolet light treatment:* The SteriPen is a pen-like device that uses ultraviolet light to purify water. It kills bacteria AND viruses. It weighs 7 ounces and runs off four AA batteries (some models use compact watch batteries which aren't available everywhere). It's safe to use, reasonably fast, and treated water has no aftertaste. It's designed to purify 1 liter of water or less at a time—it won't purify a big bucket. There are two concerns: 1) its fragile (pricey) ultraviolet bulb; 2) It only works with clear water. Still, the SteriPEN is my favorite water-purification device. I've used it for over a decade from the Boundary Waters of Minnesota to the Alaskan tundra, and when traveling abroad. It has never let me down. All you need are batteries and you're good to go!

Where Not to Get Your Drinking Water

1. Go well away from the shoreline to get drinking water. If you're camping at a spot frequented by man or animals, go upstream of the source to get water. On lakes go a minimum of 150 feet from shore—the farther (and deeper) the better.

   Tip: Place a rock in your largest cooking pot and lower it deep into the lake with a long rope. Work the bucket up and down like a yo-yo to guarantee good exchange of water. Water taken 20 feet or more below the lake surface is apt to be most trustworthy.

2. Avoid water with a greenish color, which can indicate the presence of algae and potentially harmful bacteria. Tan-colored water, however, is usually safe. Invariably, this color suggests natural runoff of tannic acid from adjacent conifer stands (quite common throughout the upper Midwest).

3. Take your drinking water from fast-moving areas; avoid backwaters, stagnant areas, and eddies, which are breeding places for microorganisms.

4. Never drink any water that has been contaminated by wastes from a paper mill. Instead, secure your water from incoming streams or springs.

5. Don't take water near beaver dams or lodges. Beavers are the favored hosts of

Giardia lamblia, a small protozoan that may cause severe discomfort. Giardia enters a water supply through the feces of the host. Its cyst can survive up to 2 months in 46°F water, and up to 1 month in 70°F water!

The infection carried by the organism is called giardiasis, characterized by severe diarrhea, cramps, nausea, and vomiting. Incubation time is 1 to 2 weeks, though some people have gone as long as 2 months without getting sick. If untreated, the disease may go on for years!

Giardiasis is usually diagnosed by stool examination, which is not always reliable. Most physicians just haven't had enough experience with the disease to correctly diagnose it. As a result, many victims suffer for months before they get the help they need. Not everyone who is exposed to the giardia parasite comes down with the disease. Indeed, most people are simply carriers.

6. Contrary to popular belief, clear water tumbling over sunny rocks may not be safe to drink. While ultraviolet light does kill microorganisms, flowing water mixes them and increases the chance they'll get in your drinking water. Better to take your drinking water from the deep sunlit pool nearby.

7. Take water from small tributaries that flow into a stream. The closer to the source of the tributary, the better.

8. Water from a still, deep pool should be taken near the surface and as far from shore as possible. Harmful microbes tend to lurk just below the surface of calm water, out of reach of sunlight.

Treatment for Giardiasis and Cryptosporidiosis

Metronidazole (Flagyl) and furazolidone (Furoxone) are the recommended prescription drugs for treating giardiasis. It's a good idea to carry a supply on long trips. There is no treatment for cryptosporidiosis, whose symptoms are similar to giardiasis. Cryptosporidiosis usually runs its course in 1 to 2 weeks.

Weather Forecasting

Every outdoors person should have a basic understanding of weather phenomena and be able to make reasonably accurate short-term weather predictions. Some campers take forecasting quite seriously; they arm themselves with min/max thermometers, barometers, cloud charts, and weather tables. Whether or not this paraphernalia will improve your short-range forecasts is debatable. After all, primitive man was right on target more than 80 percent of the time simply by looking at the sky, sensing the wind, and "feeling" the weather. You can approximate this enviable success rate by applying these time-proven principles:

1. "Red sky at night, sailor's delight; red sky in the morning, sailor take warning."

"Red sky at night, sailor's delight." Tomorrow will be a grand day!
Mike Rapatz

Translation: A red morning sky indicates possible rain that day; a red evening sky suggests the next day will be clear. The color difference relates to the reflective value of the low-lying cloud cover.

2. Check the grass, tent, canoe bottom, or whatever for the presence of dew in late evening or early morning. A heavy dew at either of these times usually suggests 8 to 12 hours of good weather.

3. Watch the smoke from your campfire. If it hangs low to the ground (a function of low pressure), rain is on the way. If it rises high into a nice vertical column (high pressure), count on good weather.

4. Check out the air bubbles in your coffee cup. They'll ring the edges of the cup when a low pressure (rain) system sets in.

5. You can sometimes smell a coming storm, as the low pressure allows methane (swamp gas) to rise and drift with the current. In boggy areas the odor is quite pronounced.

6. "When the peacock loudly bawls, there'll be both rain and squalls." Translation: Birds sing loudly just before a storm.

7. Geese and seagulls usually won't fly just before a storm. Low-pressure air is thin and it's hard for them to get airborne.

8. The ears of many animals are sensitive to low pressure. Wolves will howl before a storm. Dogs will become nervous and emit howls or howl-like sounds.

9. To determine the distance of a lightning strike, count the seconds between the flash and the thunder boom. Divide by five and you'll have your answer in miles.

10. Noises all become louder and more vibrant just before a rain, because the sound is reflected and magnified by the low clouds. The croaking of frogs, yodel of loons, etc., will echo loudly if rain is imminent.

11. Be alert for changes in wind direction. Storms are whirlpools of wind that rotate counterclockwise in the Northern Hemisphere (remember high school science?). The adage "Wind from the south brings rain in its mouth" is the keystone here, as the wind that precedes a storm usually blows from the south. Counterclockwise wind shifts therefore usually bring rain, while clockwise movements indicate fair weather. You can keep these directional changes straight by remembering the rhymes . . .

     "Wind from the east brings weather that's a beast." (This suggests a counter-clockwise wind shift from south to east, east to north, and so on.)

     "Wind from the west brings weather that's best." (This suggests a clockwise wind shift from south to west, north to east, etc.)

12. Most everyone knows that frogs emerge from the water just before a storm and croak their fool heads off. Frogs breathe partly through their skin (which must be kept moist), so when the humidity rises just before a storm, they climb ashore and sing happily.

13. If you're a canoeist, you know that about 8 to 12 hours before a storm, mosquitoes

Nature foils a well-planned camp. The author and his friends were camped on a gravel bar along the Noatak River in Alaska when this 70 mph+ Williwaw (sudden blast of powerful wind) struck. The only warning was an abruptly blackened sky followed seconds later by the freight-train roar of the wind. The tundra tarp in the background flattened instantly (but no damage). Surprisingly, the Eureka! Tundraline tents held. Our huge blazing campfire just disappeared!

and blackflies begin to swarm and bite more than usual. Up to 2 hours before the storm they quit biting altogether.

14. Check out the rainbow: A heavy red may mean more rain; vibrant rich blue suggests clear skies ahead.

15. Here's an old Down East proverb: "Filly tails make lofty ships wear low sails." Translation: Thin, hairlike clouds forecast rain within the day. These "filly tails" are really streaks of ice thrown skyward by the rising air of a coming storm.

16. "A mackerel sky [tiny scalelike clouds that resemble a mackerel's back], just 24 hours dry." Translation: Expect rain within the next day!

17. Do you see any fireflies around? When rain approaches, these little insects light up the woods, according to this rhyme: "When the little glow bug lights his lamp, the air around is surely damp."

18. Listen for the rustle of leaves as the wind precedes the storm.

19. If you can't see the sharp points on a half moon, rain may be on its way. Translation: Low clouds and haze distort sharp images.

20. Bright, twinkling stars usually indicate high altitude winds, which may be bringing in a storm.

21. There's a good chance that foul weather (rain or snow) will fall within 3 days of a new moon phase.

22. "The weather out west had best be best, for tomorrow will bring it to you to test!" This means that in all likelihood, the weather

system to your west will be at your location tomorrow.

23. In summer a sun dog, or halo around the sun, generally predicts the coming of rain. Sun dogs are caused by sunlight streaming through the ice particles of high cirrostratus clouds. A halo around the moon may also indicate rain.

24. "Evening fog will not burn soon, but morning fog will burn before high noon." Invariably, a fog-borne day will become perfectly clear (an ideal day) by noon. Fog forms when water vapor reaches the dew point and condenses on dust particles near the ground. When the day heats up, the fog evaporates and turns to invisible water vapor.

25. "Short notice, soon it will pass. Long notice, expect it to last." Watch the clouds. If they take several days to build, a warm front—and prolonged rain—is usually in the offing. If the storm system builds suddenly, it will probably pass quickly.

26. And of course everyone knows: "Rain before seven, dry by eleven."

Y

Yard Goods and Repair Materials
Tools You'll Need to Make Repairs

Sewing machine: From time to time you'll have to mend tears in tents, sleeping bags, tarps, and clothing. Of course you can send things out for repair, but it's less expensive—and frankly more fun—to do it yourself. By and large you'll be sewing lightweight fabrics, so any light-duty sewing machine will do. Many years ago I purchased a coal black, 1958 Singer. It sews forward and backward, that's all. I've used the old Singer to patch countless packs and tarps and to build more than twenty nylon splash covers for canoes. I paid $75 for the Singer, complete with maple cabinet. Good buys on old machines are still available.

Sailmaker's needles and waxed thread: Sailmaker's needles are available from Tandy Leather Company and others who sell leather supply products. Half a dozen heavy-duty needles and a bobbin of waxed thread should last for years. Use two needles when you sew. Figure

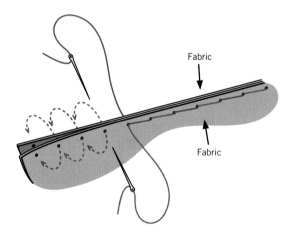

Figure Y-1. Machinelike stitching

Y-1 shows how to make a strong machinelike stitch that will never let go. *Tip:* This "double-needle machine stitch" is the one to use when sewing a knife or ax sheath. At home, use an electric drill to make the needle holes in thick leather. In the field, a thin awl will do.

Sewing awl: The awls that come on Swiss Army knives and multipurpose tools are too coarse for fine work. Get a small, sharp awl at your local fabric store.

Speedy Stitcher sewing awl: The Speedy Stitcher has been around for decades. It has a self-contained bobbin and a strong, replaceable needle. A heavy wooden handle allows you to bore through thick material. In all, the Speedy Stitcher is a solid and practical little machine, though it's a bit cumbersome for go-light trips. Two sailmaker's needles and a sharp awl are slower to use but produce results as good as the Speedy Stitcher.

Don't forget to include in your repair kit: swatches of material to match your equipment; buckles; 1-inch-wide nylon webbing; two-piece, solid brass snaps (a Tandy Leather Company item); instant epoxy; nylon filament tape; gray duct tape; tweezers; needle-nose pliers; scissors; safety pins.

Modern "Yard Goods"
Cotton

Cotton is a marvelous material for large, semi-permanent tents and for any application that requires breathability and durability. Military tents are still constructed from cotton canvas duck, as are most of the high-grade wall tents you see in western hunting camps.

Canvas breathes as it sheds water, which means that tents made of this fabric are wonderfully comfortable (no condensation) in wet weather. Worn canvas is easily restored to waterproof condition by painting on chemicals that can be purchased in most hardware stores. Mending the damaged polyurethane coatings on nylon fabrics is at best difficult.

Cotton has a nonskid surface, has a nice soft "hand," and feels good against the skin. It's ideal as a covering for foam sleeping pads and seat and boat cushions, for tent and tool bags, and for hats. A cotton-poplin parka is luxurious and will ward off quite a shower if treated with water-repellent chemicals. Cotton fabrics retain water repellents much more willingly than do nylon materials. Note that nylon *stretches* when it gets wet, whereas canvas *shrinks*.

Being a natural fiber, cotton also has considerable flex. Haul a heavy nylon pack across sharp granite and the nylon fibers won't give much. Do the same with a canvas pack and the cotton fibers will stretch and return to shape. The result is that canvas packs often outlive nylon ones, even though they are technically less strong. Some of my canvas Duluth packs are more than 30 years old and are still serviceable.

Army duck is the strongest and heaviest (and most expensive!) of the cotton fabrics. It is woven so that each warp yarn passes over (or under) a single filling yarn (similar to those loop pot holders you made as a child). "Duck" is available in weights from 7 to 15 ounces per square yard. The army prefers 12- to 15-ounce fabrics for their heavy truck tarps and bivouac tents, but 7- to 8-ounce weights are better for family campers. Army duck is the king of cotton tent fabrics.

Twill is woven so that each warp yarn passes over two or more filling yarns. It's less strong than duck and is used mostly to make military uniforms. It's tough stuff and it weighs about 8 ounces per square yard.

Drill is a three-leaf twill made from fairly coarse yarns. It's more loosely woven than duck and less expensive. The cheapest canvas tents are often made from drill.

Cotton-poplin is a tightly woven fabric that's produced by using yarns that are heavier and more coarse than the warp yarns. Poplin comes in weights of 4 to 11 ounces per square yard. Some family-size wall tents are woven from 5½-ounce fabric.

Egyptian, pima, and Supima cotton: Egyptian cotton has the longest fibers of all cottons, and it makes into the strongest and silkiest yarn. It is by far the most luxurious fabric for the interior shells of sleeping bags; no other material feels better against the skin. Pima cotton was developed by US growers to compete with the Egyptian product, and it is nearly as good. Supima is the top of the pima crop. Tightly woven high-grade cotton isn't used much in its pure form anymore (it's very expensive). However, it is a marvelous material for sleeping bags, wind shells, and summer shirts.

Ventile cotton was originally developed by the British to keep downed RAF fliers from freezing in the North Sea. It is so tightly woven that it will repel a shower for 20 minutes or more without the aid of chemical water repellents. Until the advent of Gore-Tex, all the best parkas in the world were made from Ventile. Unfortunately, this fabric is heavy when dry, heavier when wet, very expensive, and difficult to find. It is a wonderfully luxurious and long-lived material.

Waxed cotton: Wax or oil is applied to densely woven cotton duck—a method of waterproofing that dates from the days of iron men and wooden ships. Now scores of fashionable parkas—notably Australian Outback riding garments—are waterproofed by this method. Pluses include a soft, draping hand and luxurious texture, good breathability and durability, an attractive natural odor, and a techy but traditional look. Waxed-cotton garments must be periodically maintained by rubbing in more oil. These garments work well in moderate rains but not in bad storms. They are no match for today's best rain gear. Waxed-cotton parkas have become a cult thing among outdoor enthusiasts: They are quite expensive.

Microfibers

Microfibers (nylon, polyester, and acrylic) are extremely fine—about one hundred times thinner than human hair! Their small diameter gives them unique properties that thicker, conventional fibers can't match. For example, they have the ability to bend more easily than thicker fibers, so they feel soft and luxurious against the skin. They resist pilling, keep their shape through many washings, and dry almost instantly.

Microfiber liners are widely used in wind- and raincoats because they're very effective at wicking moisture away from the skin. A microfiber lining will make any garment feel less clammy in damp weather. A drawback is their sensitivity to heat—campfires (especially, sparks!) and hot clothes dryers are deadly.

Nylon Fabrics

Nylon is used for everything from tents to boots. Nylon is strong, light, and relatively inexpensive. On the negative side it degrades rapidly in ultraviolet light and stretches considerably when wet. It also shrinks over the years.

Taffeta is a flat-woven fabric that weighs between 2.5 and 3.5 ounces per square yard. Taffeta is more prone to tear than ripstop, but it has greater resistance to abrasion, the reason why most tent flies and floors are made of this material.

Polyurethane-coated nylon taffeta is the fabric of choice for lightweight rain gear, stuff sacks, and backpack tarps. Uncoated (porous) taffeta is a popular fabric for garments. Uncoated taffeta has no water repellency. Waterproof coatings last for years, not decades. It's best to toss your rain gear at the first sign of a leak than to attempt repairs with the expensive paint-on chemicals sold at camping stores.

Ripstop has a gridwork of heavy threads woven in at quarter-inch intervals to increase fabric strength. It weighs 1.5 to 2.0 ounces per square yard. Ripstop is widely used for lightweight tent canopies, sleeping-bag shells, and wind garments. Coated ripstop makes a nice lightweight rain tarp.

Vinyl-coated nylon is a heavy-weight plastic-coated nylon used largely for heavy-duty tent floors and tarps. It's much stronger and more resistant to abrasion than coated taffeta, but its vinyl coating may soften or peel if it is exposed to heavy doses of harsh solvents, such as those used in some insecticides.

Silicone-treated nylon is the hot new fabric for ultralight rain tarps and tent flies, but not for tent canopies because the material does not meet US fireproof specifications. This is a non-issue in Europe. Once again, America is behind the curve. Cordura is the toughest nylon of all. It resists abrasion and puncture far better than any other fabric of equal weight. Many of the best backpacks are made from it, and it's widely used in the manufacturing of lightweight hiking boots. However, heavyweight Cordura does not accept waterproofing compounds very well. Invariably, tiny pinholes (which you can see when the fabric is held up to a strong light) of untreated material remain, which will admit some water.

Packcloth is a medium-weight nylon weave with a heavy polyurethane coating. Packcloth is lighter, less abrasion resistant, and more waterproof than Cordura. It also costs less than Cordura.

Coated oxford cloth (which weighs about 6 ounces per square yard) is a strong, absolutely watertight fabric used in the manufacture of lightweight backpacks. This is the same stuff that Eureka uses for flooring in their outfitter Timberline tents. It is the best material I've found for making fabric splash covers for canoes.

Taslan nylon: Nylon yarn is textured with jets of air to make it feel soft and cottony. Taslan nylon fabrics are lightweight, durable, and very resistant to abrasion. Taslan nylon is much less "slippery" than regular nylon.

Ballistics cloth is a 1050+ denier nylon. The yarn was originally developed as a tire cord then later refined into cloth for military flak vests. Ballistics cloth is exceptionally strong and abrasion resistant. It is less flexible than Cordura or cotton canvas. Like all synthetic fibers, ballistics cloth must be coated with polyurethane to make it waterproof.

Note: All these nylon fabrics can be had with or without waterproof coatings. Weight and cost of the fabrics will vary depending upon the type and amount of coating applied.

Polyethylene and Polypropylene

Polyethylene-coated polyethylene is a tough polyethylene fabric with a polyethylene plastic coating on both sides. The material is mildewproof and is commonly used for heavy-duty tent floors and tarps. Both vinyl-coated nylon and polyethylene-coated polyethylene are much more dimensionally stable (less wet stretch/dry shrinkage) than polyurethane-coated nylon.

Propex (Condessa) is a woven polypropylene that is designed for use in luggage. It resists solvents, stains, molds, abrasion and tears. The (coated) material weighs about 12 ounces per square yard and looks and feels almost exactly like 18-ounce canvas. Tough stuff . . . and very beautiful.

Blends

Sixty/forty cloth (60 percent cotton/40 percent nylon) is woven with nylon threads in one direction and cotton in the other. The nylon supplies strength, the cotton provides water repellency and a luxurious feel. A lot of great mountain parkas are built from 60/40 cloth.

Sixty-five/thirty-five cloth: Cotton and polyester yarns are blended together then woven into the garment. Threads of each yarn run in both directions. This fabric is supposed to be more water repellent and have greater strength than 60/40 cloth.

There are also a number of exotic blends that feature cotton, polyester, and nylon in varying weaves and amounts. Generally, the higher the nylon content, the stronger, lighter, and less water repellent the garment. More cotton and polyester mean a softer hand, higher water repellency, and heavier weight. In practice, the differences between these similar fabrics are relatively insignificant.

Here are some other common fabric terms you may encounter:

- *Acrylic:* The generic name for fibers made from polyacrylonitrile. Acrylics are soft, washable, nonallergenic, and quick drying. In the days before fleece, acrylics were the substitute for wool. They are still a good choice for growing kids and those on a budget.

- *Olefin (polypropylene):* A paraffin-based fiber that doesn't absorb water. See the discussion of polypropylene long underwear in the Clothing section.

- *Spandex* (Dupont calls it Lycra) is very stretchy but has a good memory for shape. It's always used in combination with other fibers like cotton or nylon.

- *Triblend:* Three different fibers woven together—like cotton/nylon/polyester. Each fiber contributes something special to the blend.

- *Tricot:* A strong double-thread weave that doesn't easily tear or fray.

Appendix A

Recommended Reading

Basic Illustrated: Knots for the Outdoors (First Edition). Cliff Jacobson. FalconGuides, 2008. All the knots and hitches you need to know for camping. Includes left-handed illustrations of every knot and hitch.

Basic Illustrated: Map and Compass (First Edition). Cliff Jacobson. FalconGuides, 2008. All you need to know to navigate by map and compass and GPS. Widely used by schools, scouts, and summer camps.

Bear Attacks: The Deadly Truth. James Gary Shelton. Pallister Publishing, 1998. This book examines the lives of people who have survived bear attacks. Emphasis is on what went wrong.

Bear Attacks: Their Causes and Avoidance (Revised Edition). Stephen Herrero. Lyons Press, 2002. The most authoritative guide available. All the research is here!

Bear Attacks II: Myth and Reality. James Gary Shelton. Pallister Publishing, 2001. Firsthand accounts of bear attacks are ana-lyzed to determine cause.

Bear Aware (Fourth Edition). Bill Schneider. FalconGuides, 2012. Solid advice for those who camp in western national parks like Yellowstone.

Bear Encounter Survival Guide. James Gary Shelton. Pallister Publishing, 1997. A refreshing look at bearhavior from a British Columbia woodsman who has spent the better part of his life around bears.

Camping and Woodcraft. Horace Kephart. Facsimile edition: University of Tennessee Press, 1988. First published in 1917, this classic started the camping revolution. There's still much to learn from this old camping book.

Camping in the Old Style. David Wescott. Gibbs Smith Publisher (www.gibbs-smith.com), 2000. If you love traditional camping—or just want to learn about it—you'll love this book, which details the methods used by campers before the "nylon age." Includes more than one hundred classic photos and illustrations. Wescott's book *Primitive Technology: A Book of Earth Skills* is another great read. Mr. Wescott kindly contributed many of the traditional camping photos used in this book.

Canoeing and Camping: Beyond the Basics (Third Edition). Cliff Jacobson. FalconGuides, 2007. Skills, equipment, and sage advice for canoeing wilderness waters—beginners through experts.

Cooking the Sourdough Way: Tips, Stoves, and Recipes. Scott Power. ICS Books, 1994. Not just for bread anymore, sourdough can be used in a variety of recipes, all wilderness tested by Chef Scott.

Canoeing Wild Rivers, (Fifth Edition/30th Anniversary Edition). Cliff Jacobson. FalconGuides, 2015. Experts consider this the premier guide to canoeing and explor-ing North America's waterways. Includes advice from the world's top paddlers.

GPS Land Navigation. Michael Ferguson. Glassford Publishing, 1997. The most complete and intuitive text for learning about global positioning and coordinate systems.

Justin Cody's Race to Survival. Cliff Jacobson. 10,000 Lakes Publishing (10KLP.com), 2019. A unique teen book that mixes a fictional wilderness survival adventure with practical outdoor skills everyone should know—a first for books of this type. Adults love it too!

The New Way of the Wilderness: The Classic Guide to Survival in the Wild, reprint. Cal Rutstrum. University of Minnesota Press, 2000. A must read for every serious camper, written by a master who spent long periods in the wilderness. I am proud to admit that Rutstrum was my mentor.

Wilderness Medicine: Beyond First Aid (Sixth Edition). William W. Forgey, MD. FalconGuides, 2012. The most practical and useful first-aid text for those who don't have much medical knowledge. Offers prescription and nonprescription advice and describes innovative first-aid kits you can assemble.

The Prepper's Medical Handbook. William W. Forgey, MD. Lyons Press, 2020. Packed with useful medications and procedures for when the zombies come.

Woodcraft and Camping. George W. Sears ("Nessmuk"). Dover, 1963. This camping classic was first published in 1920. "Nessmuk" canoed the Adirondacks alone in the early part of the 20th century. His wisdom and sage advice continues today. If you love camping, you'll love this book!

Appendix B

Sources for Recommended Products

Agawa Canyon: www.agawacanyoninc.com. State-of-the-art folding camp saws. Parts are connected; no need to touch the blade during assembly/disassembly. All toothed (no rakers!) blade for cutting dead wood. Assembles in seconds!

aLOKSAK waterproof plastic bags: www.loksak.com. Waterproof and odor-proof ziplock bags. Used by government agencies and the military.

Badger Healing Balm:; www.badgerbalm.com. Heals cracked skin fast. Its alcohol-free formula won't irritate cuts.

The Biffy Bag: www.biffybag.com. Compact toilet system in a bag. Convenient and odor-proof.

Bound Tree Medical: www.boundtree.com. Strong, leak-proof sterile water for irrigation bottles in sizes from 250ml to 1,000ml. Type "Sterile Water For Irrigation" into their search box.

Chota: www.chotaoutdoorgear.com. Terrific boots for canoeing and wet-weather camping.

Cooke Custom Sewing: (651) 784-8777; www.cookecustomsewing.com. Superior tarps, packs, winter mukluks, and specialized canoeing gear.

Council Tool: www.counciltool.com. Terrific US-made axes. Council Tool has been making fine axes and fire-fighting tools since 1886. Their Wood-Craft Camp Carver, with 16" Curved Handle is exquisite!

Counter Assault: www.counterassault.com. Pepper spray that will discourage bears.

Duluth Pack: www.duluthpack.com. Traditional canvas canoe packs and camping accessories.

Eagles Nest Outfitters (ENO): www.eaglesnestoutfittersinc.com. Modern, well-designed hammocks for camping.

Emberlit Stove: www.emberlit.com. Constructed from ultralight titanium or stainless steel. Five "playing-card thin" pieces snap together. When packed it consumes about as much space as a large postcard. The stove is remarkably strong for its weight—it easily supported my 20-pound Dutch oven!

EfferSan Sanitizer by Activon Products: (800) 841-0410; www.activon.com. Dry chlorine tablets that you add to rinse water to purify camp dishes.

Empire Canvas Works: www.empirecanvasworks.com. Canvas summer and winter tents, mushing clothes, canoeing accessories, and more.

Fast Bucksaw www.fastbucksaw.com. Best folding camp saw I've found. Made by hand in small batches. Expect to wait weeks for delivery. Questionable availability.

FITS sock company: www.fitssock.com. Wonderfully soft and warm and fits better than any sock I've worn. My favorite socks!

FoodSaver by Tilia: www.foodsaver.com. Vacuum-sealing machine with enough power to crush a tin can.

Frost River: www.frostriver.com. McAllister waxed canvas packs (the tiny Nessmuk is my favorite), tents, garment bags, brief-cases, and more.

Go-Girl.com. A reusable device that allows women to urinate in a standing position.

Granite Gear: www.granitegearstore.com. Impeccable packs and paddling accessories that will stand up to the hardest use.

Gransfors Bruk axes:; www.gransforsbruk.com. Superb hand-made axes.

Grohmann Knives: www.grohmannknives .com. The #1 Original, the flat-ground carbon camper, is my favorite factory knife.

Icebreaker pure merino wool underwear and outerwear: www.icebreaker.com. Supersoft, itch-free, 100 percent merino wool–layered garments.

Idaho Knife Works: www.idahoknifeworks .com. Source of the Cliff knife I designed and other terrific knives with carbon-steel blades. Questionable availability.

Klar Ullfrotté merino wool-polyamide underwear and outerwear: www.woolpower.se. Merino wool–layered garments. Warmest and softest underwear I've found. Widely worn by police, military personnel, and rescue teams.

Littlbug Stove: www.littlbug.com. My favorite wood-burning trail stove. It's light (the Junior model weighs 5 ounces!), compact, and burns brightly with very little wood. Stainless steel construction. An optional 9-ounce stainless steel fire pan ("Fire Bowl") contains embers.

L.L. Bean Classic "Bean boots" and other great outdoor gear. Really, is there anyone who hasn't heard of L.L. Bean?

MIOX water purifier from MSR.; www.miox .com. A fast and simple purifier in a compact size.

Mytopo.com: Online map company with full coverage of North America. You choose the map scale, coordinate system(s), and location of map center. Print from your computer or order finished maps on waterproof Tyvek paper.

Nalgene bottles by US Plastics Corporation: www.usplastic.com The secret to Nalgene's popularity is their toughness and unique seal, which absolutely, positively will not leak.

N/R Laboratories-Allegro Medical. www.allegro medical.com. No-Rinse shampoo and body bath:. Ideal products for trips where clean water is hard to find.

NRS: www.nrs.com. Top shelf specialty gear for paddlers. I especially like their NRS Boundary Boot.

The Original Bug Shirt: www.bugshirt.com. Highly recommended if bugs drive you batty.

Sawyer repellents: wwwsawyer.com. Insect repellents, insecticides.

Smartwool: www.smartwool.com. Supersoft, pure merino wool socks and underwear.

Smith Abrasives: www.smkw.com. The finest natural oil stones, diamond hones, and accessories for sharpening knives and precision tools.

Steger mukluks: www.mukluks.com. The most comfortable and beautiful mukluks on the planet.

SteriPEN: www.katadyn.com. Water-purification "pen" that uses ultraviolet light to purify water. My favorite!

Surefire: www.surefire.com. Ultra-high-powered tactical flashlights (bulb and LED)—many times more powerful than traditional lights. They are widely used by law-enforcement personnel and are so bright they can disable an attacker—or a determined wild animal.

Tandy Leather Company: www.tandyleather.com. Leather and tools for working leather.

Tear-Aid: www.tear-aid.com. Fabric and vinyl repair tape that really works!

Tentsmiths: www.tentsmiths.com. Old-time tents made from traditional canvas.

Thermax and Thermistat long underwear from Cabela's: www.cabelas.com. A comfortable and odor-free alternative to wool.

Tingley rubber boots: www.tingleyrubber.com. Inexpensive knee-high rubber boots that fit over running shoes.

UDAP Industries: www.bearspray.com. Source for field-proven Pepper Power bear-repelling pepper spray and lightweight electric bear fences.

WAG Bags: www.cleanwaste.com/wag-bag. Government-approved, sanitary toilet-in-a-bag system.

World of Maps. www.worldofmaps.com. A great place to order Canadian topo maps.

Glossary of Common Camping Terms

A-frame tent: An inverted V-shaped tent with one or two poles at each end.

agonic line: A line of zero compass declination along which the compass needle points to both true and magnetic north.

anorak: A shell parka that goes on over the head. Anoraks have a chest-length zipper or snaps. They conserve heat better than full-zip parkas.

Arkansas stone: A medium-hard mineral stone used for putting a fine edge on knives.

azimuth: Commonly used to indicate a directional bearing in degrees or mils. Technically, azimuth relates direction to one (or a fraction of one) of the 360 degrees of the compass rose. A bearing (often used synonymously with azimuth) relates direction to the north or south cardinal point. Example: An azimuth of 330 degrees equals a bearing of north 30 degrees west. An azimuth of 160 degrees equals a bearing of south 20 degrees east, etc.

baffle: Fabric panels sewn to the inner and outer shell of a sleeping bag. Baffles keep the insulation in place. Down bags must be baffled. Most synthetic bags feature quilted insulation.

bannock: The traditional trail bread. Usually made in a skillet by a combination of frying and reflective baking.

bathtub floor: A tent floor that wraps 6 inches or more up sidewalls of the tent before it is sewn in. This construction eliminates ground-level perimeter seams, which can leak.

Bean boots: Slang for Maine Hunting Shoe, the leather-top/rubber-bottom boots invented by Leon Bean.

bearing: A compass direction (see *azimuth*).

billy can: A straight-sided cooking pot with a wire bail.

bivouac: Technically, a temporary encampment. Modern usage connotes an emergency or bush camp made where no other camp has stood.

blousing bands: Elastic bands used by the military to secure pant-leg bottoms around boots. Blousing bands are useful for sealing trouser legs against mosquitoes and blackflies.

breathable: Refers to the porosity of fabrics. Breathable materials are not waterproof.

bug jacket: A fabric mesh jacket impregnated with insect repellent.

cagoule: A waterproof, ankle-length, over-the-head parka used by mountaineers for bivouacking. Cagoules have tailored hoods and drawstring hems. The wearer pulls his legs inside, draws the hem tight, and "outlasts" the elements.

canopy: The (usually porous) roof of a tent. Not to be confused with the waterproof tent fly.

cap fly: Three-quarter-length tent fly. Tents with cap flies are not as weatherproof as those with full-length flies.

catenary cut: The natural curve formed by a rope tightly strung between two trees. A tent that has a catenary cut rigs tighter (has less sidewall sag) than one without catenary cut. Catenary cut is a feature of the best tents.

chute cord: Slang for parachute cord.

contour lines: Thin brown lines on maps connecting points of equal elevation.

cord lock: Spring-loaded nylon clamp used to secure the drawstring closures of stuff sacks.

crash out: To bushwhack out of a forested area to a trail, road, or meadow.

cruiser compass: A needle compass that has the numbers on the dial reversed (running counterclockwise rather than clockwise) to permit reading bearings in the same plane as the observer's eye. Cruiser compasses are still used by some professionals, but there are better choices for campers. The design of these instruments originated in the 19th century, and they are now outdated.

cryptosporidium: A protozoan you won't want in your drinking water! Causes symptoms similar to giardiasis. Cryptosporidium cysts may be killed by boiling or removed by filtering. They resist most chemicals.

declination: The difference between true or geographic north and magnetic north. Declination (also called *variation* by mariners) is expressed in degrees east or west of the agonic line.

Deet: N,N-diethyl-meta-toluamide, the active ingredient in most insect repellents.

diamond stone: A type of man-made sharpening stone that contains powdered diamonds. Diamond stones are lubricated with water (not cutting oil). They remove metal much faster than traditional oil stones.

differential cut: When the inner shell of a sleeping bag is cut smaller than the outer shell to produce a Thermos-bottle effect. The merits of this construction are still being argued by equipment freaks.

dining fly: An overhead tarp (fly) used for protection from rain. Usually erected just before meals, hence the descriptive name.

double-wall tent: A tent with a double-layered wall. All modern nylon tents are built this way, featuring a breathable taffeta canopy (inner wall) and a watertight ripstop fly (outer wall). Double-wall canvas tents are sometimes used in winter (with a sheepherder stove) to conserve heat.

draft tube: A down-filled tube that runs the length of a sleeping bag zipper to prevent cold air from filtering through the zipper teeth.

dropped-point knife: The favored style for hunting knives. The point is centered (similar to a spear point) on the blade. Dropped-point knives are ideal for skinning game animals but are not the most suitable style for camp knives.

Duluth pack: A voluminous envelope-style pack (usually canvas) popular with canoeists.

Dutch oven: A unique oven consisting of a heavy-walled pot and cover with a large retaining rim. Coals from the fire are placed on top of the pot lid and the affair is set into the hot ashes. Heat from the top does most of the baking.

EVA (ethyl vinyl acetate): Strongest, most resilient, and most expensive of the closed-cell foams. EVA makes an excellent trail mattress.

fanny pack: Small, zippered nylon pack that's attached to a waist belt.

ferrule: The metal sleeve attached to fiberglass tent poles. Ferrules form a joint between pole sections.

filling power (of down): Same as *loft*. It's the thickness of a sleeping bag lying flat and fluffed. Generally speaking, the greater the loft of a sleeping bag, the warmer it will be.

fisherman's shirt: Same as a *cagoule*, only calf length and without a drawstring hem.

flat-fell seam: Overlapping construction. The seam goes through four layers of material.

fleece: See *pile*.

floating dial compass: A compass in which the needle is part of the numbered compass dial, which rotates as a unit. This allows the instrument to be read in the same plane as the eye of the user. Some styles are very accurate.

foam pad: A sleeping mattress made of either open- or closed-cell foam.

frame pack: A pack with an exterior aluminum or fiber framework.

frost liner: A detachable inner roof for a tent. Absorbs moisture that could otherwise condense, freeze, and drop on sleeping occupants. Frost liners are made from cotton or cotton-polyester fabric and are needed only in below-freezing conditions.

fuel bottle: Traditionally refers to Sigg aluminum bottles, which are used for the storage of gasoline and kerosene.

gators: Nylon anklets (usually with side zippers) used by skiers and mountaineers. Gators prevent snow from getting in your boot tops, and they add extra warmth.

gelatin-mold oven: An oven made from a large-ring aluminum gelatin mold.

geodesic dome: A dome-shaped tent with a strong faceted framework of tubular aluminum. Geodesic domes are the Cadillac of domes!

giardia: The causative pathogen of giardiasis.

giardiasis: A waterborne disease carried by the protozoan giardia. Giardia is commonly carried by beavers. Incubation time is 1 to 2 weeks.

GPS (Global Positioning System) unit: An electronic unit that receives positioning information from twenty-four orbiting satellites. With a civilian-model GPS, you can locate your position anywhere on Earth in a matter of minutes. Accuracy is 3 meters or less! Most units run on small batteries.

hip belt: A padded waist belt that secures to a backpack—makes carrying the pack much more comfortable.

hollow-ground knife: A knife with an edge ground to a concave bevel, which produces a thin, razor-sharp edge and a stiff spine.

hood closure: The tie cord and fastener that secure the hood of a sleeping bag around the sleeper's face.

hypothermia: A potentially lethal physical state caused by lowering of the body's core temperature due to exposure to cold, wet weather. Also called exposure sickness.

internal frame pack: A hiking pack with internal stays. The stays give the pack shape and make it more comfortable to carry than a traditional soft pack.

I-pole tent: A tent with a single vertical pole at each end.

kindling: Pencil-thin pieces of wood used to nurture a fire to a reliable blaze.

layering: Wearing several thin layers of clothes, one over the other. Layering is the most efficient clothing system for cold weather.

lensatic compass: A compass that features a built-in magnifying lens for ease of reading directions. The old army lensatic compass (no longer used) is the best example of this type of instrument. Lensatic compasses are impractical for camping (they don't have built-in protractors), slow to use, and no more accurate than modern orienteering instruments.

lock-back knife: A folding knife with an integral lock that secures the blade when open. Some modern lock backs are really side locks or front locks. Lock-back knives do not have pressure springs like ordinary jackknives, so they can be opened easily with one hand while wearing mittens.

loft: Thickness of a sleeping bag while laying flat and fluffed. Generally speaking, the higher the loft, the warmer the bag.

map index: A specially gridded small-scale map that lists maps in print, how and where to get them, and their cost.

millar mitts: Fingerless gloves used by mountaineers for technical climbing. Millar mitts are great for fishing, canoeing, and general hiking.

mocha: A popular camp drink of hot chocolate and coffee.

moleskin: Soft-surfaced bandaging material used to protect blisters. The sticky side of moleskin is placed over the unbroken blister; the cushioned surface absorbs the friction from socks and boots.

mountain parka: A generic name for full-zipper, thigh-length parkas. Mountain parkas usually have lots of pockets. They're traditionally constructed from 60/40 (60 percent nylon, 40 percent cotton) cloth, which is doubled for added warmth. The US Army field jacket is a true mountain parka.

orienteering: An international sport that combines the skills of map and compass reading with cross-country running.

orienteering compass: A compass with a built-in protractor that allows you to determine directions from a map without orienting the map to north. This is the most practical compass style for outdoor use.

overlapping V-tube construction (sleeping bags): A type of baffle construction in which down is secured into V-shaped tubes that overlap one another. Some very warm winter sleeping bags are built this way.

pack basket: A basket pack traditionally woven from splints of black ash. This original American Indian–made item is still going strong in the New England area and is available from L.L. Bean. Pack baskets are ideal for berry picking, picnicking, canoe trips, and auto camping. They will protect your breakables. Compared to fabric packs, they are quite inexpensive.

parka: A thigh-length shell garment with integral hood. Parkas may be lined or filled with down, polyester, or other insulation for use in cold weather.

pelican case: Hard plastic, absolutely waterproof case that comes in many shapes and sizes—the Cadillac of waterproof cases.

pile: A luxuriously soft fabric made from polyester. Pile absorbs little water and it dries quickly. Pile—also called "fleece"—has almost replaced wool as the material for cold-weather camping.

Polarguard: A synthetic polyester material widely used in sleeping bags and parkas. Polarguard is considered one of the best synthetic insulators.

poly bottle: Short for polyethylene bottle.

poncho: A rectangular, hooded rain garment. Ponchos provide good ventilation and can be worn over a hiking pack. They do not supply reliable protection from rain.

prime (as in priming a gasoline or kerosene stove): Stoves are usually primed by filling an integral spirit cup with gasoline or alcohol, then setting the fuel aflame. Stoves can be overprimed. If too much gasoline is forced into the spirit cup, the unit may ignite into a ball of uncontrollable flames.

prismatic compass: A compass with a built-in sighting prism. Prismatic compasses are a step up from lensatic types. They're expensive but not very versatile.

Quallofil: A synthetic material developed for use in sleeping bags and parkas. Each filament has four longitudinal holes that trap air and add warmth. Quallofil is one of the best synthetic insulators.

quick-release knot: A knot that can be removed by a simple pull of the tail. The most common quick-release knot is the bow used for tying your shoes.

quilt construction: A type of sleeping-bag construction in which the insulation is sewn (quilt-like) in place. This is an inexpensive way to make a summer-weight sleeping bag. This construction is suitable for winter use if the bag is double-quilted.

reflector oven: An aluminum sheet-metal oven that bakes by means of reflected heat. Reflector ovens are hard to keep clean and are cumbersome. They require an open flame for baking and cannot be used on stoves or over charcoal. They are very efficient if you have a nice bright fire.

ridge vent: The triangular window at the ridge of A-frame tents.

ripstop nylon: A lightweight nylon fabric that has heavier threads sewn in at approximate ¼-inch intervals. Ripstop is less likely to tear than taffeta but it has less resistance to abrasion.

seam sealer: A special glue, available at all camping shops, used to waterproof the stitching on tents and rain gear.

self-supporting tent: Theoretically, a tent that needs no staking. However, all self-supporting tents must be staked or they'll blow away in the wind.

semimummy bag: A sleeping bag with a barrel shape and no hood. A good choice for those who feel confined by the mummy shape but want lighter weight and more warmth than that supplied by standard rectangular sleeping bags.

sewn-through construction: Same as *quilt construction.*

shell (garments): Refers to unlined garments, or the interior or exterior wall of a sleeping bag.

sidewall baffle: A baffle that is opposite the zipper on a sleeping bag; it keeps the down from shifting along the length of the bag.

sixty/forty parka: A parka made from fabric that consists of 60 percent nylon and 40 percent cotton. The term 60/40 is now generic; it defines any mountain-style parka, regardless of the fabric composition. See *mountain parka.*

snow flaps: Earlike flaps sewn to the perimeter of a tent floor. Snow flaps are folded outward then piled with snow, eliminating the need for staking the tent. Snow flaps are an extra-cost feature of special-purpose winter tents.

sou'wester: The traditional rain hat of sailors and commercial fishermen. The sou'wester was developed centuries ago and is still the best of all foul-weather hats. The best sou'westers have ear flaps, a chin strap, and a flannel lining.

space blanket: A Mylar-coated blanket used in survival kits. Space blankets are waterproof and are very warm for their size and weight. Every camping shop has them.

space-filler cut: Where the inner and outer shells of a sleeping bag are cut the same size. This construction allows the inner liner and fill to better conform to the curves of your body than the Thermos-bottle shape of the differential cut. The merits/demerits of space-filler versus differential cut are still being argued by sleeping-bag manufacturers.

spreader bar: Same as a wand. Used for spreading out a portion of a tent.

sternum strap: A short nylon strap that connects the shoulder straps of a hiking pack. A properly adjusted sternum strap transfers some of the pack load to the chest.

storm flap: A panel of material that backs the zipper of a parka and prevents the storm from getting in.

stuff sack: Traditionally a nylon sack in which a sleeping bag is stored. The term now defines any nylon bag with drawstring closure.

Svea: Brand name of the venerable Svea stove.

Swiss Army knife: Originally the issue knife of the Swiss Army. Now generic for any scout-style multitool pocket knife.

tinder: Ultrafine dry material used for starting a fire.

Tingleys: Tingley brand rubber boots slip over street shoes. They grip like iron, even on wet rocks, wear like steel, weigh almost nothing, and are inexpensive. Most construction supply stores have them.

topo map: A topographic map that shows the lay of the land by means of contour lines.

trenching (also called "ditching"): Digging a trench around a tent to carry away groundwater that accumulates during a heavy rain. This form of guttering is illegal in all wilderness areas. Ground cloths and tent floors have eliminated the need to trench tents.

tumpline: A head strap used to carry heavy loads. Voyageurs carried hundreds of pounds of furs with only a tumpline. Today this feature is found only on traditional canvas Duluth packs, which are used for wilderness canoeing.

UTM (Universal Transverse Mercator): A metric coordinate map grid that is universally used by the US and Canadian military. UTM grid lines are always 1 km (0.62 mile) apart. UTM coordinates are easier to use than latitude/longitude grids because their "easting" and "northing" values are decimal based.

vapor-barrier liner (VBL): A waterproof fabric that's worn next to the skin. Warm clothes are layered on top. You stay warm because perspiration can't get through the waterproof fabric to dampen your clothes and reduce their insulation value.

vestibule: An alcove or extension that secures to one or both ends of a tent. Vestibules provide a place to store gear out of the weather.

Wachita stone: A medium-hard mineral oil stone used for sharpening knives.

Wellies: Short for "Wellingtons"—the traditional knee-high (green) British rubber boot used by gardeners, hunters, and just about everyone else—a cult boot.

white-print map: A provisional map that's similar to a blueprint. White prints are up-to-date maps that show the location of logging and mining roads and man-made structures. These maps are designed for professional use; they are not listed in standard map indexes.

Index

About the Author

Cliff Jacobson is one of North America's most respected outdoors writers and wilderness paddlers. He is a retired environmental science teacher, an outdoors skills instructor, a canoeing and camping consultant, and the author of more than a dozen top-selling books and a popular video on canoeing and camping. He is a distinguished Eagle Scout, a recipient of the American Canoe Association's prestigious Legends of Paddling Award, and a member of the ACA Hall of Fame.